DK EYEWITNESS TOP 10 TRAVEL GUIDES

NEW YORK

ELEANOR BERMAN

Left **Brooklyn Bridge** Right **New York taxis**

LONDON, NEW YORK,
MELBOURNE, MUNICH AND DELHI
www.dk.com

Reproduced by Colourscan, Singapore
Printed and bound in Italy by Graphicom

First American Edition, 2002
06 07 08 09 10 9 8 7 6 5 4 3 2 1

Published in the United States by
DK Publishing, Inc., 375 Hudson Street,
New York, New York 10014

Reprinted with revisions 2004, 2005, 2006
**Copyright 2002, 2006 © Dorling
Kindersley Limited**

ISSN 1479-344X
ISBN 0-78948-351-3
ISBN 978-0-78948-351-5

Within each Top 10 list in this book, no hierarchy
of quality or popularity is implied. All 10 are,
in the editor's opinion, of roughly equal merit.

Contents

New York's Top 10

The information in this DK Eyewitness Top 10 Travel Guide is checked annually.
Every effort has been made to ensure that this book is as up-to-date as possible at the time of
going to press. Some details, however, such as telephone numbers, opening hours, prices,
gallery hanging arrangements and travel information are liable to change. The publishers
cannot accept responsibility for any consequences arising from the use of this book, nor for
any material on third party websites, and cannot guarantee that any website address in this
book will be a suitable source of travel information. We value the views and suggestions of
our readers very highly. Please write to: Publisher, DK Eyewitness Travel Guides,
Dorling Kindersley, 80 Strand, London, Great Britain WC2R 0RL.

Cover: CORBIS: front tc; Bruce Burkhardt front blb; Joseph Sohm; Chromosohm Inc back tl; Lawrence
Manning front ca; Mortin Beebe, S.F front bl.

Left **View of the Empire State Building** Right **Pier 17, South Street Seaport**

Left **Statue of Liberty** Right **Street Entertainers, Washington Square**

NEW YORK'S TOP 10

NEW YORK'S TOP 10

New York Highlights

With its skyscrapers, great museums, and bright lights of Broadway, New York is a city of superlatives. There are countless sights that have to be seen, but a handful are truly definitive of the city. The following chapter illustrates the very best of these.

1 Empire State Building

This soaring Art Deco skyscraper is one of the most widely recognized symbols of the city, and star of countless movies. It offers unforgettable panoramas of New York from its 86th floor Observatory *(see pp8–9)*.

2 Fifth Avenue

A heady mix of fashionable shops and world-class architecture makes for an avenue of endless pleasures, and some of New York's best-known addresses *(see pp10–11)*.

3 Rockefeller Center

An urban wonder in the city's center, with gardens, restaurants, an underground shopping concourse, office space, a skating rink, and over 100 works of art, from murals to statues *(see pp12–15)*.

4 Statue of Liberty

The symbol of freedom for millions seeking a new life in America, the lady holding the torch of liberty is ensconced on her own island *(see pp16–17)*.

6 Times Square and the Theater District

An explosion of neon illuminates Broadway and Times Square, where more than 40 famous theaters play host to a changing parade of hit shows *(see pp22–5)*.

5 Ellis Island Immigration History Center

Carefully restored buildings bring to life the experience of the immigrants who have poured into New York over the years, helping to build the multi-ethnic city of today *(see pp18–21)*.

Lo Manha

Hudson River

New Jersey

5 Ellis Island

Liberty Island

4

Upper

Hudson River

Central Park
7 The vast swath of green provides an 843-acre respite from the concrete of the city. The man-made park took 16 years and more than 500,000 trees to complete *(see pp26–7)*.

Metropolitan Museum of Art **8**
It would take weeks to see all the treasures of this museum. It houses one of the greatest collections of the Western world and spans 5,000 years of culture *(see pp28–31)*.

Guggenheim Museum **9**
This Frank Lloyd Wright building is a work of art in itself, and a fitting frame for a major collection of contemporary art *(see pp32–3)*.

American Museum of Natural History
10 Long famous for its dinosaurs, the museum moves into the space age with the dramatic Rose Center for Earth and Space *(see pp34–7)*.

Harlem

Morningside Heights

Upper West Side

Central Park

Upper East Side

9

10 **7** **8**

Roosevelt Island

2

3

Midtown

6

Herald Square **1**

Chelsea

Flatiron

Gramercy Park

Union Square

Greenwich Village

East Village

SoHo

Little Italy

TriBeCa

Chinatown

Civic Center

Lower East Side

South St Seaport

Lower Manhattan

Battery Park

Harlem River

Hudson River

East River

1 ⟞————— miles ⟝ 0 ⟞ km ————⟞ 1

7

⑩ Empire State Building

The Empire State Building is the tallest and most famous skyscraper in New York. More than 120 million visitors, including the rock group Kiss and Queen Elizabeth II, have gazed down on the city from the Observatory since it opened in 1931. Planned in the prosperous 1920s by the architectural firm of Shreve, Lamb, and Harmon, this Art Deco classic was completed during the Depression and was largely vacant for several years, giving rise to the nickname "Empty State Building." It has been featured in countless movies; when King Kong

View of the Empire State Building

🍽 There are two restaurants, an ice cream parlor, and a coffee shop to choose from.

✪ Visit at the end of the day to watch twilight descend and city lights go on, a memorable sight.

- 350 Fifth Avenue, at 34th Street
- Map K3
- www.esbnyc.com
- Open 9:30am–midnight daily
- Adults $13, seniors and youths (12–17) $12, children (6–11) $8, children under 5 free
- New York Skyride $25
- Audio tours $5

returned to celebrate the 50th anniversary of the classic film in 1983, fans the world over cheered the triumphant ascent by a huge inflatable ape.

Top 10 Features

1. The Building
2. Elevators
3. 102nd Floor Observation Deck
4. 86th Floor Observatory
5. Spire
6. Wonders of the World
7. Fifth Avenue Gallery Windows
8. Valentine's Day
9. New York Skyride
10. Empire State Run-up

The Building ▮1

A mooring mast for airships, now the base of a TV tower, was built to ensure the 102-story, 1,454 ft (443 m), building would be taller than the Chrysler Building.

Elevators ▮2

Visitors can ride to the 86th floor in 45 seconds – 1,400 ft (427 m) per minute – in one of 73 Art Deco elevators. The last elevator leaves at 11.15pm.

102nd Floor Observation ▮3 Deck

Visibility on a clear day from the deck on the 102nd floor is up to 80 miles (130 km), but this has been closed to the public since 1999.

For more New York Skyscrapers **See pp44–5**

Spire 5
The spire is lit to honor holidays, seasons, and the many ethnic groups of New York: red, white, and blue for national holidays; green for St. Patrick's Day; blue and white for Chanukah.

86th Floor Observatory
4 Breathtaking views from the 86th floor's glass-enclosed pavilion 1,050 ft (320 m) above the city attract more than 3.5 million visitors each year. For visibility updates call 1888 NYC VIEW.

Wonders of the World
6 The 34th Street lobby houses eight 3D panels, created in 1963 by Roy Sparkia and Rene Nemerov, depicting the seven wonders of the ancient world, and a wonder of the modern world, the Empire State Building.

Fifth Avenue Gallery Windows 7
Five display windows in the lofty marble-clad Fifth Avenue lobby exhibit art and memorabilia from New York City's many museums, galleries, and artists. The exhibits are changed on a regular basis.

Valentine's Day 8
Several couples are married in the 80th floor Sky Lobby on February 14 and become members of the Empire State Wedding Club, with free entry every Valentine's Day.

New York Skyride
9 A virtual reality, big-screen simulation of a helicopter ride takes viewers over, under, and through some of the city's best-known landmarks.

Empire State Run-up
10 Each February, following a tradition dating to 1978, 50 runners race up the 1,576 steps from the lobby to the 86th floor. The record is 9 minutes, 33 seconds.

Building the Empire State

The Empire State Building was designed by William F. Lamb following a brief to "make it big." It took only 410 days to build this 102-story, 365,000-ton limestone and granite skyscraper, with an average of four and a half stories added every week. However, in one outstanding ten-day period, the 3,500-strong construction team completed no fewer than ten stories. Due to the building's relatively shallow foundations, 60,000 tons of steel beams were used to support the tower.

⑩ Fifth Avenue

Midtown Fifth Avenue is New York's best-known boulevard and home to three of its most famous buildings. In the late 1800s, it was lined with mansions belonging to prominent families, but as retailers moved north in the 1900s, society fled uptown. The one remaining mansion is the Cartier building, reputedly acquired from banker Morton F. Plant in 1917 in exchange for a string of pearls. Although commercial enterprises now share the avenue, it has remained a mecca for luxury goods. Fifth Avenue is at its best on Easter Sunday when traffic is barred and the street is filled with New Yorkers in elaborate hats.

Cartier façade, decorated for Christmas

🕐 Free tours of the New York Public Library: 11am and 2pm Tue–Sat, and 2pm on Sun; there's no need to book.

St. Patrick's Cathedral is open to visitors 7:30am– 8:30pm daily.

• The heart of Fifth Avenue is from the Empire State Building (see pp8–9) on 34th Street, to the Grand Army Plaza, 59th Street, an easily walkable stretch of just over one mile (1.6 km)
• Map H3–K3
• Tourist Information: 212 484 1200
• New York Public Library: 212 930 0800

Top 10 Exhibits

1. Grand Army Plaza
2. Bergdorf Goodman
3. General Motors Building
4. Tiffany and Company
5. Trump Tower
6. Cartier
7. St. Patrick's Cathedral
8. Saks Fifth Avenue
9. New York Public Library
10. Lord and Taylor

Grand Army Plaza 1
This ornamented plaza is presided over by the 1907 Plaza Hotel and Augustus Saint-Gaudens' statue of General William T. Sherman. Hansom cab rides through Central Park can be boarded here.

Bergdorf Goodman 2
Founded in 1894 as a small ladies' tailoring and fur shop, the most élite department store has been here since 1928. A separate shop for men was opened in 1990 across Fifth Avenue.

General Motors Building 3
Edward Durrell Stone's 1968 marble skyscraper is of interest not for its architecture but for the CBS studio in the plaza area and the F.A.O. Schwarz toy store adjacent.

Tiffany and Company 4
Truman Capote's 1958 *Breakfast at Tiffany's* made this the most famous jewelry store in New York. The window displays are works of art.

Trump Tower
5 A six-story open interior space, the Trump Tower Atrium is graced by hanging gardens and a spectacular 80-ft (24-m) water wall. There are also several exclusive shops, a restaurant and a great coffee shop.

Cartier
6 Look up to admire what remains of the fine 1905 Beaux Arts mansion housing this famous luxury jeweler. During the Christmas season, the whole building is wrapped in a giant red ribbon.

St. Patrick's Cathedral
7 In 1878 James Renwick, Jr. designed New York's grandest religious building in French Gothic style *(above)*. The bronze doors, the baldachin over the high altar, the Lady Chapel, and the rose window are among its notable features.

Saks Fifth Avenue
8 One of New York's most attractive stores, Saks is famous for the changing seasonal decor on the main floor of its 1924 building, as well as for its exclusive fashions for men and women.

New York Public Library
9 The epitome of Beaux Arts elegance, this 1911 landmark *(right)* features vaulted marble halls and a paneled reading room that glows with light from great arched windows.

Lord and Taylor
10 Retailing on Fifth Avenue since 1914, Lord and Taylor has a mix of fashions for budgets low and high. The store is known for its animated Christmas windows.

Millionnaires' Row

From its inception in the early 19th century, Fifth Avenue has been the territory of New York's well-heeled society, with homes costing the princely sum of $20,000 after the Civil War. As retail and commercial ventures, albeit exclusive ones, encroached on the wealthy's patch toward the end of the 19th century, they moved their palacial residences further north along Fifth Avenue. This trend was set by Mrs Astor who moved up to 65th Street after her nephew, William Waldorf Astor, built the Waldorf Hotel next to her former home.

For more on New York shopping See pp64–5

Rockefeller Center

A city within a city and a National Historic Landmark, this is the largest privately owned complex in the world. Begun in the 1930s, it was the first commercial project to integrate gardens, dining, and shopping with office space. Rockefeller Center is the hub of midtown New York, alive with activity day and night. The number of buildings has grown to 19, though the newer buildings do not match the Art Deco elegance of the original 14 structures. Over 100 works of art lie within the complex, including a major mural in each building. Still growing, this is one of the most outstanding public art collections in America.

 Starting on Fifth Avenue, walk through the Channel Gardens to the Sunken Garden.

Pick up a self-guided tour leaflet from the lobby of the G.E. Building while looking at the Sert Murals.

• Rockefeller Center extends from Fifth to Sixth avenues, between 48th and 51st streets
• Map J3
• www.rockefeller center.com
• NBC Studios: 30 Rockefeller Plaza, 212 664 7174, tours: open 8:30am–5:30pm Mon–Sat, 9:30am–4:30pm Sun, admission charge, reservations advised
• Today Show, Rockefeller Plaza at 49th Street, open 7–9am Mon–Fri

Top 10 Exhibits

1. Channel Gardens
2. Sunken Garden
3. Prometheus Statue
4. Atlas Statue
5. G.E. Building
6. NBC Studios
7. Today Show Studio
8. Shopping Concourse
9. Radio City Music Hall
10. Paine Webber Art Gallery

1 Channel Gardens
Named after the English Channel because they separate the French and British buildings, the gardens change with the calendar and are lined with glowing angels at Christmas. The six fountainhead figures are by René Chambellan *(below)*.

2 Sunken Garden
A skating rink in winter and leafy outdoor café in summer, the Sunken Garden is a bright spot year round. It is surrounded by colorful flags that represent the members of the United Nations.

3 Prometheus Statue
An 18-ft (5.5-m) bronze and gold leaf statue *(below)* by Paul Manship presides over the Sunken Garden. The pedestal represents Earth and the circle containing the signs of the zodiac represents the heavens.

Atlas Statue

Sculpted by Lee Lawrie, this 14,000-lb (6,350-kg), 15-ft (4.5-m) figure is perched on a 9-ft (3-m) pedestal. One of 15 works by Lawrie at the Center, it stands at the entrance to the International Building.

Rockefeller Center Plan

G.E. Building

The centerpiece of Rockefeller Center is a slim, 70-story limestone tower. The design features gradual setbacks as the building rises to ensure that no office is more than 27 ft (8 m) from a window.

NBC Studios

Backstage tours of a major television network's studios are popular. Visitors can now buy tickets online or write ahead for shows (see p166); tickets may also be available in the lobby of the G.E. building.

Today Show Studio

This morning TV show can be viewed live every weekday morning from the sidewalk in front of the studio. A camera often films the fans watching the show.

Shopping Concourse

A variety of stores are found in the underground concourse, also known as the catacombs, of the G.E. Building, including a branch of the Metropolitan Museum shop.

Radio City Music Hall

Guided tours of this Art Deco masterpiece and former movie palace are a chance to admire the decor, the stage, and the legendary Wurlitzer organ.

Paine Webber Art Gallery

Opened in 1985, this gallery (above) mounts four or five shows a year. Changing exhibits are eclectic, ranging from Mayan art to sports photography.

John D. Rockefeller, Jr.

The legendary philanthropist and multimillionnaire, John D. Rockefeller, Jr. (1874–1960) was son and heir to Ohio oil magnate John Davison Rockefeller's fortunes and took over the family oil business in 1911. Rockefeller, or John D., as he was known, strongly believed his inheritance should be used for the public good. Among his philanthropic donations were contributions to the building funds of the United Nations Headquarters (see pp124–5), the Cloisters (see p31), and the Riverside Church (see p145).

Left **Mural by Thomas Hart Benton** Right **Gaston Lachaise's panel**

Rockefeller Center Artworks

1 America's Progress
Jose Maria Sert's (1876–1945) mural depicts America's development over 300 years by uniting two forces, brain and brawn. Sert's *Time* mural adorns one of the ceilings.

2 Wisdom
The striking central figure of *Wisdom* by Lee Lawrie (1877–1963) grasps a compass pointing to light and sound waves and is carved on a screen made of 240 glass blocks.

3 Gaston Lachaise's panels
This two-panel work by the noted American sculptor (1882–1935) honors the contribution made by workmen to the Rockefeller Center's construction, depicting them at their labors.

4 News
This heroic sculpture by Isamu Noguchi (1904–88) is cast in stainless steel. The 10-ton panel illustrates the tools of the press, including camera, telephone, pad, and pencil.

News, Isamu Noguchi

5 Industries of the British Commonwealth
Cast in bronze and finished in gold leaf, this panel by Carl Paul Jennewein (1890–1980) depicts nine major industries of the British Empire, including sugar cane, salt, and tobacco.

6 Intelligence Awakening Mankind
Some one million tesserae (pieces of glass enamel) in more than 250 shades create Barry Faulkner's (1881–1966) mosaic representing spoken and written words.

7 Portals
Josef Albers' 1961 work of thin, highly polished, milky-white and ivory Carrara glass creates a surface of receding squares that gives the mural a sense of depth.

8 America Today
This nine-panel mural painted in 1931 by Thomas Hart Benton was commissioned for the New School University and was on view there until 1984, when it was purchased by the Equitable Group.

9 Mural with Blue Brushstrokes
A sign of the continuing emphasis on art within Rockefeller Center's newer buildings is this giant, five-story, 70-ft (21-m) mural by the late master of Pop Art, Roy Lichtenstein, c.1984–5.

10 Wall Drawing 896
The newest mural, a site-specific, geometric design created in 1999 by Sol Lewitt, covers four walls of the entrance to the headquarters of Christie's on 48th St.

Top 10 Statistics

1. Tallest building: 850 ft (259 m), 70 floors
2. Elevators: 388
3. Passenger rides per day: more than 400,000
4. Fastest elevator speed: 1,400 ft (427 m) per minute (37 seconds non-stop to 65th floor)
5. Number working in the complex: 65,000
6. Telephones: 100,000
7. Office windows: 48,758
8. Restaurants: 45
9. Shops: 100
10. Daily visitors: 250,000

The Building of Rockefeller Center

John D. Rockefeller driving in final rivet

When the Depression made John D. Rockefeller Jr.'s original plan for a new opera house impractical, he instead developed a large, creative-commercial complex. The innovative Art Deco design, lead by Raymond Hood, included a mid-block street (Rockefeller Plaza) and an underground concourse. The 14 buildings constructed in 1931–40 provided 225,000 jobs during the worst of the Depression. Artworks were an essential element; over 30 artists contributed work for foyers, façades, and gardens as part of the "New Frontiers" program.

Early Radio Broadcast

The young network-broadcasting industry, made up of RCA, RKO, and NBC, became the primary tenants of the Rockefeller Center. The entire complex was originally named "the Radio City."

Rockefeller Center construction workers, 1932

📖10 Statue of Liberty

The figure presiding over New York harbor, officially titled "Liberty Enlightening the World," has been a harbinger of freedom for millions since her inauguration by President Grover Cleveland in 1886. The statue, a gift of friendship from the French to mark the U.S.'s 100th birthday in 1876, was designed by the French sculptor Frédéric-Auguste Bartholdi, who devoted 21 years to the project. Slow fundraising on both sides of the Atlantic delayed the unveiling by 10 years, but no problem was encountered financing the $100 million restoration for the statue's 100th birthday. Her unveiling on July 3, 1986, was the occasion for the largest fireworks display ever seen in the U.S.

Restoration celebrations, July 3, 1986

🟢 **Crowds can be heavy, so an early departure is advised. A cafeteria is available on site.**

For the best photos, sit on the right of the boat going out, the left coming back.

• Take the 1 or 9 train to South Ferry, 4 or 5 train to Bowling Green, or the R or W train to Whitehall Street to get to Battery Park by subway.
• Ferries leave from Castle Clinton, Battery Park, every 30–45 minutes between 8:30am–3:30pm daily.
• www.nps.gov/stli

Top 10 Features

1. Castle Clinton National Monument
2. Battery Park
3. Boat Ride
4. Close-up View of the Statue
5. Pedestal
6. Crown
7. Torch and Book
8. Frame
9. Views
10. Historical Exhibits

4 Close-up View of the Statue

A close-up view reveals the awesome size of the Statue of Liberty. Dominating New York harbor, she stands 305 ft (93 m) tall and weighs 225 tons. Her right arm carrying the symbolic torch is 42 ft (13 m) long while her index finger measures 8 ft (2.4 m) and dwarfs most men.

2 Battery Park

With statues and monuments honoring everyone from New York's first Jewish immigrants to the U.S. Coast Guard, the park is also a great spot for sea-gazing.

3 Boat Ride

The views from the ferries that carry a constant stream of visitors from Manhattan and Jersey City to the Statue of Liberty and on to Ellis Island are dramatic.

5 Pedestal

Richard Morris Hunt, one of America's most prestigious architects, was chosen to design the 89-ft (27-m) pedestal of the Statue of Liberty. The pedestal sits on a concrete foundation within the 11-pointed, star-shaped walls of Fort Wood, a fortress erected for the War of 1812.

1 Castle Clinton National Monument

Built as a fort in 1807, it is now a visitor center for Statue of Liberty and Ellis Island visitors. The building exhibits panoramas of New York history.

Crown 6

Legend says that Bartholdi's mother was the model for Liberty, but the face was actually based on his early drawings for a never-commissioned statue in Egypt. The seven rays of her crown represent the seven seas and seven continents.

Torch and Book 7

The new torch, with its 24-carat gold leaf-coated flame, was added during a 1984–86 restoration. The original is on display in the main lobby. The book in the statue's left hand is inscribed July 4, 1776, in Latin.

Frame 8

Gustave Eiffel, best known for his Paris tower, created the inner framework. The copper sheeting shell, weighing 31 tons, is hung on iron bars from a massive central iron pylon that anchors the statue to the base.

Views 9

The lofty observation decks in the pedestal and crown of the Liberty Statue, which offered spectacular views of Manhattan, are now closed because of security concerns since the events of September 11, 2001.

Gateway to the New World

The Statue of Liberty has symbolized the beginning of a new way of life for millions of immigrants fleeing poverty and hardship. She is an enduring symbol of the freedom and hope offered by the U.S. and the subject of Emma Lazarus's poem *The New Colossus:* "...Give me your tired, your poor, Your huddled masses yearning to breathe free... Send these, the homeless, tempest-tost to me, I lift my lamp beside the golden door."

Historical Exhibits 10

The museum inside the base documents the complete history of the Statue of Liberty using photos, prints, videos, oral histories, and full-scale replicas of the face and foot. A pass is required to visit the base and observation platform.

 To reserve a pass to visit the statue's base, contact: 1-866-STATUE 4, or visit www.statuereservations.com

🔟 Ellis Island Immigration Museum

Ellis Island is the symbol of America's immigrant heritage. From 1892 to 1954, it was the arrival point for over 12 million people fleeing religious persecution, poverty, or unrest in their homelands. Their descendants, more than 100 million people, comprise almost 40 percent of today's population. First and second class passengers were processed for immigration on board ship, but the poor traveling in steerage class were ferried to the crowded island for medical and legal examinations. It was a frightening prospect after an exhausting journey to a land where few newcomers could speak the language. As many as 5,000 passed through in a day. The museum not only retraces their experience here, but is a picture of the total immigrant experience in America.

The vast interior of the Great Hall

🍴 **The island's cafeteria and picnic areas are great for lunch or snacks.**

🕐 **Catch an early ferry from Battery Park to avoid crowds on the island.**

Stop at the museum information desk for tickets to the free 30-minute film "Island of Hope, Island of Tears."

• For a map of Ellis Island see Lower Manhattan to Midtown inset on p6
• 212 363 3200
• www.nps.gov/elis
• Ferries from Battery Park: 212 269 5755
• Ferry rides to Statue of Liberty and Ellis Island: adults $10, seniors $8, children (4–12) $4, children under 4 free
• Open 8:30am–5:15pm daily
• Free

Top 10 Features

1. Arrival Area
2. Great Hall
3. Medical Examining Line
4. Dormitory
5. Railroad Ticket Office
6. Baggage Room
7. The Peopling of America
8. Immigration History Center
9. American Immigration Wall of Honor
10. Immigrants' Living Theater

1 Arrival Area
Crowds of steerage passengers *(below)* entered through the original gateway here after being ferried from arrival vessels. Instructions were given by interpreters in a babel of languages.

2 Great Hall
Huddled on benches, immigrants awaited examinations that would determine whether they would be granted entry. A doctor watched as they ascended the stairs and marked letters in chalk on those who showed signs of conditions needing special inspection.

3 Medical Examining Line
Interpreters guided immigrants through their medical examinations. The most dreaded were the "eye men," looking for symptoms of trachoma, a disease that caused blindness. It was the reason for more than half the medical detentions and meant sure deportation.

4 Dormitory
Immigrants who were detained for further examinations slept here in separate quarters for men and women. Although the process was nerve-wracking, only two percent of those seeking refuge were sent back.

5 Railroad Ticket Office
Those traveling beyond New York were ferried to railroad terminals in New Jersey to continue their journeys. Agents could sell as many as 25 tickets per minute.

Key to Floor Plan
▓ First Floor
▒ Second Floor
▓ Third Floor

6 Baggage Room
Here newcomers checked the boxes, trunks, and baskets that held the meager belongings they carried, now all their worldly possessions.

7 The Peopling of America
400 years of immigration history are displayed in more than 30 galleries. Exhibits such as *The Peopling of America* have artifacts, heirlooms, posters, maps, and photos donated by immigrants' families.

8 American Family Immigration History Center
Using computer and multimedia technology, visitors can access passenger arrival records of more than 22 million people entering New York between 1892 and 1924.

New Jersey's Ellis Island
Although federal property, a long-fought battle over territorial jurisdiction of Ellis Island was settled in 1998. Originally a 3-acre site, Ellis Island's landmass was increased in the 1900s with landfill to more than nine times its original size, to over 27 acres. A US Supreme Court ruling decided the added landfill to be within the territory of New Jersey, and the original portion to be in New York. New Jersey officials launched a restoration program that includes saving the derelict hospital buildings.

9 American Immigration Wall of Honor
To honor their forebears, Americans pay to have their names inscribed on this list. Including the families of John F. Kennedy and Barbra Streisand, this is the world's largest wall of names; over 600,000.

10 Immigrants' Living Theater
Daily theatrical productions that are based on actual immigrant accounts are given by actors who recreate the experiences of Ellis Island. The museum has two movie theaters, a Library and an Oral History Studio with taped reminiscences.

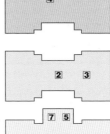

For more museums See pp40–41

Left **Italian immigrants** Center **Arrivals to the island** Right **French West Indian arrivals**

Milestones in Immigration History

1
1624
First Dutch arrived in New Amsterdam, which thrived as a trading center, attracting settlers from many other nations. By 1643, the 500-strong population spoke 18 different languages.

2
1664
The dislike of Dutch governor Peter Stuyvesant and unpopular tax demands by the Dutch West India Company meant little resistance to the ousting of the Dutch by the British, who renamed the city New York.

3
1790
For the first U.S. Census, New York's population of 33,131 was the second largest in the Colonies. The make-up was mostly British and Dutch.

4
Mid-1800s
Ireland's 1845–8 Great Famine and economic hardship in Germany led many to seek new lives in New York, where rapid growth as a seaport and manufacturing center opened many jobs.

Polish woman at Ellis Island c.1910

5
1880–1910
Thousands of Russian and Polish Jews and Italians arrived, fleeing persecution or hard economic times.

6
1892
When Castle Island, an immigrant depot set up in 1855, could no longer handle the inflow, Ellis Island took over. "Settlement Houses" were set up in the city to help those living in squalid tenements, and "Americanization" programs encouraged assimilation.

7
1924
Nearly 40 percent of New York's population was foreign-born. U.S. laws set national quotas on immigration; Great Britain's Caribbean colonies benefited from the British quota and arrived in large numbers.

Asian women in a garment factory in Chinatown

8
1965
The Hart-Cellar Act ended discrimination based on national origin; a new wave of immigration began.

9
1980s
One million mainly Asian and Latin American newcomers arrived. The Chinese population topped 300,000, Koreans became visible elements in the city, and Dominican numbers grew.

10
1990–present
Another one million newcomers entered, swelling the foreign-born population to over 40 percent of the total population – the highest since 1910. Immigrants from more than 160 nations now live in New York.

Top 10 Nationalities Entering Ellis Island

1 Italy: 2,502,310
2 Austria and Hungary: 2,275,852
3 Russia: 1,893,542
4 Germany: 633,148
5 England: 551,969
6 Ireland: 520,904
7 Sweden: 348,036
8 Greece: 245,058
9 Norway: 226,278
10 Ottoman Empire: 212,825

(Between 1892–7, 1901–31)

The Restoration of Ellis Island

Laws defining immigration quotas enacted in 1924 drastically curtailed the numbers of foreigners coming into the U.S., and Ellis Island was no longer needed as an immigration depot. It became a detention and deportation center for undesirable aliens, a training center for the U.S. Coast Guard, and a hospital for wounded servicemen during World War II. In 1954 the U.S. government closed the island. It remained abandoned until 1984, when a $156 million renewal project replaced the copper roof domes, cleaned the mosaic tiles, and restored the interior, preserving any surviving original fixtures in the largest historic restoration in U.S. history.

The restoration included the establishment of the Ellis Island Immigration Museum (see pp18–19), telling the immigrant story through displays and more than 2,000 artifacts. The museum also has an oral history archive of taped interviews and an interactive children's gallery, both available to visit by appointment. Reopened to the public in 1990, Ellis Island receives almost 2 million visitors every year.

Restoration

Preservation of Ellis Island began in 1965 with the rebuilding of the seawall, but the biggest task was the restoration of the main building, which had deteriorated severely. The period of 1918–24 was chosen for reconstruction because this coincided with a peak time for immigration.

Glass canopy marking the restored main entrance to Ellis Island

For more New York museums **See pp40–41**

21

Times Square and Theater District

Known as the "Crossroads of the World," Times Square is New York's most famous intersection and the symbol of the lively surrounding theater district that includes Broadway. It was called Longacre Square until 1904, when the New York Times built a 25-story tower on the site. Its occupancy on New Year's Eve was marked with fireworks, a celebration that continues today. Currently, a giant crystal ball descends the building at midnight to herald the new year, cheered by the millions packed into the square. The reputation of Times Square was sullied when the adjacent 42nd Street grew seedy in the 1970s. The 1990s saw the peep shows and X-rated movie houses closed, and with a massive government and private effort, the street and neighborhood have again been transformed.

News Ticker, Times Square

🌀 Go to the TKTS booth in Times Square at Broadway and 47th for half-price tickets to all kinds of Broadway shows.

Discount coupons for shows are often available at the Times Square Information Center, 1560 Broadway between 46th and 47th streets.

Try to see Broadway at night, when the lights are on.

• Times Square is located where Broadway and 7th Avenue intersect at 42nd Street
• Map J3
• www.timessquare nyc.org
• Madame Tussaud's New York: 234 West 42nd Street, 1 800 246 8872, open 10am–8pm Mon–Thu, 10am–10pm Fri–Sun, admission charge, www.nycwax.com

Top 10 Exhibits

1. Broadway Lights
2. Times Square News Ticker
3. Nasdaq Headquarters
4. MTV Headquarters
5. Brill Building
6. Condé Nast Building
7. New 42nd Street
8. Madame Tussaud's, New York
9. Port Authority Bus Terminal
10. Off-Broadway

1 Broadway Lights
The city's longest street is known best for the section north of 42nd Street dubbed the "Great White Way" for its dazzle of neon.

2 Times Square News Ticker
In 1928, the *New York Times* erected the world's first moving electronic sign to post news, a fixture that remains although the *Times* has moved to 43rd Street.

3 Nasdaq Headquarters
The headquarters of this over-the-counter stock market dominates its corner with a screen that regularly broadcasts financial news.

For more entertainment venues See pp50–51

4 MTV Headquarters

It isn't unusual to find crowds of teenagers beneath the second floor studios of this music TV network hoping to spot an idol on the way in, or a camera crew descending to tape crowds in the street.

5 Brill Building

Everyone from Cole Porter to Phil Spector has produced hits in this legendary music industry building, a long-time home to famous music publishers and arrangers.

6 Condé Nast Building

The 48-story skyscraper opened in 2000 to house this magazine empire is a sign of the resurgence of Times Square.

7 New 42nd Street

With the renovation of the New Amsterdam Theater in the 1990s, 42nd Street took a dramatic up-turn. The New 42nd Street Studios and several theaters now line the block.

8 Madame Tussaud's, New York

George Washington, Fergie, and Madonna are among the wax inhabitants of 42nd Street's new tenant. The museum has exterior glass elevators and a huge hand holding the illuminated sign.

9 Port Authority Bus Terminal

One of the busiest mass transit terminals in the world, Port Authority is used by nearly 60 million commuters and bus passengers every year.

10 Off-Broadway

Before the rest of 42nd Street was rejuvenated, this block between 9th and 10th Avenues was resurrected by Off-Broadway companies needing inexpensive homes. New plays are premiered at Playwrights Horizons, one of the better known tenants.

Theater District

It was the move by the Metropolitan Opera House to Broadway in 1883 that first drew lavish theaters and restaurants to this area. In the 1920s, movie palaces added the glamour of neon to Broadway. After World War II, the popularity of movies waned and sleaze replaced glitter. Now a redevelopment program has brought the public and bright lights back to this area.

Left **Lyceum** Center **Hilton Theater** Right **Hudson Theater**

🔟 Theaters

1 Lyceum
The oldest playhouse boasts a vaulted ceiling, murals, and elaborate plasterwork. Often used as an auxiliary for Lincoln Center *(see p139)*. 🚇 *149–157 West 45th Street • Map J3*

2 New Victory Theater
Built for Oscar Hammerstein in 1900, this had resorted to X-rated films until restored in 1995 to present family entertainment. 🚇 *209 West 42nd Street • Map K3*

3 Hilton Theater
The rundown Lyric and Apollo were combined to form this showcase for musicals in 1998, marking the arrival of corporate sponsorship for theaters. 🚇 *213 West 42nd Street • Map K3*

4 Shubert Theater
Constructed in 1912–13 as a lavish site for big musicals and headquarters for the Shubert Organization. The intimate Booth, opposite, was built at this time. 🚇 *221–33 West 44th Street • Map J3*

5 New Amsterdam Theater
This Art Nouveau beauty housed the famous Ziegfeld Follies. Restored by Disney, it is home to the popular *The Lion King*. 🚇 *214 West 42nd Street • Map K3*

6 Hudson Theater
A restrained façade belies the lavish interior, including an inner lobby with a classical arcade and domes of Tiffany glass. 🚇 *139–141 West 44th Street • Map J2*

7 Belasco Theater
A 1907 monument to impresario David Belasco, who supervised the unusual Georgian Revival design. The rooftop duplex was his personal residence. 🚇 *111–121 West 44th Street • Map J3*

8 Lunt-Fontaine Theater
Originally the Globe (finished in 1910); part of the roof of this venue could be removed to create an open-air auditorium. 🚇 *203–217 West 46th Street • Map J3*

9 Palace Theater
Sarah Bernhardt inaugurated the stage, and playing the Palace became the ultimate assignment. Now restored as a venue for musicals. 🚇 *1564 Broadway • Map J3*

10 Winter Garden Theater
Originally the American Horse Exchange in 1885, this was acquired by the Shuberts in 1910 and remodeled in 1922. Until 2000, it was the home of *Cats*. 🚇 *1634 Broadway • Map J3*

24 *For more New York theaters See pp50–51*

Top 10 Enduring Broadway Shows

1. *The Phantom of the Opera*
2. *Beauty and the Beast*
3. *Rent*
4. *Chicago*
5. *The Lion King*
6. *The Producers*
7. *Mamma Mia!*
8. *Hairspray*
9. *Movin' Out*
10. *Avenue Q*

A Brief History of New York Theater

Oscar Hammerstein

The first of countless theaters built in New York is thought to have been the New Theater, erected in lower Manhattan in 1732. The city's theatrical center steadily moved uptown to the Bowery, then Astor Place, Union Square, and Herald Square, until it settled for good around Longacre Square (now Times Square),
following the opening of Oscar Hammerstein's Olympia Theater on Broadway in 1895. Some 85 theaters were built over the next three decades, many with grand Beaux Arts interiors by architects such as Herbert J. Krapp, and Herts and Tallant, the latter responsible for designing cantilevered balconies that eliminated the need for columns. Impresarios like the Shuberts and the Chanins made theater-going more democratic by blurring the class distinction between orchestra and balconies, using a single entrance for all. As modern theaters replaced them, more than 40 of these beauties have been demolished. Fortunately, the rest have now been designated landmarks.

Show stoppers

Although Broadway musicals are as popular as ever, *Cats* finally closed in 2000. It was the longest-running show in history, having played to packed theaters for 18 years.

42nd Street

TOP 10 Central Park

New York's "backyard," an 843-acre swathe of green, provides recreation and beauty for over two million visitors each year. Designed by Frederick Law Olmsted and Calvert Vaux in 1858, the park took 16 years to create and involved the planting of over 500,000 trees and shrubs, the hauling in of vast amounts of stone and earth to form hills, lakes, and meadows, and the building of 30 stone-and-iron bridges and arches.

Bethesda Terrace
2 Overlooking the lake and Ramble, the ornate terrace and its fountain are the focal point of the park. On the adjacent tree-lined Mall inline skaters often show off acrobatic stunts.

The Beresford apartments on Central Park West

🍴 Refreshments and light lunches are available at the Boat House snack bar; The Boat House restaurant serves gourmet meals.

🌳 Make your first stop The Dairy, a Victorian Gothic building housing the Visitor Center. Ask about the free nature workshops and guided walks.

Rent bicycles, row-boats, and gondolas from the Boathouse, and skates at the Wollman Rink.

Rent horses at the Claremont Stables, 175 West 89th Street.

• From Central Park South to 110th Street & between Fifth Avenue and Central Park West.
• Map D3–H3
• www.centralparknyc.org
• Open dawn–dusk

Top 10 Features

1. Great Lawn
2. Bethesda Terrace
3. Belvedere Castle
4. The Ramble
5. Reservoir
6. Strawberry Fields
7. Conservatory Garden
8. Hans Christian Andersen Statue
9. Wildlife Center
10. Delacorte Theater

Great Lawn
1 This is a 13-acre oval of green lawn. In summer, free concerts by the Metropolitan Opera and New York Philharmonic draw as many as 100,000 people.

Belvedere Castle
3 A 19th-century stone castle atop a rock, complete with towers and turrets, offers peerless views in all directions. Inside is the Henry Luce Nature Observatory with exhibits covering the surprisingly diverse wildlife found in the park.

The Ramble
4 This wooded 37 acres of land is crisscrossed by paths and streams and is a paradise for bird-watchers. Over 270 species have been spotted in Central Park, which is on the Atlantic migration flyway.

The Visitor Center is open 10am–5pm Tue–Sun, and can be contacted on: 212 794 6564

5 Reservoir
The 106-acre lake is rimmed by a 1.6-mile (5-km) running track used by joggers. It is the largest of the park's five lakes and ponds, which include Conservatory Water, where model boat races are held each Saturday.

6 Strawberry Fields
This peaceful garden area *(above)* was created by Yoko Ono in memory of John Lennon, who lived in the nearby Dakota apartments. Gifts for the memorial came from all over the world.

7 Conservatory Garden
An elegant 6-acre formal garden with fountains and beautiful displays of flowering trees, bulbs, annuals, and perennials is at its best in the spring, when crab-apples, tulips, and azaleas are in bloom.

8 Hans Christian Andersen Statue
Children's storytelling sessions are held here in the summer. Other activities for youngsters include nature workshops, a vintage carousel, and a marionette theater.

9 Wildlife Center
This conservation center and children's zoo has three climate zones. The space features a rainforest and over 100 species, including seals, monkeys, and penguins.

Creating Central Park

Central Park was the first landscaping project for Frederick Law Olmsted, who was already 43 years old. Rejecting the usual formal plantings, he created passages of contrasting scenery, calm and pastoral against the rugged and picturesque. Areas for active and passive recreation were separated, and dense raised plantings shut out the surrounding city. The park brought Olmsted high praise and set a pattern for landscapes that followed. He went on to become America's most prolific designer of parks.

10 Delacorte Theater
The New York Public Theater presents two "Shakespeare in the Park" productions in July and August. Free tickets are available on the day, but get in line early. Other free park entertainment includes a SummerStage series of popular music and dance.

🔟 Metropolitan Museum of Art

One of the world's great art museums, the Metropolitan is a veritable collection of museums, spanning 5,000 years of culture from every part of the globe. Each of its specialized galleries holds an abundance of treasures. It was founded in 1870 by a group who wanted to create a great art institution in America, and began with three private European collections and 174 paintings. The present holdings number over two million. The original 1880 Gothic Revival building by Calvert Vaux and Jacob Wrey Mould has been expanded many times. Recent additions include courts with huge windows overlooking Central Park.

Entrance, Metropolitan Museum of Art

🄾 There is a cafeteria, bar, and two cafés inside. The Roof Garden Café is accessed from the first floor.

🄾 If time is short, the European Paintings on the second floor, Egyptian Art on the first, and the American Wing will give you a sense of the greatness of this enormous institution.

Weekend evenings are less crowded and offer the advantage of bar service and live music.

• 1000 5th Avenue at 82nd St
• Map F3
• 212 535 7710
• www.metmuseum.org
• Open 9:30am–5:30pm Tue–Thu & Sun, 9:30am–9pm Fri & Sat (galleries cleared 15 mins before closing time)
• Adults $15, seniors $10, students $7, children under 12 and members free

Top 10 Exhibits

1. European Painting
2. Egyptian Art
3. Michael C. Rockefeller Wing
4. American Wing
5. Robert Lehman Collection
6. Costume Institute
7. Asian Art
8. Lila Wallace Wing
9. European Sculpture and Decorative Arts
10. Roof Garden

1 European Painting

The museum's 2,500 Old Master and 19th-century European paintings form one of the greatest collections in the world and include many instantly recognizable masterpieces. Special strengths include the Rembrandts and Vermeers, and the many Impressionist and Post-Impressionist canvases.

2 Egyptian Art

The largest collection of Egyptian art outside Cairo includes masks, mummies, statues, jewelry, the Tomb of Perneb, and the spectacular Temple of Dendur, c.15B.C., re-assembled as it appeared on the banks of the Nile.

Key to Floor Plan

▨ Ground Floor
▨ First Floor
▨ Second Floor

3 Michael C. Rockefeller Wing

Masks, wooden sculpture, gold and silver ornaments, Pre-Columbian gold, ceramics and stone from Mexico and Peru, and works of art from the Court of Benin in Nigeria are highlights among 1,600 objects of primitive art covering 3,000 years, and three continents.

For more New York museums See pp40–41

Robert Lehman Collection

5 This extraordinary private collection, includes Renaissance masters, Dutch, Spanish and French artists, Post-Impressionists and Fauvists, plus ceramics and furniture.

American Wing
4 Several floors display Tiffany glass, paintings, and period rooms spanning the 17th to 20th centuries, including one by Frank Lloyd Wright.

Costume Institute
6 Women's fashions from ballgowns to miniskirts, and menswear from the French courts to the present day; annual shows draw the crowds.

Asian Art
7 The most comprehensive collection in the West features paintings, sculpture, ceramics, and textiles.

Lila Wallace Wing
8 The Metropolitan has a growing display of art from 1900 to the present day, with works from Picasso to Jackson Pollock.

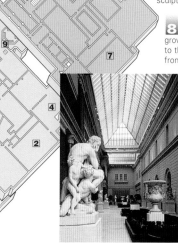

European Sculpture and Decorative Arts
9 One of the museum's largest collections reflects the development of art in Western Europe, and includes architectural settings, French and English period rooms, tapestries, and sculptures by Rodin and Degas.

Gallery Guide
The Costume Institute and part of the Robert Lehman Collection are on the ground floor. The 1st floor includes the American Wing (also on the 2nd), European Sculpture and Decorative Arts, and Egyptian Art; the 2nd floor contains European Paintings, and 19th-Century European Paintings and Sculpture.

Roof Garden
10 From May to October the Iris and B. Cantor Roof Garden boasts outstanding annual displays of 20th-century sculpture. The garden also offers a fine opportunity to enjoy a drink with a peerless view of Central Park and the surrounding skyline.

Left *The Card Players*, 1890 Center *Garden at Sainte-Adresse*, 1867 Right *Gertrude Stein*, 1905

Paintings in the Met

1 Self-portrait
Rembrandt (1606–1669) painted a self portrait each decade of his career. In this moving study from 1660, when he was 54, he portrayed age very honestly.

2 View of Toledo
Darkening clouds set an eerie mood for one of El Greco's (1541–1614) most memorable paintings, depicting the capital city of the Spanish empire until 1561.

3 Young Woman with a Water Pitcher
Painted in 1660–67, this is a classic example of the subtle and sensitive use of light that has made Vermeer (1632–75) one of the most revered Dutch masters.

4 The Harvesters
One of five remaining panels of the months of the year, painted in the 1500s, this is Bruegel (1551–1569) at his realistic best, an example of the use of light and detail that set him apart.

5 Madame X
Part of the excellent American art collection, this canvas by John Singer Sargent (1856–1926) is of an American woman who married a French banker, becoming a notorious Paris beauty in the 1880s.

6 Garden at Sainte-Adresse
This resort town on the English Channel where Monet spent the summer of 1867 is portrayed with sparkling color and intricate brushwork. The work combines illusion and reality, showing why Monet (1840–1926) was considered one of the greatest Impressionists.

7 Gertrude Stein
This portrait, created when Picasso (1881–1973) was 24 years old shows the influence of African sculpture and a shift from the slender figures of his early years to Cubist forms.

8 The Card Players
Better known for landscapes and still lifes, Cézanne (1839–1906) was intrigued by a scene of peasants intent on their card game. This ambitious project emphasizes the somber concentration of the participants.

9 Cypresses
Painted in 1889, soon after Van Gogh's (1853–90) voluntary confinement at an asylum in Saint-Remy, it shows the swirling and heavy brushwork typical of his work from this period.

Cypresses, 1889

10 Autumn Rhythm
This work by Jackson Pollock (1912–1956), the Abstract Expressionist famous for his drip paintings, is part of the Met's modern collection.

For more New York art galleries **See pp42–3**

Top 10 Cloister Sights

1. Gothic Chapel
2. Boppard Room, lives of the saints in stained glass
3. Merode Triptych, Annunciation altarpiece
4. *Nine Heroes* tapestries
5. *Hunt of the Unicorn* tapestries
6. The Treasury
7. The Elizabeth Shrine
8. Virgin statue from Strasbourg Cathedral
9. Altar Angel
10. Medieval Gardens

The Cloisters

Stained-glass window detail

In addition to the medieval treasures in the main building, the Metropolitan oversees a spectacular branch, The Cloisters, built in medieval architectural style and set on four acres of land overlooking the Hudson River in Fort Tryon Park in northern Manhattan. Opened in 1938, the complex consists of elements from five medieval cloisters and other monastic sites in southern France. The collections are noted for Romanesque and Gothic architectural sculptures and include illuminated manuscripts, tapestries, stained glass, enamels, ivories, and paintings. The Cloister gardens are a serene escape from the city. John D. Rockefeller, Jr. (see p13), who gave items from his own collection, is largely responsible for funding the grounds, building, and collections.

The Unicorn in Captivity, 1495

Cloisters Arcades
These arcades are from the Bonnefont-en Comminges Cloister in southern France. They date back to the late 13th and early 14th century.

Annunciation altarpiece by Robert Campin, 1425

🔟 Solomon R. Guggenheim Museum

One of the great architectural achievements of the 20th century, Frank Lloyd Wright's 1959 spiral interior alone would make this museum a must. Solomon Guggenheim's core collection of Abstract art has been widened by donations of several important collections. The museum owns a host of work by Brancusi, Calder, Klee, Chagall, Miró, Leger, Mondrian, Picasso, Oldenberg, and Rauschenberg. Only a small portion, changed periodically, is displayed, as the main gallery is used for temporary exhibits. Sections of the Thannhauser collection, which includes masterpieces by Cézanne, Gauguin, van Gogh, and Picasso, are always on view. The Guggenheim has the largest collection of Kandinsky's works in the U.S.. The Kandinsky Gallery contains permanent displays.

Façade of the Guggenheim Museum

🍴 The café on the main floor is a good spot to rest your feet.

🎫 The best way to see the museum is to take the elevator to the skylighted top and wind your way back down.

Free jazz concerts take place on Saturday evenings.

There is a regular weekly program of talks and tours. Check the main desk for current schedules.

• 1071 5th Avenue at 89th St • Map E4
• 212 423 3500
• www.guggenheim.org
• Open 10am–5:45pm Sat–Wed, 10am–8pm Fri
• Adults $15, students and seniors (with valid ID) $10, children under 12 and members free, 6–8pm Fri donation only.

Top 10 Exhibits

1. *Woman Ironing* (Thannhauser Collection)
2. *Woman with Yellow Hair* (Thannhauser Collection)
3. *Mountains at Saint-Remy* (Thannhauser Collection)
4. *Before the Mirror* (Thannhauser Collection)
5. *Haere Mai* (Thannhauser Collection)
6. *Still Life: Flask, Glass, and Jug* (Thannhauser Collection)
7. *Bibémus* (Thannhauser Collection)
8. *The Hermitage at Pontoise* (Thannhauser Collection)
9. *Black Lines*
10. *Paris Through the Window*

1 Woman Ironing
Picasso's early paintings showed sympathy for the working class. This striking 1904 canvas uses angular contours and a bleak palette of whites and grays to make the subject a symbol of the misfortunes of the poor.

2 Woman with Yellow Hair
In this memorable portrait from 1931, Picasso portrays the supple body and golden tresses of his mistress, Marie-Thérèse, one of his favorite subjects. He employed the continuous arched line from forehead to nose that he would often repeat in the many paintings of his young muse.

For more New York museums See pp40–41

4 Before the Mirror

Edouard Manet scandalized Paris with his paintings of prostitutes and courtesans. This private scene is of a partially undressed woman, an actress perhaps, contemplating her image.

3 Mountains at Saint-Remy

Van Gogh was recovering from an attack of mental distress when he painted this scene in July 1889, one year before his suicide. The subject was the low range of the Alpilles mountains in southern France, visible from his hospital grounds. The bold brush strokes are characteristic of van Gogh's later work.

6 Still Life: Flask, Glass, and Jug

Paul Cézanne's later style, based on the interplay of surface and depth, is shown in this 1877 painting. His mastery of space and depth, as seen in the mottled apples in the foreground, make him the foremost precursor of Cubism.

5 Haere Mai

Gauguin made his first trip to Tahiti in 1891 in search of a paradise untainted by Western culture. This idyllic village landscape *(below)* was painted during that trip; the rich hues and flattened forms show the simplicity he sought. The phrase "Haere Mai," ("Come Here") is painted into the left corner.

7 Bibémus

In Bibémus, the abandoned quarries outside Aix-en-Province, France, Cézanne found a manmade landscape that suited his increasingly geometric style. He painted many variations of this scene from 1895–9.

Frank Lloyd Wright

Though Wright (1867–1959) designed many public buildings, he was best known for residential designs, "organic architecture" that followed the natural contours of the land, and tradition-breaking open interior spaces that have had lasting worldwide influence. The Guggenheim, one of his last projects, was a complete departure. So intent was Wright on his spiral design that when told some walls were too short for large works, he reportedly responded, "cut the paintings in half."

8 The Hermitage at Pontoise

This unsentimental rendering *(above)* of the village where Pisarro lived on and off from 1866–83 emphasizes the use of light and shade. The depiction of villagers was thought vulgar by some painters of the day.

Black Lines 9

Kandinsky wanted the undulating, richly-colored ovals and animated black brushstrokes to elicit specific reactions from viewers. *Black Lines* (1913) is one of his best-known nonobjective works.

10 Paris Through the Window

Painted after Chagall moved to Paris from Russia in 1910, the scene reflects the latest avant garde styles. The Eiffel Tower seen in the distance is a metaphor for Paris and for modernity.

For more on New York's art scene **See pp42–3**

TOP 10 American Museum of Natural History

Few city children grow up without visiting the dinosaurs, the life-size dioramas of animal life, and other natural wonders in this popular museum patronized by over 4 million people each year. Since its founding in 1869, the museum has grown to 45 permanent exhibition halls spanning four city blocks, 13 of them opened in the past 10 years. Holdings include 30 million specimens and cultural artifacts, many unique in the world. Newer exhibition areas such as the Hall of Biodiversity, the renovated Fossil Halls, and the Rose Center (see pp36–7), bring constantly updated research to visitors through multimedia installations.

Museum seen from 77th Street

○ If you don't mind the crowds, eat at the lower-level food court, or one of the three cafés.

○ Don't miss the great dinosaurs and African mammals, or the fabulous collection of minerals and gems.

Join a free tour of the museum's highlights or enjoy free jazz concerts on the first Friday of each month.

- Central Park West, between 77th and 81sts
- Map F2
- 212 769 5100
- www.amnh.org
- Open 10am–5:45pm daily; Rose Center open until 8:45pm on Fri
- Adults $13, students and seniors $10, children $7.50, members free
- For advance tickets for the Space Show call 212 769 5200.

Top 10 Exhibits

1. Dinosaurs and Fossils
2. Mammals
3. Ocean Life
4. Hall of Biodiversity
5. Hall of Asian Peoples
6. Hall of African Peoples
7. Meteorites, Minerals, and Gems
8. Northwest Coast Indians
9. Human Biology and Evolution
10. Birds of the World

2 Mammals

Dramatic dioramas of life-size animals are divided by continents and shown in accurate natural habitats. The wildlife ranges from colossal African elephants to endangered Asian species such as lions and leopards.

Key to Floor Plan

	First Floor
	Second Floor
	Third Floor
	Fourth Floor
	Rose Center

3 Ocean Life

The Milstein Hall of Ocean Life explores the waters of the earth and their inhabitants in skillful dioramas of ocean life. The hall is presided over by a 94-ft (29-m) life-size model of a blue whale.

1 Dinosaurs and Fossils

The best-known hallmark of the museum, the collection of dinosaur fossils is the world's largest. The giant Barosaurus in the rotunda is the highest free-standing exhibit.

For more New York museums See pp40–41

34

4 Hall of Biodiversity

Opened in 1998 to encourage conservation, the hall contains a rainforest with accurate sounds, plants, and inhabitants. The 100-ft (30-m) long Spectrum of Life wall displays 1,500 specimens from bacteria to mammals, as well as a giant squid overhead.

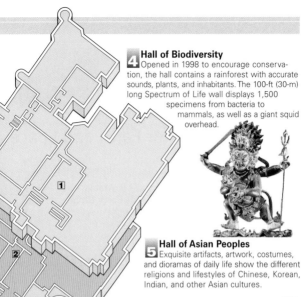

Third Floor includes the Hayden Planetarium (see pp37).

5 Hall of Asian Peoples

Exquisite artifacts, artwork, costumes, and dioramas of daily life show the different religions and lifestyles of Chinese, Korean, Indian, and other Asian cultures.

6 Hall of African Peoples

These depictions of tribes living in various environments reflect 100 years of research. The displays include dwellings, clothing, masks, textiles, weapons, and tools.

7 Meteorites, Minerals, and Gems

Wonders include the 563-carat Star of India, a 596-lb (270-kg) topaz crystal from Brazil, and the Cape York meteorite, 4.5 billion years old and weighing 34 tons.

8 Northwest Coast Indians

This area features Native American totem poles showing the woodworking skills of tribes living from Washington state to southern Alaska. Also on show is a 63-ft (19-m) Haida canoe built in 1878.

9 Human Biology and Evolution

This display of human origins and physical characteristics includes reconstructed heads of early hominids that bring you face to face with your predecessors.

10 Birds of the World

The museum has the world's largest collection of birds – more than a million specimens. The collection is organized geographically, with separate halls displaying dioramas of oceanic, North American, and other birds of the world.

Museum Guide

Enter from Central Park West onto the 2nd floor to view the Barosaurus exhibit, and African, Asian, and Central and South American peoples and animals. The Hall of Biodiversity, ocean life, and minerals and gems are on the 1st floor. North American Indians, birds, and reptiles are on the 3rd floor, and dinosaurs and fossils on the 4th.

Left **Cosmic Pathway** Center **Scales of the Universe** Right **Cosmic Pathway**

🔟 Rose Center for Earth and Space

1 The Building
Opened in 2000 to explore inner earth and the outer universe, the dramatic exhibit building is a huge glass cube enclosing a three-story, 87-ft-wide sphere containing the new Hayden Planetarium.

2 Hall of the Universe
Exhibits, divided into the universe, galaxies, stars, and planets, show the discoveries of modern astrophysics. Digital scales measure your weight on Saturn, Jupiter, and the Sun.

3 Ecosphere
A sealed spherical aquarium in the Hall of the Universe holds a complete ecosystem of plants and animals that can recycle nutrients and obtain energy solely from sunlight.

4 AstroBulletin
This large, high-definition video screen displays the latest imagery from telescope observations worldwide and from current NASA missions.

5 Hall of Planet Earth
Geological samples from around the world and videos explain the processes that formed the earth and continue to shape it.

Hayden Planetarium

6 Dynamic Earth Globe
This globe, suspended above an amphi-theater in the Hall of Planet Earth uses a projection system to re-create views of a rotating earth as seen from space.

7 Earth Event Wall
Reports on events such as earthquakes or volcanoes are broadcast on a screen as they unfold. Other video stations show scientists at work.

8 Scales of the Universe Walkway
Models show the relative size of cosmic, human, and micro-scopic objects, from galaxies, stars, and planets, to the human brain and the smallest atom.

9 Big Bang
Glass flooring around a circular opening lets visitors look down into a multisensory inter-pretation of the first movements of the universe. Explanatory narration is by Jodie Foster.

10 Cosmic Pathway
The Big Bang exits to this sloping 360-ft pathway with astronomical images tracing landmarks through 13 billion years of cosmic evolution.

For more New York museums See pp40–41

Top 10 Features

1. 3D Milky Way model
2. High speed simulators
3. In-depth study of galaxy
4. Advanced star projector
5. Up-to-date planetary data supported by NASA
6. Onyx 2 Infinite Reality supercomputer
7. 3D map of galaxy
8. Continuous calculation of star locations
9. "Flyby" of Orion Nebula
10. Simulations of current events

The Hayden Planetarium

The new Hayden Planetarium, a remarkable advance in the study of astronomy and astrophysics, boasts a highly sophisticated Digital Dome System that is the most advanced high-resolution virtual reality simulator ever built. The space shows take place in a 429-seat Space Theater and are virtual flights through a scientifically accurate universe. Currently showing are "The Search for Life: Are We Alone?" – a trip through space and time to the outer reaches of the cosmos, which explores the potential for life on other planets – narrated by actor Harrison Ford; and "Passport to the Universe", narrated by Tom Hanks. Also showing is "Sonicvision", hypnotic visuals set to contemporary music.

Virtual Nebula

The planetarium presents a virtual representation of every star and nebula in a 3D map of the galaxy. The state-of-the-art, multisensory technology creates such a realistic environment that all sense of being in a theater is lost.

The Hayden Planetarium within the Rose Center for Earth and Space

Following pages **Times Square by night**

The NEW TIMES SQUARE
Chock full o Nuts
RENT
JVC
QUALITY AUDIO AND VIDEO
PALACE

Left **Solomon R. Guggenheim Museum** Right **Frick Collection**

🔟 Museums

1 Metropolitan Museum of Art

It would take weeks to take in all the treasures of this mammoth, ever-changing museum that includes a collection of more than 3,000 European paintings. The Greek, Roman, Cypriot, and Asian halls have had striking new renovations, and the Howard Gilman Photography Gallery is a growing presence *(see pp28–31)*.

2 Museum of Modern Art

Following a $425 million expansion program, MoMA reopened in 2004. The renovation marked the museum's 75th anniversary and almost doubled the capacity of the original building. MoMA has one of the world's most comprehensive collections of modern art, including works by Picasso, Van Gogh, and Warhol. ◈ *11 West 53rd Street • Map J3 • Open 10:30am–5:30pm Wed–Mon (to 8pm Fri) • www.moma.org • Admission charge*

3 American Museum of Natural History

The largest museum of its kind in the world exhibits everything from dinosaurs to Chinese costumes and rare gems. In addition to the planetarium show in the Rose Center, there are nature films in a giant IMAX theater *(see pp34–7)*.

4 Solomon R. Guggenheim Museum

The Guggenheim has expanded its collection with several major donations, including Justin Thannhauser's Impressionist masters, Peggy Guggenheim's Cubist, Surrealist, and Abstract Expressionist works, a collection of American Minimalist and Conceptual art, and the most extensive collection of Kandinsky's works in the U.S. *(see pp32–3)*.

5 Whitney Museum of American Art

The entire range of 20th-century American art can be seen in the permanent collection housed in this striking Marcel Breuer building, along with changing exhibitions of contemporary art. ◈ *945 Madison Avenue at 75th St • Map G4 • Open 11am–6pm Wed–Thu, 1–9pm Fri, 11am–6pm Sat & Sun • www.whitney.org • 1-800-WHITNEY • Admission charge*

6 Frick Collection

The mansion of industrialist Henry Clay Frick, with indoor garden court and reflecting pool, is the setting for his exceptional collection of Old Masters, French furniture, and Limoges enamels. Look for Rembrandt, Vermeer, and Hals in the West Gallery; Holbein, Titian, and Bellini in the Living Hall. ◎ *1 East 70th Street at 5th Av • Map G4 • Open 10am–6pm Tue–Sat, 1–6pm Sun • www.frick.org • Admission charge*

7 Brooklyn Museum
A world-class museum in a fine Beaux Arts building exhibiting cutting-edge contemporary work alongside permanent collections of Asian, Egyptian, African, and American art. There are also Rodin sculptures, and decorative arts that include period rooms. ◎ *200 Eastern Pkwy, Brooklyn • Subway Eastern Pkwy • Open 10am–5pm Wed–Fri, 11am–6pm Sat & Sun, 11am–11pm first Sat of month • www.brooklyn museum.org • Admission charge*

8 Morgan Library
This *palazzo* was designed in 1902 to hold the collection of billionaire J. Pierpont Morgan, an extraordinary assemblage of rare manuscripts, books, and prints, and galleries with changing exhibits. His original opulent study and library are highlights. ◎ *29 East 36th Street, between Madison & Park avs • Map K4 • www.morganlibrary.org • Admission charge*

9 Museum of the City of New York
New York City's history is illustrated with photographs, paintings, costumes, toys, silver, period rooms, and a large collection of Currier & Ives hand-colored lithographs. There is also an exhibition that celebrates the work of Broadway theater composer Richard Rogers. ◎ *1220 5th Avenue at 103rd St • Map D3 • Open 10am–5pm Tue–Sun • www.mcny.org • Admission charge*

Museum of the City of New York

10 American Folk Art Museum
The first New York museum built from the ground up in 30 years, the eight-level, innovative, skylit structure shows off a great collection of this whimsical, all-American art form. Paintings, sculptures, quilts, weathervanes, samplers and furniture are among the items on show. ◎ *45 West 53rd Street between 5th and 6th avs (Branch: 2 Lincoln Square at Columbus Av) • Map J3 • 10:30am–5:30pm Tue–Sun, 10:30am–7:30pm Fri • Admission charge*

Left **Mary Boone Gallery** Right **Paula Cooper Gallery**

🔟 Art Galleries

1 Gagosian

Expect big names and equivalent price tags at this blue-ribbon gallery with two locations, two floors uptown and a Chelsea address with the lofty spaces necessary for exhibiting large-scale art. Damien Hirst, Anselm Kiefer, Richard Serra, and Cy Twombly are among the contemporary artists represented. ◈ *980 Madison Avenue (& Chelsea: 555 West 24th Street) • Map E4 • Open 10am–6pm Tue–Sat • www.gagosian.com*

2 Marlborough

This top-of-the-art-world gallery, representing artists including Larry River, Red Grooms, R.B. Kitaj, and Marisol, has opted for two locations. The Midtown gallery has shown work by sculptors such as Anthony Caro and Jacques Lipschitz. New sculpture and paintings are found at the Chelsea location. ◈ *40 West 57th Street, Floor 2 (& Chelsea: 211 West 19th Street) • Map H3 • Open 10am–5:30pm Mon–Sat • www.marlboroughgallery.com*

3 Mary Boone

One of the art world's big names has deserted SoHo for a sleek Chelsea gallery where work on show still has a downtown edge and talented newcomers share space with established artists. Occasional intriguing group shows, assembled by independent curators, include sculpture, photography, and painting. ◈ *4th floor, 541 West 24th St between 10th & 11th sts (745 Fifth Ave) • Map L2 • Open 10am–6pm Tue–Sat (by appointment only on Sat in summer) • www.maryboonegallery.com*

Contemporary works at the Pace Wildenstein Gallery

4 Pace Wildenstein

Expect the likes of Picasso, Rothko, Chuck Close, or Julian Schnable at this ultra-prestigious gallery showing modern masters of the 20th century and living artists. At 57th Street the galleries are for photographs and prints, as well as fine art. The gallery in Chelsea shows large-scale pieces. ◈ *32 East 57th Street, Floor 4 (& Chelsea: 534 West 25th Street) • Map M3 • Open 9:30am–6pm Tue–Fri, 10am–6pm Sat • www.pacewildenstein.com*

5 Sperone Westwater

This is an excellent place to see some of the most creative work being produced today. The gallery was set up in 1975 to showcase European artists who had little recognition in the US. Exhibitions have included works by many notable international artists, including Bruce Nauman and his wife Susan Rothenberg. ◈ *415 13th Street, West Village • Map M3 • Open 10am–6pm Tue–Sat (open Mon in summer) • www.speronewestwater.com*

The spacious Paula Cooper Gallery

6 The Drawing Center

Formed in 1976 to promote the art of drawing, the non-profit center displays the drawings of more than 1,800 emerging artists, as well as the work of the Old Masters. The Center also hosts monthly readings to present new writing. ◎ *35 Wooster Street • Map P4 • Open 10am–6pm Tue–Fri, 11am–6pm Sat, closed Nov 25–26, Dec 24–Jan 1 • www.drawingcenter.org*

7 Dia Center for the Arts

A trenchant supporter of large-scale works of art since the 1970s, the non-profit Dia Center for the Arts opened this spacious facility in 1987 in a four-story renovated warehouse. The galleries are currently closed for renovation until 2006, but exhibitions continue to be held at the branch gallery in Beacon, NY *(see p120)*.

8 Matthew Marks

This was the first commercial gallery to open in Chelsea, in a converted garage, in 1994. Marks specializes in displaying the work of big-name artists such as Ellsworth Kelly, Willem de Kooning, Lucian Freud, and Brice Marden. There is now a second two-story location in a former knife factory on 24th Street. In this building, new works by painters, photographers, and sculptors are currently being exhibited *(see p120)*.

9 Paula Cooper

This vast, creatively-designed space filtering natural light through a cathedral ceiling is a superb setting for conceptual and minimalist art by Donald Judd, Sol Lewitt, Joel Shapiro, and others. Paula Cooper, a SoHo pioneer, deserted in 1996 to move to the Chelsea district *(see p120)*.

10 Paul Kasmin

Kasmin is the son of a bohemian London dealer and continues the family tradition of taking chances on new artists. He features these artists in group shows that often turn the artists into rising stars. More established names, including those of sculptors and photographers, regularly appear in solo exhibitions. Kasmin joined the popular exodus to Chelsea in 1999 *(see p120)*.

Left **Chrysler Building** Right **View of the World Financial Center from the yacht harbor**

New York Skyscrapers

1 Empire State Building

The Empire State Building (1930–31) is the tallest structure in New York. For 27 years its dominance was eclipsed by the World Trade Center, but the latter was destroyed in September 2001 during a terrorist attack on the city. With an 86th-floor observatory, the building receives some 3.5 million visitors each year *(see pp8–9)*.

2 G.E. Building

Soaring 70 stories into the sky, this dramatic skyscraper *(see p13)*, designed by Raymond Hood in 1931–3, has shallow setbacks that recede into the distance. Part of the greatness of Hood's design is the contrast between the building's height and surrounding Rockefeller Center. ◈ *30 Rockefeller Plaza, between 50th & 51st sts • Map J3 • Closed to public*

3 Chrysler Building

The gleaming, stainless steel, tiered spire of the Chrysler Building adds grace to the city skyline. William Van Alen fashioned this Art Deco classic in 1928–30 as a whimsical tribute to the automobile. The building has a decorative frieze of stylized hubcaps and silver gargoyles, much like the winged radiator caps of a Chrysler car *(see p123)*.

4 Flatiron Building

This 21-story, triangular-shaped building has intrigued New Yorkers since it was built by Daniel Burnham in 1902; the shape was so unusual that people took bets on whether it would topple. The secret was in the steel frame support, which was used instead of traditional heavy stone walls: a precursor of skyscrapers to come *(see p112)*.

5 Woolworth Building

Architect Cass Gilbert was responsible for this flamboyant Gothic building of 1913, the tallest building in the world for two decades after it was completed. The rich terra-cotta ornamentation accentuates the structure's steel frame, which soars to a crown 55 stories above Broadway. The small lobby boasts one of the most luxurious marble interiors in Manhattan. ◈ *233 Broadway, between Park Pl & Barclay St • Map Q4 • Free*

6 Lever House

Gordon Bunshaft's 24-story Lever House, completed in 1952, was revolutionary; it was New York's first skyscraper built in the form of a soaring glass and steel vertical slab. It began the eventual transformation of Park Avenue into an avenue of glass towers. ◈ *390 Park Avenue, between 53rd and 54th Street • Map J4 • Open during office hours*

7 Seagram Building

The first New York building by Mies van der Rohe is this landmark "glass box" with slender bands of bronze amid walls of smoked glass rising from the horizontal open plaza. The materials in the glass-walled lobby by Philip Johnson help blur the division between indoor and outdoor space. The Four Seasons Restaurant, offering American cuisine, lies within. ◈ *375 Park Avenue, between 52nd & 53rd sts • Map J4 • Open during office hours • Free*

Citigroup Center

8 Citigroup Center

The 59-story Citigroup Center, built in 1978, was New York's first Postmodern skyscraper. The rakish, triangular top never served its original purpose as a solar panel, but it did make the building instantly recognizable. An open base on four tall columns and a reflective aluminum-and-glass exterior give the building an airy quality despite its huge size. ◈ *153 East 53rd Street at Lexington Av • Map J4 • Closed to public*

9 World Financial Center

Cesar Pelli's Postmodern complex, comprising four tall towers around a glorious palm-filled Winter Garden, gave the city an elegant business center when it was completed in 1985. In addition, there are public spaces for concerts and special events and an outdoor plaza on the water complete with boat marina and Statue of Liberty views *(see p74)*.

The Winter Garden, World Financial Center

10 World Wide Plaza

The copper roof and crown of frosted glass atop a 48-story tower by Skidmore, Owings & Merrill bring some traditional romance to a 1989 Postmodern building. There is a wraparound arcade that acts as another entrance. The building of the World Wide Plaza complex, which includes two apartment buildings and a large open plaza, transformed a decaying neighborhood. ◈ *Between 8th & 9th avs and 49th & 50th sts • Map J2*

For more on New York's Architecture **See pp46–7**

45

Left **Grand Central Station** Right **U.S. Custom House**

TOP 10 Historic Buildings

1 St. Paul's Chapel
Built in 1767–8, this church has a glorious Georgian interior lit by Waterford chandeliers. The pew where George Washington prayed after his inauguration as president has been preserved *(see p80)*.

2 City Hall
Built in 1802–12, this Georgian building with French Renaissance influences is one of New York's finest. The interior features a rotunda circled by Corinthian columns, opening to twin spiral marble staircases *(see p80)*.

City Hall's imposing façade

3 Trinity Church
This lovely, square-towered church has bronze doors designed by Richard Morris Hunt. Built in 1839–46, the spire, once the tallest in Manhattan, is now dwarfed by Wall Street towers. Alexander Hamilton *(see p48)* and Robert Fulton are buried here *(see p73)*.

4 St. Patrick's Cathedral
James Renwick, Jr. designed America's largest Catholic cathedral (built in 1878) in French Gothic style with twin 330-ft (100-m) towers. The interior has side altars dedicated to saints and holy figures, chapels, and stained-glass windows *(see p124)*.

Trinity Church

5 Carnegie Hall
Philanthropist Andrew Carnegie financed the city's first great concert hall, built in 1891. Major renovation in 1996 restored the wonderful interior bronze balconies and ornamental plaster, and added a museum. Corridors are lined with memorabilia of the great artists who have performed here *(see p50 and p125)*.

6 Cathedral of St. John the Divine
The world's largest cathedral was begun in 1892 and is still a work in progress. The part-Romanesque, part-Gothic building is impressive for its stonework, enormous nave, bay altar windows, and rose window. The seat of New York's Episcopal archdiocese, the church is the scene of many avant-garde musical and theatrical events *(see p145)*.

7 New York Stock Exchange

Built in 1903 and reminiscent of a Roman temple, the façade of this 17-story edifice is appropriately monumental for the building at the center of the U.S. economy. The figures on the pediment represent Commerce. "Black Thursday," the start of the Depression, began here in 1929 *(see p73)*.

8 U.S. Custom House

One of the city's best Neo-Classical buildings, this eight-story structure, built in 1907, features an elaborate mansard roof and fine sculptures, including four by Daniel Chester French. A 1927 nautical mural by Reginald Marsh adorns the huge, oval rotunda *(see p74)*.

9 New York Public Library

This white marble, 1911 Beaux Arts edifice is magnificent inside and out. Imposing stairways, terraces, and fountains inspire awe; Periodicals Reading Rooms invite repose. Events and talks are held here *(see p124)*.

10 Grand Central Terminal

Resplendent after restoration, this public facility from 1913 is remarkable for its beauty; the soaring main concourse is suffused with natural light. Of note is the vaulted ceiling of cerulean blue, decorated with twinkling constellations *(see p123)*.

Top 10 Churches and Temples

1 Zion St. Mark's Evangelical Lutheran Church

Built in 1888, it is a reminder of the Upper East's German past. ⊗ *339 East 84th Street • Map F5*

2 St. George's Ukrainian Catholic Church

A contemporary church built in Byzantine style. ⊗ *30 East 7th Street • Map M4*

3 St. Nicholas Russian Orthodox Cathedral

Five onion domes mark this Russian Baroque church. ⊗ *15 East 97th Street • Map E4*

4 St. Sava Serbian Orthodox Cathedral

Byzantine windows were added to this 1856 church. ⊗ *15 West 25th Street • Map L3*

5 St. Vartan Armenian Cathedral

The goldleaf dome was inspired by the churches of Armenia. ⊗ *630 2nd Avenue • Map K4*

6 St. Elizabeth of Hungary Church

This Neo-Gothic church has a painted vaulted ceiling. ⊗ *211 East 83rd Street • Map F4*

7 Greek Orthodox Cathedral of the Holy Trinity

Built in 1931 in Byzantine style as the seat of the Diocese. ⊗ *319 East 74th Street • Map G5*

8 Temple Emanu-El

The world's largest synagogue was built in 1929. ⊗ *1 East 65th Street • Map G4*

9 First Chinese Presbyterian Church

The stone sanctuary dates from 1819. ⊗ *61 Henry Street • Map P5*

10 Islamic Cultural Center

Ninety bulbs hang by brass rods from the dome. ⊗ *1711 3rd Avenue • Map E4*

Left **Alexander Hamilton** Center **DeWitt Clinton** Right **John D. Rockefeller, Jr. (left)**

TOP 10 Figures in New York History

1 Peter Minuit
Sent from the Netherlands in 1626 to govern New Amsterdam, Peter Minuit (1580–1638) was so disliked by his subjects that they welcomed British occupation.

2 Alexander Hamilton
Revolutionary leader and first Secretary of the Treasury, Hamilton's (1755–1804) business-friendly policies were instrumental in New York's emergence as the financial center of the U.S. He lost his life in a duel with political opponent Aaron Burr and is buried in Trinity Church graveyard.

3 William "Boss" Tweed
The political leader of Tammany Hall, Tweed (1823–78) became the living embodiment of political corruption, kickbacks, and payoffs. It is estimated that he and his associates took up to $200 million from the city. To hide his crime, he did good works, building orphanages, public baths, and hospitals, but died in prison.

5 Jacob Riis
Appalled by immigrant living conditions, Riis (1849–1914), a social reformer, writer, and photographer, used photos taken in tenements to illustrate his stories, shocking the middle class and motivating them to act. His 1888 article, *Flashes from the Slums*, and his book, *How the Other Half Lives*, brought national attention.

6 John D. Rockefeller, Jr.
The largess of John D. Rockefeller, Jr. (1874–1960) helped support housing in Harlem, the Bronx, and Queens, created Fort Tryon Park and the Cloisters, and provided land for the United Nations. The construction of Rockefeller Center (*see pp12–15*) employed thousands at the height of the depression and gave the city an enduring landmark.

William "Boss" Tweed

4 DeWitt Clinton
Mayor of the city, governor of the state, and U.S. senator, Clinton (1769–1828) is best remembered for negotiating the construction of the Erie Canal in 1817–25. By connecting the Great Lakes to the Hudson River, he helped to secure New York's future as a predominant seaport.

7 Fiorello LaGuardia
Considered the city's best mayor, after his election in 1933 LaGuardia (1882–1947) modernized and centralized a chaotic city government, eliminated waste, unified the transit system, and obtained federal funds to help the city. A man of the people, he is remembered for reading the comics on the radio during a city newspaper strike.

8 Robert Moses

Powerful and controversial, as construction supervisor and parks commissioner from the 1930s–1950s, Moses (1888–1981) vastly enlarged and upgraded the city's recreational areas, but he also covered the city with highways rather than develop a public transport system and was responsible for urban renewal projects that razed many neighborhoods in favor of high-rises.

9 Donald Trump

"The Donald" (b. 1946), the flamboyant real estate wheeler-dealer, has left an indelible mark on New York. The huge Trump Place development overlooks the Hudson River, while the cheapest condo in the world's highest residential building, Trump World Tower, costs close to $1 million.

10 Rudolph Giuliani

Mayor Rudy Giuliani (b. 1944) is widely credited with reducing crime, making the city cleaner, and upgrading quality of life for most New York citizens during his tenure, 1993 to 2001. Once controversial for his strong personality, and for getting rid of anyone who disagreed with him, his leadership following the attack on the World Trade Center rallied a stunned city and won praise at home and abroad.

Top 10 Dates in New York History

1 1626
Peter Minuit buys Manhattan from the natives. Beads and trinkets worth about $24 accomplished this ultimate real estate deal.

2 1664
The British take Manhattan from the Dutch. New Amsterdam becomes New York.

3 1789
George Washington is inaugurated as first president and takes his oath of office in Federal Hall. New York serves as the first U.S. capital.

4 1792
New York Stock Exchange opens; 24 traders sign an agreement beneath a tree on Wall Street, and the city becomes a financial center.

5 1876
Central Park opens and the city gains a green center enjoyed by millions every year.

6 1886
The Statue of Liberty is unveiled, becoming the symbol of freedom for millions of immigrants, who form a "melting pot" of nationalities.

7 1898
The five boroughs unite to form New York, the world's second largest city.

8 1931
The Empire State Building establishes New York as the world's skyscraper capital.

9 1952
The city becomes home to the United Nations headquarters.

10 2001
Terrorists use hijacked planes to destroy the towers of the World Trade Center.

Left **Madison Square Garden** Center **Radio City** Right **Brooklyn Academy of Music**

🔟 Performing Arts Venues

1 Carnegie Hall
The world's greatest visiting musicians play in this historic concert hall that opened in 1891 with Tchaikovsky making his U.S. debut on the podium. A campaign led by violinist Isaac Stern saved the building from demolition after Lincoln Center (see p139) was completed in 1969, and it entered its second century with old-world style intact after an extensive, lavish renovation (see p125).

2 Metropolitan Opera House
Lincoln Center's most elegant performance venue shows off glorious oversize murals by Marc Chagall inside great arched windows. The interior boasts exquisite starburst chandeliers that are raised to the ceiling before each performance. The theater presents the American Ballet Theater and many traveling groups, as well as its famous opera company (see p139).

3 Avery Fisher Hall
Thanks to the generosity of benefactor Avery Fisher, the former Philharmonic Hall is now, after early acoustics problems, worthy of the New York Philharmonic, the oldest symphony orchestra in the U.S.. A bust by Rodin of composer and former Philharmonic Music Director Gustav Mahler, on the west side of the building, is one of the best pieces of public sculpture in Lincoln Center (see p139).

4 New York State Theater
The stage was built in 1964 to the specification of legendary choreographer George Balanchine, the founder of the New York City Ballet company, which dances here in winter and spring. The New York City Opera Company is also based here, presenting laudable productions that are far more affordable than the neighboring Metropolitan (see p139).

5 Alice Tully Hall
Built for the Chamber Music Society of Lincoln Center, the hall has a pleasant, intimate feel. Besides chamber and vocal concerts, it is used for shows by the Julliard School students and faculty, many of which are free to the public (see p139).

For more entertainment venues **See pages 24 and 52–3**

6 City Center Theater

The ornate, Moorish-style building with a dome of Spanish tiles was designed in 1924 as a Shriner's Temple. Saved from developers by Mayor LaGuardia (*see p48*), it survived after losing its companies to Lincoln Center, and has become a major venue for touring dance companies. *131 West 55th Street, between 6th & 7th avs • Map H3 • 212 581 1212 • Admission charge • www.citycenter.org*

City Center Theater

7 Joyce Theater

A 1941 Art Deco movie theater was carefully converted to become an intimate home for dance. Small and medium-sized modern dance companies from around the world present an exciting range of work that can't be seen elsewhere in Manhattan. Question-and-answer sessions with the artists follow some Wednesday night performances. *175 8th Avenue at 19th St; Joyce Soho: 155 Mercer Street • Map L2 • 212 242 0800 • Admisson charge • www.joyce.org*

8 Radio City Music Hall

Opened in 1932, the largest theater in the U.S. has an opulent, Art Deco interior. Once a movie palace, it now hosts musical performances and special events. The annual Christmas show starring the Rockettes, 36 long-legged dancers, is a New York tradition.

1260 6th Avenue at 50th St • Map J3 • 212 247 4777 • Tours: 11am–3pm Mon–Sat • Admission charge • www.radiocity.com

9 Brooklyn Academy of Music (BAM)

This stately, Neo-Italianate 1908 building draws city-wide audiences for New York's most avant garde program of international music, theater, and dance, most notably the Next Wave Festival, a fixture since 1981. *30 Lafayette Avenue, Brooklyn • Subway Atlantic Av • 718 636 4100 • Open noon–6pm Mon–Sat • Admission charge • www.bam.org*

10 Madison Square Garden

Home court for New York Knicks basketball and New York Rangers hockey, the 20,000-seat Garden is also used for rock concerts, ice shows, tennis, boxing, dog shows, and the circus. *7th Avenue at 32nd St • Map K3 • 212 465 6741 • Admission charge • www.thegarden.com*

Left **Birdland** Center **Blue Note** Right **Iridium Jazz Club**

⑩ Music Venues

1 Beacon Theatre
Name the stars and they've probably been on stage at the Beacon, where the likes of Bob Dylan, Sting, and B.B. King have performed. The Allman Brothers Band is a regular, and it's always worth checking the current schedule. ◈ Broadway at 74th St • Map G2 • Open 1 hour before show • Admission charge

2 Village Vanguard
Since 1935, this basement club has featured a "who's who" of jazz. The early years were eclectic, launching folk singers like Harry Belafonte. Since the 1950s it has been all jazz. ◈ 178 7th Avenue South • Map M3 • Open 8pm–late • Cover charge

Jackie McLean at the Vanguard

3 Birdland
Another legend, although no longer in the location opened by Charlie Parker in 1949. After ups and downs, the club is ensconced near Times Square in new quarters built in three tiers to ensure good sightlines. The food is decent, and big bands play from Tuesday to Sunday. ◈ 315 West 44th Street, between 8th & 9th avs • Map J2 • Open 5pm–3am Mon–Sun • Cover charge

4 Blue Note
Tony Bennett, Natalie Cole, and Ray Charles have all played this Greenwich Village venue. The emphasis is on jazz, but blues, Latin, R&B, soul, and big band also feature. ◈ 131 West 3rd Street, between MacDougal St & 6th Av • Map N3 • Open 7pm–2am Sun–Thu, 7pm–4am Fri & Sat • Admission & cover charge

5 S.O.B.s
The initials stand for Sounds of Brazil, but the music ranges from African to reggae via soul or jazz. The beat is contagious, and the dance floor gets crowded. Monday is salsa night. ◈ 204 Varick Street at Houston St • Map N3 • Opening times vary • Cover charge

6 Jazz Standard
This stylish club has first-rate acoustics and plays traditional to avant garde music. The loft restaurant, Blue Smoke, is recommended. ◈ 116 East 27th St, between Park Av 5th & Lexington Av • Map L4 • Open 7pm–3am Tue–Sat (from 6pm Sun) • Admission charge

7 Iridium Jazz Club
A fine follow-up to a Lincoln Center performance, Iridium has funky decor, good food, a varied wine list, and excellent established and new jazz groups. The great guitarist Les Paul plays here Monday nights. ◈ 1650 Broadway at 51st St • Map J3 • Open 7pm–2am Fri–Sat, 5pm–midnight Sun–Thu • Admission charge

8 Joe's Pub
This swanky oasis attached to the Public Theater hosts an eclectic range of well-known and emerging artists, from jazz to rock, hip hop, and lounge. A DJ usually finishes the night. ✆ *425 Lafayette Street, between East 8th and East 4th sts • Map N4 • Open 6pm–4am daily • Admission & cover charge*

9 Knitting Factory
This multilevel complex has four bars and four performance spaces, the variety drawing an eclectic crowd to TriBeCa. The café and the bars, serving microbrew beers, are popular spots. ✆ *74 Leonard Street, between Broadway & Church St • Map P3 • Open 6pm–4am daily • Admission charge*

10 Bowery Ballroom
The opening of Bowery Ballroom in 1998 helped spearhead a Lower East Side renaissance. Thanks to a former life as a vaudeville hall (and shoe store), the spacious venue boasts great acoustics and sightlines. Well-known touring acts, mid-scale indie rockers, and local bands are featured. ✆ *6 Delancey St, between Bowery and Chrystie St • Map N4 • Opening times vary • Admission charge*

Top 10 Dance Clubs

1 Avalon
The former Limelight is a hip club in a converted church. ✆ *660 Sixth Avenue • Map L3*

2 Coral Room
No pretension, and a 35-ft (11-m) aquarium featuring mer-people. ✆ *512 West 29th Street • Map L2*

3 Lotus
A mix of dining room, bars, lounges, and dance floor. ✆ *409 West 14th Street • Map L2*

4 Crobar
Built from scratch, this mega club is an offshoot of a Miami hotspot. ✆ *530 West 28th Street • Map L2*

5 Marquee
Tough to get in if you're not with a model – but worth it. House and hip hop. ✆ *289 Tenth Avenue • Map L2*

6 Copacabana
Serious dancers come to one of the best clubs for Latin music from Tuesday to Saturday. No sneakers. ✆ *560 West 34th St • Map K2*

7 Roxy
Star D.J.s make this a late-night favorite; Saturday brings queens, Wednesday is roller skating night. ✆ *515 West 18th Street • Map M2*

8 Don Hill's
Celebs and cross-dressers join the throngs at this dark SoHo dive with D.J.s or live bands. ✆ *511 Greenwich Street • Map P3*

9 Cielo
The beautiful set come for soulful and deep house. ✆ *18 Little West 12th St • Map M2*

10 Discotheque
Eighties decor and a great sound system attract party-loving club kids. ✆ *17 West 19th Street • Map L3*

Left **Mark's Bar** Center **McSorley's Ale House** Right **Monkey Bar**

🔟 Bars and Lounges

1 King Cole Bar and Lounge

Maxfield Parrish's famous mural of Old King Cole, rich mahogany paneling, and sumptuous seating set the stage for New York's most famous hotel bar, which has only been admitting women since 1950. Lush, luxurious, and very expensive, the soft piano music sets a mood that makes it easy to clinch a deal or spark a romance.
⊗ *St. Regis Hotel, 2 East 55th Street, between 5th and Madison avs • Map H4 • 212 753 4500*

King Cole bar

2 44 at the Royalton

Located in the heart of Manhattan's Midtown, this chic bar and restaurant is situated in the lobby of the Royalton Hotel. The interior boasts the sleek lines of Phillippe Starck's Postmodern interior designs, and this, combined with an air of total luxury, makes it a highly sought-after bar. ⊗ *Royalton, 44 West 44th St • Map J3 • 212 944 8844*

3 Monkey Bar

A sophisticated spot with a whimsical theme – monkey murals and light fixtures, even a Purple Monkey cocktail. A long-time favorite recently restored, the bar attracts a well-heeled, well-dressed crowd.
⊗ *Hotel Elysee, 60 East 54th Street, between Madison and Park avs • Map J4 • 212 838 2600*

4 Flute

Proudly stocking 100 types of champagne, several of which are available by the glass, this former speakeasy successfully blends high-end opulence and a sumptuous menu with a romantic atmosphere and friendly service.
⊗ *205 West 54th Street, between 7th Av and Broadway • Map H3 • 212 265 5169*

5 Campbell Apartment

This is a gem hidden in Grand Central Terminal. These richly paneled, former offices of 1920s railroad tycoon John W. Campbell feature leaded glass, a beautiful painted ceiling, and a carved wood balcony, all inspired by a Florentine palazzo. Single-malt scotches or vintage wines enjoyed with a good cigar are appropriate choices to complement this setting.
⊗ *West balcony, Grand Central Terminal, 15 Vanderbilt Avenue at 42nd St • Map J4 • 212 953 0409*

6 Pen-Top Bar and Terrace

There are few places in Manhattan to be outdoors and enjoy a city view, hence the popularity of this chic bar. It has peerless night-time panoramas of the city from the 23rd floor terrace or the glass-walled bar but you'll pay a high price for the privilege. However, entranced patrons don't seem to mind. ◈ Peninsula Hotel, 700 Fifth Avenue at 55th St • Map H3 • 212 956 2888

7 Rhône
Deep in Manhattan's west-side meatpacking district lies this revamped former garage, now an industrial-edged yet sophisticated wine bar. Its extensive wine list specializes in the reds and whites of France's Rhône Valley and is complemented by a rich menu that includes *foie gras*, truffle risotto, and charcuterie. ◈ 63 Gansevoort Street at Greenwich St • Map M2 • 212 367 8440

8 Boathouse Bar
Watch the sun set and the lights come on in the surrounding skyline at this outdoor bar beside the lake in Central Park, a location worthy of a movie set. The setting is particularly romantic on warm nights when rowboats and gondolas glide by. ◈ Central Park near East 72nd St • Map G2 • 212 517 2233

Park View at the Boathouse

9 Double Happiness
The cavernous Double Happiness bar situated in the heart of Chinatown is a union of Italian and Chinese cultures exemplified by the special house drink, a Green Tea Martini. The clientele reflects the neighborhood, but the choice of music is far more wide-ranging, including old jazz, soul, funk, 80s Chinese pop, and trip-hop drum and bass. ◈ 173 Mott Street at Broome St • Map P4 • 212 941 1282

10 Ñ
Head for this out-of-the-way block in SoHo to discover an absolute gem: a raffish bar with polka dot walls, reasonably priced drinks, and Spanish tapas to be enjoyed with a choice of sherries, fruity sangria, or Spanish wines. Flamenco music adds to the atmosphere. Get there early to get a seat: this place is small and popular. ◈ 33 Crosby Street, between Broome and Grand sts • Map P4 • 212 219 8856

Left **Danny's Skylight Room** Center **Chicago City Limits** Right **Stand Up New York**

🔟 Cabarets

Look around the Algonquin, too, a hotel famous for the "round table" of writers who met here. ⊗ *Algonquin Hotel, 59 West 44th Street, between 5th & 6th avs • Map J3 • Cover charge*

1 Café Carlyle

Chic and classy Café Carlyle is New York at its best and is well worth the steep cover charge; Bobby Short can be seen here, and Woody Allen is often part of Monday night jam sessions. Bemelmans Bar features pianists like Barbara Carroll, and a cheaper tab. ⊗ *Carlyle Hotel, 35 East 76th Street at Madison Av • Map G4 • Cover charge*

2 Café Pierre

An elegant setting for the talented singer-pianist Kathleen Landis and occasional guests, performing Broadway and pop favorites. The food, while pricey, is first rate. ⊗ *Pierre Hotel, 5th Avenue at 61st Street • Map H3 • No cover*

The Oak Room

3 The Oak Room

Settle into a banquette and look forward to top entertainers like Maureen McGovern or Julie Wilson. The repertoires usually favor American classics, such as Gershwin, Berlin, or Cole Porter.

4 Don't Tell Mama

No telling who will be at this fun spot in the Theater District – singers, comics, or magicians. There are no big names, and abilities range from amateur to destined-for-stardom. Sometimes even the waiters get into the act. ⊗ *343 West 46th Street, between 8th & 9th avs • Map J2 • Cover charge*

5 Feinstein's at the Regency

This is a swank spot to hear artists like guitarist John Pizzarelli, as well as Grammy-nominated vocalist and song writer, co-owner Feinstein. ⊗ *Regency Hotel, 540 Park Avenue at 61st St • Map H4 • Cover charge*

6 Café Sabarsky

On Thursday nights, this Viennese confection becomes the city's most beautiful and atmospheric setting for contemporary cabaret. Shows are at 9pm; a *prix-fixe* dinner is available at 7pm. Check for current dates and reserve tickets at the museum. ⊗ *Neue Galerie, 1048 5th Avenue at 86th Street • Map F3 • No cover*

7 Danny's Skylight Room

Inside this Thai restaurant in the Theater District, there's no quibbling with the entertainment on stage, from mellow jazz to Broadway favorites. Old timer Blossom Dearie is often featured. ◈ 346 West 46th Street, between 8th & 9th avs • Map J2 • Usually a cover charge

8 The Hideaway Room @ Helen's

Refurbished restaurant, cabaret, and lively piano bar with singing waitstaff. The venue books award-winning cabaret performers with an emphasis on comedy. ◈ 169 8th Avenue, between 18th & 19th sts • Map L3 • Cover charge

The Duplex

9 The Duplex

The oldest cabaret in town features entertainment from early versions of *Nunsense* or *Mark Twain Tonight*, to singers, comedians, drag diva Lady Bunny, or the troupe Funny Gay Males. The raucous shows attract straight and gay. ◈ 61 Christopher Street at 7th Av South • Map N3 • Cover charge

10 Reprise Room at Dillons

The ambience here is reminiscent of a 1950s nightclub, and it attracts cabaret enthusiasts and evokes a warm vibe. Open mix nights are popular, when you can bring your own prerecorded music, or sheet music for the in-house musician. ◈ Dillons Restaurant, 245 West 54th Street • Map J2 • Admission charge

Top 10 Comedy Clubs

1 The Comic Strip Live
A leading venue for up-and-comers; Eddie Murphy and Jerry Seinfeld are alumni. ◈ 1568 2nd Avenue • Map E4

2 Caroline's Comedy Club
In the heart of the theater district, Caroline's features big names as well as beginners. ◈ 1626 Broadway • Map J3

3 Dangerfield's
One of the oldest and best; owner Dangerfield sometimes tries out material here. ◈ 1118 1st Avenue • Map G5

4 Gotham Comedy Club
An intimate setting with comics from Comedy Central and other shows. ◈ 34 West 22nd Street • Map L3

5 Comedy Cellar
Everyone from Robin Williams to Ice T has appeared in this Village landmark. ◈ 117 MacDougal Street • Map N3

6 Boston Comedy Club
Another cellar spot with up to ten acts per night. ◈ 82 West 3rd Street • Map N3

7 Stand-up New York
Novices and pros feature in this intimate space. ◈ 236 West 78th Street • Map F2

8 NY Comedy Club
Top NYC comics and a low cover charge. Two rooms of stand-up. ◈ 241 East 24th St • Map L4

9 Upright Citizens Brigade Theater
One UCBT founder is now a Saturday Night Live regular. ◈ 307 West 26th Street • Map L2

10 Chicago City Limits Theater
Timely improvization in this long-running review. ◈ 318 West 53rd Street • Map H2

Left **Carriage rides through Central Park** Right **Staten Island Ferry**

🔟 Romantic Settings

1 Carriage Ride through Central Park

The horse-drawn hansom cabs lined up at the edge of Central Park are romance personified. The driver, appropriately attired in fancy dress and top hat, will help you up as you nestle in for a 20-minute trot past park landmarks *(see pp26–7)*.

2 Dinner at the River Café

The Manhattan skyline is never more dazzling than when seen from this barge restaurant just across the East River in Brooklyn. The food is worthy of the setting; the package is worth the price *(see p157)*.

River Café, nestling beneath Brooklyn Bridge

3 View from the Empire State Building at Twilight

It has been the setting for dozens of romantic movies and countless proposals have taken place here. At dusk you can watch the sun set over the city as a million lights go on in its towers *(see pp8–9)*.

4 Drinks at the Top of the Tower

The 26th floor of this Art Deco landmark building affords unsurpassed views of the city lights and the East River from its wrap-around terraces. Order champagne and enjoy the scene and each other. ⊛ *Beekman Tower Hotel, 3 Mitchell Place at 1st Av & 49th St • Map J5*

5 Gondola Ride on Central Park Lake

Relax aboard the authentic, Venetian gondola as you glide out on the water and revel in the beauty of the park reflected in the lake and the city buildings ringing the park like a crown – the gondolier may break into song. ⊛ *Loeb Boat House, Central Park at East 74th St • Map G3 • Charge*

6 Walk in the Cloister Gardens

Away from the city's clatter, this branch of the Met is an oasis of serene beauty, a chance to glory in the past while planning the future. More than 250 kinds of plant grown in the Middle Ages are found in these gardens. The Trie Cloister features plants shown in the Unicorn Tapestries *(see p31)*.

 For more special days out in New York See pp62–3

7 Dinner at One if by Land...

A restored 18th-century Greenwich Village carriage house, candlelight, and soft piano music make for Manhattan's most seductive setting. *17 Barrow Street, between 7th Av 5th & West 4th St • Map N3 • 212 228 0822 • www.oneifbyland.com*

8 Staten Island Ferry Ride

Stand on the top deck to watch Manhattan's skyscrapers recede as you sail past Liberty, Ellis, and Governors Islands. Take the car deck coming home for close-up photos of the skyline *(see p155)*. *Whitehall Terminal, Whitehall and South sts • Map R4 • Boats every 15mins–1 hr, 24 hours daily • Free*

9 Brooklyn Bridge Stroll

A classic experience, the walk across the Brooklyn Bridge yields thrilling vistas of city skyscrapers through the intricate bridge cable work. Bring the camera to record unparalleled views. *The bridge begins behind City Hall, Broadway and Park Row • Map Q4*

10 Concert at St. Paul's Chapel

Just to walk into this chapel, New York's oldest public building, is to enter a world of grace and reverent serenity. The concerts held on Mondays at 1pm offer a chance for visitors to revel in the beauty of the setting and the music *(see p80)*.

Top 10 City Oases

1 Samuel Paley Plaza
Respite from Midtown bustle with its own waterfall. *3 East 53rd Street • Map J4*

2 Greenacre Park
A "vest pocket" park donated by the daughter of John D. Rockefeller, Jr. *217–21 East 51st Street • Map J4*

3 Bryant Park
A swath of green with formal plantings behind the Public Library. *6th Avenue, between 41st & 42nd sts • Map K3*

4 Metropolitan Museum Roof Terrace
Have a drink or just admire the prime views of Central Park and city towers beyond. *Fifth Avenue and 82nd Street • Map F3*

5 Conservatory Garden
Three formal gardens inside Central Park. *105th Street and 5th Avenue • Map D4*

6 Theodore Roosevelt Park
A shady patch of green behind the American Museum of Natural History. *Columbus Avenue, between 77th & 81st sts • Map F2*

7 John Jay Park
Past the playgrounds is a placid seating area with East River views. *East 77th Street and FDR Drive • Map F5*

8 Wave Hill
Former estate with gardens and greenhouses. *675 West 252nd Street, Bronx*

9 Grace Church
A Renwick masterpiece, this beautiful 1846 church is a calm respite in the Village. *802 Broadway • Map M4*

10 St. John the Baptist Church
Sanctuary and Prayer Garden with statuary and fountain. *210 West 31st Street • Map K3*

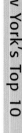

Left **Lesbian and Gay Community Services Center** Center **Big Cup** Right **Next**

🔟 Gay and Lesbian New York

1 Stonewall Pub

Next door to the Stonewall Inn, where a police raid on June 27, 1969, turned into a riot as gays rose up against constant police harassment, the present bar is far more peaceful, a sociable place for a drink or a game of pool.
◈ *53 Christopher Street • Map N3*

2 Christopher Street

The profusion of bars, shops, and cruisers between 6th and 7th avenues is the epicenter of gay Greenwich Village. The crowd is a bit older since so many younger gay men have defected to Chelsea.
◈ *Map N3*

3 Oscar Wilde Memorial Bookshop

New York's oldest gay and lesbian bookshop opened in 1967 before the Gay Rights movement began. It has survived smashed windows and open hatred to provide a center and aid for gays. Current free publications on gay events are available here, as well as videos, music, and gifts. ◈ *15 Christopher Street • Map N3*

4 Bluestockings Book Store

Named after an 18th-century feminist group, this Lower East Side lair is not only a comprehensive source for women's literature but a social center with a café, gallery, readings, and events. Women of all ages and races are welcome.
◈ *172 Allen Street at Stanton St • Map N5*

5 Lesbian and Gay Community Services Center

A nucleus of the gay community, headquarters for organizations and event notices, active in public education, health, and emotional counseling, and center for social events, the Center also maintains history archives and an extensive library. An informative welcome pack is available for tourists.
◈ *1 Little West 12th Street • Map M2*
   • Open 9am–11pm daily

HX and Time Out magazines

6 Publications

HX and *Next* are weeklies reviewing the club and entertainment scene. Other publications include *Gay New City News*, a newspaper covering politics, health, and arts; the *New York Blade*, a free tabloid; and *Metro-Source*, a glossy lifestyle magazine. *Time Out New York*, a general entertainment weekly sold at all newsstands, has a big section on gay and lesbian events from lectures to clubs.

7 Club Nights
Many clubs have party nights. Sunday nights, for example, are big at Splash, Friday nights at Crobar, Saturday at The Roxy, Sunday at Avalon. The Cock is lively all week. Venues and days change, so consult the press for current happenings.
⊗ *Check listings publications for details*

8 Lesbian Herstory Archive
The world's largest and oldest lesbian archive, founded in 1973, is located in Park Slope, a popular lesbian neighborhood. The volunteer-run archive houses art, books, photos, periodicals, video, and films recording lesbian lives and holds events supporting lesbian writers and artists in all media.
⊗ *484 14th Street, Brooklyn • Subway 15th St, Prospect Park • 718 768 3953 • Open by appointment*

9 American Fitness Center
The muscle boys in Chelsea favor this two-story gym with the latest weights and circuit training equipment and fitness classes. It also offers sauna, massage facilities, and a café serving healthy meals and snacks. The gym actively supports gay causes from AIDs walks to Gay Pride organizations.
⊗ *128 8th Avenue at 16th St • Map M2 • Open 6am–midnight Mon–Fri, 8am–9pm Sat & Sun • Admission charge*

10 Drag Shows
A transgender waitstaff and drag shows in the basement make Lucky Cheng New York's most unusual Chinese restaurant, drawing tour buses as well as gay patrons. Also check out the drag queens lip-synching songs at Lips, performing to a Latin beat at La Nueva Escuelita, and serving and entertaining at Stingy Lulu's.
⊗ *Check listings publications for details.*

Top 10 Eating and Meeting Places

1 Big Cup
The coffee house hangout to meet and greet, day and night. ⊗ *228 8th Avenue • Map L2*

2 Food Bar
The food and the well-muscled clientele are attractions at this Chelsea standby.
⊗ *149 8th Avenue • Map M2*

3 Therapy
Chic two-level lounge with cabaret shows and nightly DJs.
⊗ *348 West 52nd Street • Map H2*

4 G
Trendy lounge with a live D.J., round stainless steel bar, and conversation pit. ⊗ *225 West 19th Street • Map L3*

5 Splash Bar
Enjoy the go-go guys working on the shower stage and erotic videos above the urinals.
⊗ *50 West 17th Street • Map M3*

6 Boiler Room
A favorite East Village cruising destination. Weeknights are mellow, weekends packed.
⊗ *86 East 4th Street • Map N4*

7 XL Lounge
Trendy, soaring space with changing light scheme.
⊗ *375 West 16th Street • Map M2*

8 The Works
Gay Upper West Siders gather here in various states of dress and undress. ⊗ *428 Columbus Avenue • Map F2*

9 Henrietta Hudson
Warm, down-to-earth, lesbian lair in Greenwich Village.
⊗ *483 Hudson Street • Map N3*

10 The Cubby Hole
Cozy, unpretentious lesbian bar where regulars sing along to the jukebox. ⊗ *281 West 12th Street • Map M2*

New York's Top 10

Left **Easter Parade** Right **Feast of San Gennaro**

🔟 Festivals and Events

1 St. Patrick's Day Parade
People wear Irish green for this big day when marching bands, politicos, and lovely lasses march down 5th Avenue to proclaim their love of the Emerald Isle. Millions come to watch and the celebrations last way into the night.
🚇 5th Avenue • 11am Mar 17 • Check press for exact route

2 Easter Parade
Following a long-time tradition, 5th Avenue closes to traffic in Midtown, and New York families in their Sunday best stroll up the avenue, with ladies sporting amazing hats, both traditional and outrageous. 🚇 5th Avenue • Map H3–J3 • 11am Easter Sunday

3 9th Avenue Food Festival
New York's biggest food extravaganza began in 1974. Vendors come from all over and more than a million people jam the streets to sample a United Nations of food from burritos to samosas.
🚇 9th Avenue, 37th to 57th sts • Map H2–K2 • Mid-May

4 4th of July Fireworks
River drives close to traffic and huge crowds come out to see this pyrotechnic spectacular over the East River. Macy's spends over $1 million for this salute to the red, white, and blue.
🚇 East River • Map R3 • 9:30pm Jul 4

4th of July fireworks over the East River

5 West Indian Day Carnival
Brooklyn's West Indian population celebrates its heritage with a parade of enormous floats, lavish, feathered costumes in rainbow hues, and contagious Caribbean music. Street stands offer Caribbean specialties. 🚇 Eastern Parkway, Brooklyn • Subway to Franklin Av • Labor Day (1st Mon in Sep)

West Indian Day Carnival

6 Feast of San Gennaro
The patron saint of Naples is carried through the streets of Little Italy, and Mulberry Street is packed day and night with music, game booths, and tons of tasty, traditional food. Sausage and pepper sandwiches are the trademark of this 10-day event, but there is an Italian treat for every taste. 🚇 Mulberry Street • Map P4 • 3rd week in Sep for 10 days

7 New York City Marathon
An amazing 30,000 entrants run the 26.2-mile (42-km) marathon that starts on Staten Island, takes in all five boroughs, and finishes in Central Park. New Yorkers line the route, cheering and offering water to the runners. Ⓢ *1st Avenue above 59th Street is a good viewpoint • Map H5 • 10:45am 1st Sun in Nov*

8 Macy's Thanksgiving Day Parade
New Yorkers take to the streets and America watches on television as cartoon character balloons, marching bands, lavish TV and movie star-laden floats, and the dancing Rockettes announce the start of the Christmas season. Santa Claus in his sleigh is the last float. Ⓢ *Central Park West at 77th Street along Broadway to 34th Street • Map G2 • 9am Thanksgiving Day*

9 Christmas Tree Lighting Ceremony
America's tallest Christmas tree, festooned with miles of lights, stands next to the skating rink in Rockefeller Center. Trumpeting angel statues in the Channel Gardens and animated windows in 5th Avenue department stores add to the holiday spirit.
Ⓢ *Rockefeller Center • Map J3 • 1st week in Dec*

10 New Year's Eve Ball Drop
Crowds begin gathering hours before, ready to cheer when a giant, illuminated, Waterford crystal ball lowered at midnight marks the official start of the New Year. Other "First Night" events include dancing at Grand Central Station or the Empire State Building and midnight fireworks in Central Park. Ⓢ *Times Square • Map K3 • Midnight Dec 31*

Top 10 Sports Events

1 U.S. Open Tennis Championships
The last Grand Slam of the year. Ⓢ *USTA National Tennis Center, Queens • Aug–Sep*

2 New York Yankees and Mets Baseball
Perennial rivals compete in America's favorite pastime. Ⓢ *Yankee Stadium, Bronx; Shea Stadium, Queens • Apr–Sep*

3 New York Knicks Basketball
Fast-paced games that always sell out. Ⓢ *Madison Square Garden, 7th Avenue • Oct–Apr*

4 New York Liberty
Women's professional basketball. Ⓢ *Madison Square Garden, 7th Avenue • Jun–Aug*

5 New York Jets and Giants Football
Both teams play in New Jersey; tickets are scarce. Ⓢ *Giants Stadium, New Jersey • Sep–Dec*

6 New York Rangers Hockey
Played on ice, requiring speed and skill. Ⓢ *Madison Square Garden, 7th Avenue • Sep–Apr*

7 Millrose Games
America's fastest runners compete in this indoor track meet. Ⓢ *Madison Square Garden, 7th Avenue • Feb*

8 Wood Memorial
Race featuring Kentucky Derby contenders. Ⓢ *Acqueduct Raceway, Queens • Mid-Apr*

9 Belmont Stakes
The last of racing's "triple crown." Ⓢ *Belmont Park, Long Island • 2nd Sat in Jun*

10 New York/New Jersey MetroStars
The growing popularity of soccer draws devoted fans.
Ⓢ *Giants Stadium, New Jersey. • Apr–Oct*

New York's Top 10

Left **Bloomingdale's** Center **Barney's** Right **Henri Bendel**

🔟 New York Stores

1 Macy's

What can you say about the world's largest store? Food to futons, the selection is vast. And Macy's is a major part of the New York scene, from the annual spring flower show to Tap-O-Mania, when thousands of tap dancers converge on Herald Square *(see p119)*.

2 Bloomingdale's

After Macy's, this is New York's best-known department store, renowned for high fashion for men and women. The main floor with cosmetics, jewelry, and accessories is a mob scene, but don't be discouraged; upper floors are more manageable. ◈ *1000 Lexington Avenue at 59th St • Map H4*

3 5th Avenue Department Stores

Bergdorf Goodman, Saks Fifth Avenue, and Lord and Taylor have a full range of well-known brand

Saks Fifth Avenue

clothing for men, women, and children, as well as an upscale selection of home accessories. All have seasonal window displays that make for stylish browsing. ◈ *Bergdorf Goodman, 754 5th Avenue; Saks Fifth Avenue, 611 5th Avenue; Lord and Taylor, 424 5th Avenue • Map H3–K3*

4 Barney's New York

If you have the where-withal, here's the place to find the latest designer labels to please a well-heeled, young and trendy clientele. Their semi-annual clearance sales are legendary and draw hordes of shoppers after chic on the cheap. ◈ *660 Madison Avenue at 61st St • Map H4*

5 Henri Bendel

Set up like a series of boutiques, Bendel's displays innovative, fun women's fashions for glamorous shoppers. The sales staff are particularly friendly. The signature brown and white shopping bag is such a status symbol that the pattern is used for accessories. ◈ *712 5th Avenue at 55th St • Map H3*

6 Takashimaya

In a sleek, five-story Post-modern building, this outpost of the Japanese department store sells clothing, art, linens, *objets d'art*, and furniture. All have Eastern influence, are expensive, and are chosen for excellent design.

Visit the serene Tea Box for bento box lunches and beautiful desserts. ✆ *693 5th Avenue, between 54th & 55th sts • Map H3*

7 H&M

Hennes & Mauritz, a Swedish retailer, was a smash success when the 5th Avenue store opened in New York in 2000. Their secret? Kicky, young designs for men, women, and children at rock bottom prices, creating a look that belies the price tag. ✆ *640 5th Avenue at 51st St; 34th Street and Herald Square; 558 Broadway • Map J3, K3, & N4 respectively*

8 Madison Avenue Designers

The epicenter of designer boutiques in New York used to be 57th Street between 5th and Madison avenues, where shops such as Burberry are still found. But as stores like Nike and Levi's have invaded this territory, the designers, Giorgio Armani to Yves Saint Laurent, have moved to Madison Avenue, where the exclusive shops and boutiques now run from 59th almost to 79th Street. ✆ *Giorgio Armani, 760 Madison Avenue; Yves Saint Laurent, 855–859 Madison Avenue • Map F4–H4*

9 SoHo Boutiques

The 20–30-something crowd does its shopping in trendy SoHo boutiques such as Anna Sui, A.P.C., Miu Miu, and Cynthia Rowley. Shops are concentrated between Thompson Street and Broadway, between Prince and Greene streets, though any block in this area may yield a special find. This is also prime hunting ground for home furnishings at stores such as Portico and Armani Casa. ✆ *Anna Sui, 113 Greene Street; A.P.C., 131 Mercer Street; Miu Miu, 100 Prince Street; Cynthia Rowley, 112 Wooster Street; Portico, 72 Spring Street; Armani Casa, 97 Greene Street • Map N3–N4*

10 6th Avenue Superstores

Between 18th and 23rd streets, the cast-iron buildings that comprised the late-1800s "Fashion Row" are another shopping mecca. Current occupants include superstores like Bed, Bath, and Beyond for homewares, Old Navy for casual clothing, and bargain fashion outlets such as T.J. Maxx and Filene's Basement. ✆ *Bed, Bath, and Beyond, 620 6th Avenue; Old Navy Clothing Co., 610 6th Avenue; T.J. Maxx, 620 Sixth Avenue; Filene's Basement, 620 Sixth Avenue • Map L3*

Left **Coney Island** Center **Central Park's carousel** Right **Children's Museum of Manhattan**

🔟 Places for Children

1 Central Park

Myriad activities for kids include storytelling, carousel rides, bike riding, boating, ice skating, nature workshops, and guided walks. The Wildlife Center is excellent, not too large in size, and the Tisch Children's Zoo allows petting and feeding of farm animals (see pp26–7).

2 Bronx Zoo

America's largest city zoo offers authentic environments for exhibits such as the Himalayan Highlands, African Plains, Jungle World, the Congo Gorilla Forest and the spectacular new Tiger Mountain. All enclosures are easily reached via shuttle trains and elevated rides (see p151).

Polar Bear in Central Park Children's Zoo

3 Children's Museum of Manhattan

Five floors of educational hands-on fun with exhibits like Body Odyssey, exploring a giant crawl-through body; Inventor Center, using scanners and digital images; and a TV studio where kids produce their own shows. Under-fours have their own play area (see p140).

4 American Museum of Natural History

Join throngs of New York parents introducing children to the world-famous dioramas of wild animals in realistic natural habitats and the fascinating dinosaur exhibits. The totem and giant canoe in the Northwest Coast Indian exhibit and the enormous meteorites and mineral rock specimens are also favorites. The Rose Center will intrigue older children and teens (see pp34–7).

5 New Victory Theater

The "New Vic," a 1900 landmark, has been transformed into New York's first major theater devoted to family entertainment. Troupes from around the world offer plays, circus acts, and other diversions to delight young audiences. Pre-performance family workshops with staff and cast are scheduled, offering interesting insights into how a theater functions ⑨ 209 West 42nd Street, between 7th & 8th avs • Map J3 • Open noon–7pm Tue–Sat, 11am–5pm Sun & Mon • Admission charge

6 F.A.O. Schwarz

Expect to be awed by this ultimate toy store selling giant stuffed animals to the last word in action toys. This wonderland of fun was founded by German immigrant Frederick August Otto Schwarz in 1862 and is now the flagship store for over 40 U.S. locations. Kids love looking, but be prepared to be wheeled into a purchase. ◈ 767 5th Avenue at 58th St • Map H3

7 Coney Island/ New York Aquarium

F.A.O. Schwarz

Although a bit frayed since its early 1900s heyday, Coney Island is still home to the landmark ferris wheel and roller-coaster rides, and the long sandy beach and beachside boardwalk. The excellent New York Aquarium, along the boardwalk, is an indoor and outdoor complex where whales, walruses, and dolphins play, and finny creatures range from sharks to seahorses. Worth the trip, this is a great family day's outing (see p155).

8 Tall Ship Cruises

A boat ride in Manhattan harbor is always a thrill, and what better way to go to sea than aboard the 1885 Schooner Pioneer at South Street Seaport? Ninety-minute lunch sails are good for those with short attention spans; two-hour cruises depart afternoon and evening. ◈ South Street Seaport Museum: Pier 16 at South Street Seaport • Map Q4 • Thu–Sun May–Sep • Admission charge

9 The Circus

New York's own non-profit Big Apple Circus, with a delightful one-ring show, pitches its tent from October to December in Damrosch Park at Lincoln Center. Those who want the traditional three-ring extravaganza will find Ringling Bros. and Barnum & Bailey in town in March and April. ◈ Big Apple Circus, Lincoln Center Plaza; Ringling Bros./Barnum & Bailey, Madison Square Garden, 7th Avenue at 32nd St • Map H2 & K3 • Admission charge

10 Children's Museum of the Arts

When little ones get fed up with sight-seeing, bring them to this SoHo stop where children can enjoy interactive exhibits. Those under the age of ten can create their own works of art using paint, collage, chalk, or you name it, and work off energy in the play areas. Under-fives have their own WEE (wond-rous experimenting and exploring) Artists Drop-In section. Children's art from other nations is on show. ◈ 182 Lafayette Street, between Broome & Grand sts • Map P4 • Open noon–5pm Wed–Sun, noon–6pm Thu • Admission charge • www.cmany.org

Left **Upper West Side restaurant** Right **Nobu**

🔟 Restaurants

1 Union Square Café

Danny Meyer's first restaurant has been one of New York's most popular since 1985, loved for delicious fare served by friendly staff in comfortable surroundings. Chef Michael Romano's new takes on American standards include the freshest ingredients from the neighboring Union Square Greenmarket (see p115).

Union Square Café

2 Gotham Bar and Grill

A perennial favorite. Alfred Portale was one of the first with "vertical food," delicious layers so artfully stacked you can hardly bear to disturb them. The new American fare is elegant, and the lofty, columned space is sophisticated and casual. The \$20 three-course lunch is a great buy. ⊙ 12 East 12th Street, between 5th Av & University Pl • Map M3 • 212 620 4020 • \$\$\$

3 Nobu

Reservations are hard to come by for Nobu Matsuhisa's Japanese/Peruvian fusion that produces inspired dishes. Say "Omakase" ("I leave it to you") and let the waiter choose among the surprising and always sublime offerings. David Rockwell's whimsical setting adds to the experience. Casual Nobu Next Door needs no reservations (see p103).

4 Jean Georges

Already a culinary star from his earlier Jo Jo and Vong restaurants, Jean-Georges Vongerichten in his namesake restaurant turns out food that is among the very best in New York, transformed by the French master's delicate sauces and creative combinations. Designer Adam Tihany has created a polished, almost austere, setting that does not upstage the four-star chef (see p143).

5 Daniel

Another luminary of the food world, Daniel Boulud now has a flower-filled, Venetian Renaissance-inspired dining room worthy of his extraordinary talents. Seasonal menus with choices such as roasted squab with spiced pineapple or black truffle-crusted cod are divine. Lunch is a less expensive opportunity to sample the master (see p137).

6 Danube

The chemistry is just right at David Bouley's unusual TriBeCa restaurant, offering light as air, "nouveau Austrian" food in an intimate, sensuous new spin on an old-world setting that includes Klimt-style paintings. It's all so warm and wonderful, nobody wants to leave. Wiener schnitzel and spaetzle never had it so good (see p103).

7 Per Se

You need to call two months in advance to get a seat in Thomas Keller's new restaurant. One of a handful of eateries to receive four stars from *The New York Times*, diners come for the food, service, and views of Central Park. Patrons can also visit the kitchen *(see p129)*.

8 Le Bernardin

Seafood doesn't come any better than at this quietly luxurious French restaurant lauded for revolutionizing the way fish is served in New York. Chef Eric Ripert seems to have no critics. Of course, perfection has its price and you'll pay dearly, but the meal will be memorable *(see p129)*.

9 Gramercy Tavern

Another Danny Meyer success, this is perhaps New York's most unpretentious fine dining. Tom Colicchio's inventive American cuisine is universally praised. No reservations are needed for the less expensive Tavern area *(see p115)*.

10 Four Seasons

Restaurants come and go but this New York institution with landmark decor by Philip Johnson seems to go on forever, and it is always among the top-rated for Continental food. The Grill Room is still the prime place for power lunches, and the Pool Room is a perfect setting for special occasion dinners *(see p129)*.

Top 10 Cheap Eats

1 Lombardi's Pizza

On everybody's list of best-in-town for its thin crust, coal oven pizza *(see p89)*.

2 Salaam Bombay

A top-ranked Indian restaurant with bargain lunch and brunch. ◎ *319 Greenwich Street • Map Q3 • 212 226 9400*

3 The Elephant

Café with Thai/ French fusion menu. ◎ *58 East 1st Street • Map N4 • 212 505 7739*

4 Nyonya

Good Malaysian fast food. ◎ *194 Grand Street • Map P4 • 212 334 3669*

5 Sweet-n-Tart

Asian snacks, dinners, tea drinks, and soups; Tong shui, the house soup, is said to balance ying and yang. ◎ *20 Mott Street • Map P4 • 212 964 0380*

6 Flor de Mayo

A mix of Peruvian, Cuban, and Chinese cuisine; Peruvian-style rotisserie chicken is a specialty. ◎ *2651 Broadway • Map D2 • 212 595 2525*

7 Republic

Lots of noodle dishes and noise at this Pan-Asian. ◎ *37 Union Square West • Map M4 • 212 627 7168*

8 Il Bagatto

Even uptowners head for this East Village Italian with good food and prices. ◎ *192 East 2nd Street • Map N5 • 212 228 0977*

9 La Bonne Soupe

Midtown's best bet for onion soup, fondue, and other bistro specialties *(see p129)*.

10 Pomaire

This cheerful Chilean restaurant is the Theater District's best deal. ◎ *371 West 46th Street • Map J2 • 212 956 3056*

For more restaurants and a key to price categories **See pages 77, 83, 89, 95, 103, 109, 115, 121, 129, 137, 143, 149, and 157**

69

AROUND TOWN

NEW YORK'S TOP 10

Left **Federal Reserve Bank** Center **Federal Hall National Memorial** Right **Battery Park City**

Lower Manhattan

OLD AND NEW NEW YORK *meet at the tip of the island. The city was born here under Dutch rule and became the nation's first capital after the Revolutionary War (1775–83). At the intersection of Broad and Wall streets are the Federal Hall National Memorial, marking the site where George Washington was sworn in as president in 1789, and the New York Stock Exchange, the financial giant founded in 1817, whose influence is felt worldwide. The 20th-century skyscraper era added drama to the skyline. The 2001 leveling of the World Trade Center towers damaged but certainly did not destroy lower Manhattan. Historic buildings, exciting architecture, outdoor sculptures, and waterfront promenades remain unscathed. Numerous museums and galleries add to the area's appeal.*

Battery Park City esplanade

🔟 Sights

1. New York Stock Exchange
2. Trinity Church
3. Federal Hall National Memorial
4. U.S. Custom House
5. Battery Park City
6. World Financial Center
7. Museum of Jewish Heritage
8. Federal Reserve Bank
9. Cunard Building
10. Battery Park

New York Stock Exchange

The present building opened in 1903, and behind its Neo-Classical facade is the financial heart of the U.S. The exchange has grown from a dealing with local businesses to a global enterprise. On the busiest days, over 200 million shares are traded daily for more than 2,000 companies, although the action is much calmer now that everything is computerized. There are 17 trading posts, each with 22 sections of traders handling the stock of up to 10 companies.

New York Stock Exchange

🔊 *20 Broad Street at Wall St • Map R4 • www.nyse.com • Closed to public*

Trinity Church

This much-admired Gothic building is the third church on this site for one of the U.S.'s oldest Anglican parishes, founded in 1697. The church has had notable additions since completion in 1846, including the sacristy, chapel, and Manhattan wing; the bronze doors were donated as a memorial to John Jacob Astor III. Trinity is known for its musical programs, with concerts each Monday and Thursday at 1pm and occasional Sunday concerts by the full choir. Trinity also oversees the programs at St. Paul's Chapel *(see p80)*.

🔊 *Broadway at Wall St • Map R6 • Open 7am–6pm daily (church), 7am–4pm (churchyard); tours 2pm daily and after 11:15am Sun service • Free*

Federal Hall National Memorial

Although the bronze statue of George Washington on the steps marks the site where the nation's first president took his oath of office, the original building was replaced by this handsome, columned Greek Revival structure in 1842. It served as the U.S. Custom House and a branch of the Federal Reserve Bank before becoming a museum in 1955, with exhibits of the Constitution and the Bill of Rights. An introductory video and talks detail the historic events that occurred here.

🔊 *26 Wall Street at Nassau St • Map R4 • Under renovation until 2007 • Free*

Left **New York Stock Exchange** Right **Trinity Church**

4 U.S. Custom House

A renovation in 1994 installed gleaming galleries that circle the grand rotunda of this classic building. It is now the George Gustav Haye Center of the Smithsonian National Museum of the American Indian, with changing exhibits of Native American life, including costumes and fine crafts. Baskets of ceremonial objects, toys, and musical instruments in the research room can be examined and researched further on the computer installed there *(see p47)*. ⊗ *1 Bowling Green, between State & Whitehall sts • Map R4 • Open 10am–5pm Fri–Wed, 10am–8pm Thu • Free*

5 Battery Park City

Several prestigious architects were involved in this extension of Manhattan, a commercial and residential enclave built on a 92-acre landfill created with earth displaced by excavation for the World Trade Center. A 2-mile (3-km) esplanade offers grand Statue of Liberty views. Parts of the complex were damaged by the Trade Center collapse but a brighter future is forecast since the opening of the posh Ritz-Carlton Hotel and the new Skyscraper Museum. ⊗ *Off West Street, Battery Place to Chambers St, bounded by the Hudson River • Map Q3–R3*

George Washington in New York

A statue at the Federal Hall National Memorial *(see p73)* where George Washington was sworn into office is testament to the time the president spent in New York City. So too is the pew where he worshipped at St. Paul's Chapel *(see p80)*, and the museum at Fraunces Tavern where he said farewell to his officers in 1789.

6 World Financial Center

Some of the top U.S. financial companies have headquarters in the World Financial Center, which was damaged in the September 11 attack. The center of the complex is the Winter Garden, with a 120-ft (37-m) atrium, palms and marble steps *(see p45)*. ⊗ *Battery Park City at West St • Map Q3 • Open daily •* www.worldfinancialcenter.com

7 Museum of Jewish Heritage

A memorable experience for all faiths is this chronicle of the 20th-century Jewish experience before, during, and after the Holocaust, told with over 2,000 photographs, hundreds of artifacts, and original documentary films. ⊗ *36 Battery Place, Battery Park City • Map R3 • Open 10am–5:45pm Sun–Tue, Thu, 10am–8pm Wed, 10am–3pm Fri & Jewish holiday eves • Admission charge •* www.mjhnyc.org

Left **Federal Hall interior** Center **Federal Reserve Bank** Right **U.S. Custom House**

Cunard Building

8 Federal Reserve Bank

Although gold is no longer transferred in payments between nations, much of the world's gold reserve remains stored in the five-story vault below this building. All bank notes from this branch have the letter B in the Federal Reserve seal. ◈ *33 Liberty Street, between William & Nassau sts • Map Q4 • Tours 9:30, 10:30, 11:30am, 1:30, 2:30pm, Mon–Fri • Free, reserve ahead*

9 Cunard Building

Brass doors and wrought iron gates lead into a U.S. Post Office in one of New York's grandest interiors; a Great Hall with murals, frescoes and an elaborate domed ceiling. It was once the ticket office for the Queen Mary and Cunard's other great ocean liners. ◈ *25 Broadway • Map R3 • Open 8am–6pm Mon–Fri*

10 Battery Park

Built largely on 18th- and 19th-century landfill, this park at New York harbor is usually visited for Castle Clinton, the 1811 fort that is now the embarkation point for Ellis Island and Statue of Liberty ferries. This welcome swath of green is of interest for its many monuments and statues. ◈ *Broadway and Battery Place • Map R3–4 • Open daily • Free*

A Day Exploring Lower Manhattan

Morning

Begin at **Battery Park** for a view of the waterfront, and look into **Castle Clinton** (see p16), an 1807 fort, to see dioramas of a changing New York. Then visit the **Museum of the American Indian** at the **U.S. Custom House**. Cross to **Bowling Green**, the city's first park, then turn right on Whitehall, and left on Pearl Street for the **Fraunces Tavern Museum**, a restoration of the 1719 building where George Washington bade farewell to his troops.

Head up Broad Street to Wall Street to the **New York Stock Exchange**, where there is chaos on the trading floor. Close by is **Federal Hall** (see p73), where the country's first president took his oath of office. Join Wall Street denizens at a favorite lunching spot, the impeccably French **14 Wall Street** (see p77), between Broad Street and Broadway.

Afternoon

Continue uptown on Nassau Street (a continuation of Broad Street) to see **Chase Plaza** and its famous sculptures. At the end of the Plaza on Liberty Street is the ornate **Federal Reserve Bank** and then Louise Nevelson Square, featuring the artist's *Shadows and Flags*.

Go back on Liberty and turn downtown on Broadway to find **Trinity Church** (see p73) and the **Cunard Building**. End the day with dinner at the Ritz-Carlton's restaurant, **2 West @ Battery Park Place** (see p77).

Left **The Immigrants** Center **The Four Continents** Right **Group of Four Trees**

Outdoor Sculptures

1 The Immigrants
Reflecting the diversity of newcomers to the U.S. from 1855–90, Luis Sanguino's 1973 work includes an African, a Jew, a family, a priest, and a worker. Ⓢ *Battery Park • Map R3*

2 Giovanni da Verrazzano
The first European to sail into New York Harbor in 1524 was honored by fellow Italians with this 1909 statue by Ettore Ximenes. Ⓢ *Battery Park • Map R3*

3 The Four Continents
Sculptor Daniel Chester French reflects 18th-century U.S. views – meditative Asia and exotic Africa to the sides, regal Europe and a dynamic U.S. in the center. Ⓢ *U.S. Custom House, 1 Bowling Green • Map R4*

4 Shadows and Flags
Louise Nevelson's 1977 figures enliven the traffic island they inhabit. The largest is rooted to the ground, others are on stilts. Ⓢ *Between Maiden Lane, William, & Liberty streets • Map Q4*

5 Sunken Garden
The spray from a central fountain covers the floor of the recessed circular garden. Isamu Noguchi's 1960s work suggests rocks rising from the sea. Ⓢ *Chase Manhattan Bank Plaza, between Nassau & Liberty sts • Map R4*

6 Group of Four Trees
Jean Dubuffet's 1972 mushroom-like sculptures hover over pedestrians nearby and bring a reason to smile in this busy area. Ⓢ *1 Chase Manhattan Plaza, between Nassau & Liberty sts • Map R4*

7 George Washington
Designed and cast in 1883, a bronze Washington on a massive granite pedestal lifts his hand from the Bible after being sworn in. Ⓢ *Federal Hall National Memorial, 26 Wall Street • Map R4*

8 Red Cube
Isamu Noguchi's 1967 red, 28-ft (9-m) high, metal cube balances on a corner defying gravity. Ⓢ *Marine Midland Plaza, 140 Broadway • Map Q4*

9 Double Check
The briefcase of J. Seward Johnson, Jr.'s 1982 seated bronze figure contains a stapler, calculator, and an occasional sandwich provided by a passerby. Ⓢ *Liberty Plaza, between Broadway & Church St • Map Q4*

10 Yu Yu Yang Sculpture
This untitled sculpture by artist Yu Yu Yang creates intriguing patterns with an L-shaped steel slab pierced by a circular disk. Ⓢ *Orient Overseas Building, 88 Pine Street • Map R4*

Price Categories

For a three-course meal for one with a glass of house wine, and all unavoidable charges including tax.

$	under $25
$$	$25–$50
$$$	$50–$80
$$$$	over $80

Left **St. Maggie's Café** Right **Vine**

 Restaurants

1 Battery Gardens
This restaurant offers a New American menu with Asian accents, and panoramic views of the harbor. ✆ Battery Park, opposite 17 State St • Map R4 • 212 809 5508 • $$

2 Gigino's at Wagner Park
Gigino's delivers excellent Italian food from the Amalfi coast and dazzling views from the sophisticated dining room and the waterfront terrace. ✆ 20 Battery Place, next to the Jewish Heritage Museum • Map R3 • 212 528 2228 • $$$

3 14 Wall Street
A handsome setting for fine French cuisine. Service is impeccable and there's a convivial bar. ✆ 14 Wall Street, between Broad St and Broadway • Map R4 • 212 233 2780 • $$$

4 Vine
A good wine list accompanies American dishes served in this airy room. The building is an 1898 Beaux Arts landmark. ✆ 25 Broad Street at Exchange Place • Map R4 • 212 344 8463 • $$$

5 Fraunces Tavern
This recently reopened 19th-century tavern is the former home of George Washington. The site features a restaurant and museum. ✆ 54 Pearl Street at Broad St • Map R4 • 212 968 1776 • $$

6 St. Maggie's Café
An oasis in the busy financial district, the menu features American standards. ✆ 120 Wall Street, between Front and South sts • Map R4 • 212 943 9050 • $$$

7 Bayard's
Located in the restored landmark India House. The chef uses the freshest ingredients and the wine list is good. ✆ 1 Hanover Square at Pearl St • Map R4 • 212 514 9454 • $$$$

8 Les Halles
Financial district meets Parisian bistro at this sister restaurant of the Park Avenue spot with celebrity chef Anthony Bardain. ✆ 15 John Street between Broadway and Nassau St • Map Q4 • 212 285 8585 • $$

9 Joseph's
When Wall Streeters require Italian food, they often head for Joseph's. The menu includes linguine with clam sauce and fried calamari. ✆ 3 Hanover Square • Map R4 • 212 747 1300 • $$$

10 2 West
A contemporary steakhouse with French influences. Located in the Ritz Carlton Hotel, with views across the Hudson and Battery Park. ✆ 2 West Street, at Battery Park • Map R3 • 917 790 2525 • $$$

Note: Unless otherwise stated, all restaurants accept credit cards and serve vegetarian meals

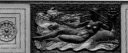

Left **Surrogate's Court** Center **Relief detail, the former AT&T Building** Right **Police Plaza**

Civic Center and South Street Seaport

SOME OF NEW YORK'S *finest architecture is found at its Civic Center, the headquarters for city government. Buildings here span the centuries, from the 18th-century St. Paul's Chapel to the pioneering 20th-century Woolworth Building. Nearby is the famous Brooklyn Bridge, and the old maritime center of the city, South Street Seaport, its piers and buildings now restored as a lively hub of cafés, restaurants, and museums.*

Sights

1. South Street Seaport
2. Brooklyn Bridge
3. Woolworth Building
4. AT&T Building
5. St. Paul's Chapel
6. City Hall
7. Municipal Building
8. New York County Courthouse
9. Surrogate's Court/ Hall of Records
10. Police Plaza

Woolworth Building

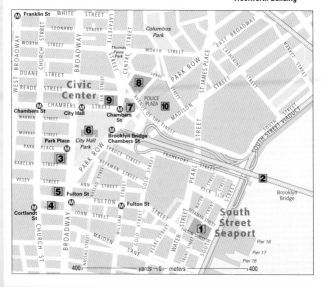

1 South Street Seaport

The cobbled streets, buildings, and piers that were the center of New York's 19th-century seafaring activity (known as "the street of sails") have been restored as a tourist center. There are shops, food stalls, restaurants, a museum with many seafaring exhibits, a fleet of tall ships for boarding, and plenty of outdoor entertainment. ⊗ Map Q4 • Open Nov–Mar: 10am–7pm Mon–Sat, 11am–6pm Sun; Apr–Oct: 10am–9pm Mon–Sat, 11am–8pm Sun • www.southstseaport.org

2 Brooklyn Bridge

When it was completed in 1883 linking Manhattan and Brooklyn, this was the largest suspension bridge in the world and the first to be built of steel. It took 600 workmen and 16 years to build, and claimed 20 lives, including that of the designing engineer, John A. Roebling. It is now a symbol of New York, and those who walk the 1-mile (1.8-km) span are rewarded with fabulous views of city towers seen through the artistic wire cablework. ⊗ (Manhattan side) Park Row near Municipal Building • Map Q4 • Free

3 Woolworth Building

Built in 1913, this has one of New York's great interiors; marble walls, bronze filigree, a mosaic ceiling, and stained glass combine to magical effect. Architect Cass Gilbert also had a sense of humor – sculptures include Five and Dime mogul Woolworth counting nickels and Gilbert himself cradling a model of the building. It set the standard for the skyscrapers that followed in the 1920s and 1930s (see p44). ⊗ Broadway, between Park Pl & Barclay St • Map Q4

4 AT&T Building

Built in 1922, this is a monument to excess but fun to see nevertheless. The façade is said to have more columns than any other building in the world, and the vast lobby is a forest of marble pillars. Close by at 120 Broadway, the former Equitable Building, built in 1915, is of note for another excess: the immense bulk of the building was responsible for the nation's first skyscraper zoning regulations. ⊗ 195 Broadway • Map Q4 • Open office hours • Free

Left **Brooklyn Bridge** Right **Bas-relief caricature of architect Cass Gilbert, the Woolworth Building**

5 St. Paul's Chapel

Manhattan's oldest church was built in 1766 as an "uptown" chapel for Trinity Church and took on added importance while Trinity was being rebuilt after the great fire of 1776. The chapel was modeled after London's St. Martin-in-the-Fields and has been kept as close as possible to its original form. ◎ *209 Broadway, between Fulton & Vesey sts • Map Q4 • Episcopal service 8am Sun • Concerts 1pm Mon, $2 donation • www.saintpaulschapel.org*

6 City Hall

The seat of city government since 1812, City Hall is considered one of the most beautiful early 19th-century public buildings in the U.S. The design, by architects Mangin and McComb, Jr., won a competition held in 1802. A statue of Justice, dating from 1887, crowns the top of the structure. The rear of the building, facing north, was not clad in marble until 1954, since the architects never expected the city to develop further north. ◎ *Broadway and Park Row • Map Q4 • Open for pre-arranged tours only • Free*

City Hall

The "Boss Tweed" Courthouse

The first New York County Courthouse at 52 Chambers Street (completed in 1881) was built by Boss Tweed *(see p48)*, a corrupt politician who spent fortunes on this grand marble monument to himself. The elaborate interior and octagonal rotunda are being restored, though its future use is uncertain.

7 Municipal Building

This building dominating the Civic Center area, straddling Chambers Street, was the first "skyscraper" by McKim, Mead, and White, a 25-story structure completed in 1914. The top is a veritable wedding-cake fantasy of towers and spires topped by Adulph Wienman's famous statue, Civic Fame. The intricate terra-cotta vaulting above the street is modeled on the entrance of the Palazzo Farnese in Rome, and the subway entrance at the south end, an arcaded plaza, is a dramatic vault of Guastavino tiles. ◎ *1 Center Street at Chambers Street • Map Q4*

Left **Interior, St. Paul's Chapel** Right **Municipal Building**

8 New York County Courthouse

Ascend the wide staircase of the 1926 New York County Courthouse (adjacent to the 31-story, pyramid-topped U.S. Courthouse dating from 1933) and enter to admire the marble columned rotunda with Tiffany lighting fixtures. Note, too, the ceiling murals depicting Law and Justice. The hexagonal building has a courtroom in each of its six wings. ◎ *60 Center Street • Map P4 • Open 9am–5pm Mon–Fri • Free*

9 Surrogate's Court/ Hall of Records

An interior inspired by the Paris Opéra is one of the glories of this 1907 Beaux Arts beauty, boasting a magnificent central hall with marble stairways and ceiling mosaics. The façade features statues representing justice, the seasons, commerce, and notable New Yorkers, as well as figures depicting the various stages of life. ◎ *31 Chambers Street • Map Q4 • Lobby open 9am–5pm Mon–Fri • Free*

10 Police Plaza

Constructed in 1973, the city's police headquarters can be found on a spacious pedestrian plaza, a welcome area in a district with very few public spaces. The 75-ton Tony Rosenthal abstract sculpture, Five in One, made of five sloping interlocked discs, symbolizes the city's five boroughs. ◎ *Park Row at Pearl St • Map Q4*

A Walk Through Civic Center and South Street Seaport

Morning

🕐 Most subway routes lead to City Hall. When you come up to street level, walk down Broadway to see the lobbies of the **Woolworth** *(see p79)* and the former **AT&T Building** *(see p79)* and the Georgian interior of **St. Paul's Chapel**.

Return via Park Row, once known as Newspaper Row because it was lined with their offices. Printing House Square has a statue of Benjamin Franklin with his Pennsylvania Gazette. West of the Row lies City Hall Park, where the Declaration of Independence was read to George Washington's troops in July 1776. The park was recently restored and has a new granite time wheel telling the city's history.

A walk along Center and Chambers streets takes you past the ornate **Municipal Building**.

Afternoon

At midday, head east for a seafood lunch at the **Bridge Café** *(see p83)*, housed in a 1794 wood-framed building. From here the East River is a short stroll away, offering excellent views of lower Manhattan.

Spend the afternoon at **South Street Seaport** *(see p79)*, visiting the museum and maritime crafts center, perhaps taking a cruise on one of the ships. Have dinner on Pier 17, enjoying Caribbean fare at the lively **Cabana** *(see p83)*, or New American fare at **Harbour Lights** *(see p83)*.

Around Town – Civic Center & South Street Seaport

Left **Schermerhorn Row** Center **South Street Seaport Museum** Right **Pier 17**

🔟 Maritime Sights

1 South Street Seaport Museum

The city's maritime heritage is celebrated in art, photographs, workshops, and ships. 🚢 *12 Fulton St • Map Q4 • Open Apr–Oct: 10am–5pm daily; Nov–Mar: 10am–5pm Fri–Sun • Admission charge*

2 Schermerhorn Row

Federal-style houses built by Peter Schermerhorn in 1811–12 have restaurants and shops. They will house the World Port New York exhibition. 🚢 *Fulton St, between Front & South sts • Map Q4 • Free*

3 Historic Ships

Seven classic ships, several open for boarding, include the 1885 square-rigger *Wavertree*, and the landmark, four-masted *Peking*, built in 1911. 🚢 *Piers 15, 16, South Street Seaport • Map Q4 • Open 10am–6pm daily • Admission charge*

4 Bowne & Company

Recreation of a 19th-century print shop with working printing presses. 🚢 *211 Water Street • Map Q4 • Open 10am–5pm Tue–Sat • Free*

5 Maritime Crafts Center

Marvel at the skill of woodcarvers at work, creating model ships and figureheads. 🚢 *Pier 15, South Street Seaport • Map Q4 • Open 10am–6pm daily • Free*

6 Pilot House

The South Street Seaport ticket and information center is housed in this pilot house, taken from a steam tugboat built in 1923 by the New York Central Railroad. 🚢 *South Street Seaport • Map Q4 • Open 10am–6pm daily*

7 Pier 17

A pier with three floors of restaurants, food stands and sweeping views of the East River and Brooklyn Bridge. 🚢 *South Street Seaport • Map Q5*

8 Harbor Excursions

The 1885 schooner *Pioneer* offers 90-minute family sails and two-hour cruises in the afternoon and evening. 🚢 *Pier 16, South Street Seaport • Map Q4 • Admission charge*

9 Titanic Memorial

This lighthouse was built to commemorate the sinking of the Titanic – the largest steamship ever made – in 1912. 🚢 *Fulton Street at Water St • Map Q4*

10 Seaman's Church Institute

Established in 1834, the institute is in a stunnning 1991 building with a gallery plus water views. 🚢 *241 Water Street, between Beekman St & Peck Slip • Map Q4 • Free*

Price Categories

For a three-course meal for one with a glass of house wine, and all unavoidable charges including tax.

$	under $25
$$	$25–$50
$$$	$50–$80
$$$$	over $80

Left **Bridge Café** Right **Little Italy Pizza**

🔟 Restaurants

1 Bridge Café
Opened in 1791, this is one of the oldest establishments in the city. Inside the quaint building, there are checked tablecloths, and a surprisingly sophisticated American menu. ☏ 279 Water Steet at Dover St • Map Q4 • 212 227 3344 • $$

2 Harbour Lights
Incomparable views of the harbor and bridge account for the crowds, although the seafood-oriented fare is only average. The sirloin steak is a good alternative to fish. ☏ Pier 17, 3rd level, South Street Seaport • Map Q5 • 212 227 2800 • $$$

3 Sequoia
Nautical décor, a seafood menu, and breathtaking harbor views make this informal American restaurant a top choice. ☏ Pier 17, South Street Seaport • Map Q5 • 212 732 9090 • $$

4 Quartino
Convivial Italian wine bar, with a big selection of wines by the quartino (carafe). The rustic Osteria serves pizza, pasta, cured meats, and imported cheese. ☏ 21–23 Peck Slip • Map Q4 • 212 349 4433 • $$

5 Cabana at the Seaport
A Latin flavor enlivens this Seaport favorite, serving a Cuban/Caribbean menu. Expect pitchers of sangria and spontaneous samba. ☏ Pier 17, 3rd level, South Street Seaport • Map Q5 • 212 406 1155 • $$

6 Heartland Brewery
Pub grub, with a menu strong on seafood. But the real attraction is the selection of seasonal beers brewed at Heartland's own microbrewery. ☏ 93 South Street • Map Q4 • 646 572 2337 • $

7 Cosi Sandwich Bar
Pita bread warm from the oven laden with your choice of fillings, including ham, chicken, or roasted peppers. Part of a chain. ☏ 54 Pine Street at William St • Map Q4 • 212 809 2674 • $

8 Café Europa
Another chain found all over the city, this café offers a selection of hot drinks, soups, salads, inventive sandwiches, and pizzas. ☏ 199 Water Street, between Fulton & St. John sts • Map Q4 • 212 422 0070 • $

9 Red
Wall Street suits and tourists alike can be found enjoying the famous blood orange margaritas at this colorful Tex-Mex spot. ☏ 19 Fulton Street, between Front & Water sts • Map Q4 • 212 571 5900 • $

10 Pacific Grill
A Pan-Asian restaurant serving mostly seafood dishes, including tempura and coconut shrimp. The outside seating area boasts ideal harbor views of Brooklyn Bridge. ☏ Pier 17, South Street Seaport • Map Q5 • 212 964 0707 • $$

Note: Unless otherwise stated, all restaurants accept credit cards and serve vegetarian meals

Left **Police Headquarters Building** Center **Church of the Transfiguration** Right **Food shopping**

Chinatown and Little Italy

THESE TWO ETHNIC ENCLAVES are among the most colorful parts of the city. Each was settled by early immigrants, who preserved their own language, customs, and food in the midst of the new and foreign land. Little Italy has dwindled to a few blocks, but it is still an atmospheric center of authentic Italian food and shops, especially on a warm night, when cafés set out sidewalk tables and the songs of Napoli fill the air. Chinatown, however, continues to grow. More than 200,000 Chinese live there, in crowded quarters. The shops and sidewalk markets overflow with exotic foods and herbs, as well as gifts ranging from backscratchers to fine antiques; and it has been estimated that Chinatown contains an astounding 200 restaurants.

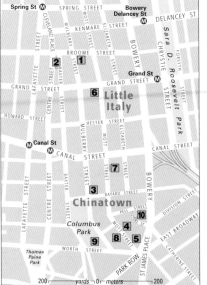

Street scene, Chinatown

🔟 Sights

1. Mulberry Street
2. Police Headquarters Building
3. Museum of Chinese in the Americas
4. Mott Street General Store
5. Mott Street Shopping
6. Pearl River Chinese Products Emporium
7. Eastern States Buddhist Temple
8. Church of the Transfiguration
9. Columbus Park
10. Bloody Angle

Il Palazzo, Little Italy *(see p89)*

fits a wedge-shaped lot. Empty for more than a decade after the department relocated in 1973, the building has since been converted into luxury cooperatives, the Police Building Apartments.
⊗ *240 Centre Street • Map P4 • Closed to public*

1 Mulberry Street

There are many trendy shops on Mulberry Street from Houston down to Spring Street and though Chinatown is overrunning much of Little Italy, the block between Broome and Canal remains strictly Italian. It is filled with restaurants, coffee shops with tempting Italian pastries, and stores selling pasta implements, statues of saints, and T-shirts saying "Kiss Me, I'm Italian." The Feast of San Gennaro packs the street each September *(see p62)*. ⊗ *Mulberry Street, between Broome & Canal sts • Map P4*

2 Police Headquarters Building

After the boroughs merged into Greater New York in 1898, the city's police department expanded rapidly. This 1905 headquarters near Little Italy was the result, a monumental, columned Baroque structure fit for "New York's Finest," with an ornate dome tall enough to be seen from City Hall. The strange shape of the building

3 Museum of Chinese in the Americas

Small but fascinating, this first floor museum, devoted to the Chinese experience in the West, features an exhibit called "Where is Home?," with personal stories, photographs, and poetry culled from the community. Among the topics explored are women's roles, religion, and the "bachelor society." Changing exhibits range from art to the experience of gay Chinese. Books, area guides, and free flyers on cultural events are available. ⊗ *70 Mulberry Street at Bayard St • Map P4 • Open noon–6pm Tue–Thu, Sat–Sun, noon–7pm Fri • Admission charge, free Fri • www.moca-nyc.org*

4 Mott Street General Store

Originally known as Quong Yeun Shing & Company, this is the oldest store in Chinatown, established in 1891. The store was a social hub for Chinese men, who were not allowed to bring their wives to the U.S. under old immigration laws.
⊗ *32 Mott Street • Map P4*

Left **Detail, Police Headquarters Building** Right **Museum of Chinese in the Americas**

5 Mott Street Shopping

Clustered on this block are shops with a wonderful selection of Chinese goods. China Silk and Handicrafts has vases, figurines, bowls, tea sets, and Buddhas by the dozen. Lamps made from attractive Oriental vases are the specialty of Pearl of the Orient Gallery, while New Age Designer makes clothing to order in your choice of jewel-hued silks. Serious antiques collectors should head to the Sinotique Gallery. ✆ *China Silk and Handicrafts: 18 Mott Street • Sinotique Gallery: 19A Mott Street • Pearl of the Orient Gallery: 36 Mott Street • New Age Designer: 38 Mott Street • Map P4 for all*

6 Pearl River Chinese Products Emporium

The largest department store in Chinatown has two locations and a fascinating potpourri of goods for sale. There are Chinese musical instruments, paper lanterns, kites, dried herbs, embroidered silk tops, dresses and pajamas with mandarin collars, purses, dolls, pillows, and sandalwood and jasmine soaps. ✆ *477 Broadway & 200 Grand Street • Map P4*

7 Eastern States Buddhist Temple

Step into the incense-scented interior, where offerings of fresh fruit are piled high, and more than 100 gold Buddhas gleam in

Chinatown's Early Days

The 1882 Chinese Exclusion Act prevented Chinese workers from bringing their families to New York, so the original Chinatown, bounded by Pell, Doyers, and Mott streets, was mostly male and dominated by *tongs*. These were sometimes social clubs and sometimes rival criminal fraternities, giving the old locale its dangerous reputation.

the candlelight. The temple takes advantage of Chinatown's tourist traffic by offering $1 fortunes for sale near the front. ✆ *64B Mott Street • Map P4 • Open 9am–6pm daily • Free*

8 Church of the Transfiguration

Built by the English Lutheran Church in 1801 and sold to the Roman Catholic Church of the Transfiguration in 1853, this Georgian-style stone church with Gothic windows is typical of the influence of successive influxes of immigrants in New York. The church has changed with the nationalities of the community it serves, first Irish, then Italian, and now Chinese. As the focal point of today's Chinese Roman Catholic community, it offers classes and services to help newcomers and holds services in Cantonese and Mandarin. ✆ *29 Mott Street • Map P4 • Open 7:30–9am & 11:30am–1pm daily, 5:30–7pm Sat, 8am–2pm Sun • Free*

Left **Pearl River Chinese Products Emporium** Right **Eastern States Buddhist Temple**

Bloody Angle, Chinatown

Columbus Park
9 Chinatown's only park was created in the late 1890s as a result of the campaigning of newspaper reporter Jacob Riis and other social reformers. It filled a stretch of the city that at the time was New York's worst slum, where Riis reported a stabbing or shooting at least once a week. Though it features more concrete than greenery, the park is popular today, filled with Chinese kids at play, *mah jong* players, and people practicing *tai chi* and martial arts. On the weekends, Chinese fortune-tellers sometimes set up shop in the park. ✎ *Bayard and Mulberry sts • Map P4*

Bloody Angle
10 The name for this sharp curve on Doyers Street was coined by a newspaper because this was the site of so many gangland ambushes during the 1920s. It was a period when the Hip Sing and On Leong *tongs*, groups similar to criminal gangs, were fighting for control of the opium trade and gambling rackets in Chinatown. The *tong* wars continued off and on until at least the 1940s, and their rivalries continue in the present-day youth gangs. ✎ *Doyers Street near Pell St • Map P4*

A Stroll Around Chinatown and Little Italy

Morning

🕐 Take the No. 6 train to Spring Street, walk past Lafayette, and turn down Mulberry Street *(see p85)* for a stroll through Little Italy. Don't miss the old-fashioned food shops on Grand Street, such as cheese specialist Alleva Dairy (188 Mulberry Street at Grand) and Piemonte Co. (190 Grand Street), where two dozen shapes and varieties of pasta can be bought. At 206 Grand is DiPalo Dairy, where you can watch fresh mozzarella being made. Take a break at a classic Italian café, like Caffè Roma, 385 Broome Street, or Ferrara's, 195–201 Grand Street.

Continue on Mulberry to Bayard, and you'll find an introduction to what's ahead, the **Museum of Chinese in the Americas** *(see p85)*. Walk east one block to Mott Street, the center of Chinatown. Enjoy a dim sum lunch at **Jing Fong** or the **Golden Unicorn** *(see p89)*.

Afternoon

Remaining on Mott Street, spend some time browsing the many shops, exotic food stores, markets, and galleries that line the street. Step into Saint's Alp Teahouse, 51 Mott Street, to sample a current fad imported from Taiwan: tall glasses of flavored teas served with "pearls" of tapioca in the bottom.

End the afternoon with a visit to the golden Buddhas of the **Eastern States Buddhist Temple** and have your fortune read.

Left **Street market** Center **Ten Ren Tea & Ginseng Company** Right **Chinatown Ice Cream Factory**

Chinatown Food Shops

1 Street Markets
Canal Street and Hester Street are among the many blocks crowded with outdoor stands selling exotic Chinese vegetables, fruits, and dried foods. Ⓢ *Chinatown, including Canal & Hester sts • Map P4*

2 Egg Cake Lady
Constant lines attest to the talents of Cecilia Tam, who sells the neighborhood's best custard cakes at a little red street stand. Ⓢ *Mott Street at Mosco St • Map P4*

3 Kamwo Herb and Tea
One of the better-known shops offering Chinese herbs said to cure anything from arthritis to impotence. Ginseng is available in teas or supplement form. Ⓢ *209–11 Grand Street • Map P4*

4 Fay Da Bakery
Sample a delicious soft bun filled with roasted pork or beef for less than $1, then try almond cookies, red bean cakes, custard tarts, or cream buns for dessert. Ⓢ *83 Mott Street at Canal St • Map P4*

5 Ten Ren Tea & Ginseng Company
An array of golden canisters holds many varieties of Chinese teas; knowledgeable clerks will explain the properties of each and how to brew them properly. Ⓢ *75 Mott Street • Map P4*

6 Kam Man Food Products
One of the largest food emporiums in Chinatown stocks tonics, teas, jellies, ginseng, vegetables of every shape, and row upon row of sauces. Ⓢ *200 Canal Street • Map P4*

7 Dynasty Supermarket
This calm, modern market is in marked contrast to the raucous street scene, a place for comfortable browsing where all the strange vegetables you've seen elsewhere are neatly labeled. Ⓢ *68 Elizabeth Street • Map P4*

8 Kam Kuo Food Corp.
Another wide selection of foods and an upstairs laden with woks, kitchen tools, steamers, teapots, and other utensils. Ⓢ *7 Mott Street • Map P4*

9 May May Gourmet Chinese Bakery
On one of the streets of old Chinatown is this cheerful, modern shop best known for dim sum, to be enjoyed on the spot or to go. Ⓢ *35 Pell Street • Map P4*

10 Chinatown Ice Cream Factory
Ginger, lychee, pumpkin, mango, and red bean are among the flavors that can be sampled at this popular dessert stop, a favorite with young visitors. Ⓢ *65 Bayard Street at Mott St • Map P4*

For more on New York shopping See p165

Left **Great N.Y. Noodletown** Right **Golden Unicorn**

🔟 Restaurants

1 Great N.Y. Noodletown
The decor is simple and so is the menu, with wonderful soups, noodles, meat dishes, and creative ways with seafood. ⊛ 28¹/₂ Bowery Street at Bayard St • Map P4 • 212 349 0923 • No credit cards • $

2 Joe's Shanghai
The Chinatown branch of the Flushing restaurant famous for its soup dumplings (look for steamed buns on the menu). ⊛ 9 Pell Street at Bowery • Map P4 • 212 233 8888 • No credit cards • $$

3 Grand Sichuan
For the spicy flavors of China's Sichuan province, this is a no-frills bargain storefront with authentic specialties. ⊛ 125 Canal Street at Broadway • Map P4 • 212 625 9212 • No credit cards • $$

4 New Pasteur
A tiny Vietnamese hole-in-the-wall offering fast and cheap noodles and a range of Asian beverages. Avoid the spicy dishes unless you like to sweat. ⊛ 85 Baxter St, between Bayard & Canal sts • Map P4 • 212 608 3656 • No credit cards • $

5 Golden Unicorn
Dim sum is the star but all the dishes are well prepared in this crowded, third-floor restaurant. Go in a large group to enable more sampling. ⊛ 18 East Broadway at Catherine St • Map P4 • 212 941 0911 • $

6 Jing Fong
This enormous, glittery room is packed on weekends for the amazing selection of dim sum. Point at your choices as the carts roll by and ignore the din. ⊛ 20 Elizabeth Street, between Bayard & Canal sts • Map P4 • 212 964 5256 • $$

7 Canton
Cantonese food at its best lures locals even though the prices are high for Chinatown. ⊛ 45 Division Street at Bowery St • Map P4 • 212 226 4441 • No credit cards • $$$

8 Lombardi's
Pizza doesn't come much better than at this unpretentious old-timer that turns out delectable thin-crust pies. ⊛ 32 Spring Street, between Mott & Mulberry sts • Map P4 • 212 941 7994 • No credit cards • $

9 Da Nico
A rustic setting and a wonderful courtyard garden make this family-run restaurant with 16 kinds of pizza a favorite. ⊛ 164 Mulberry Street, between Broome & Grand sts • Map P4 • 212 343 1212 • $$

10 Il Palazzo
One of the better choices on Mulberry Street; cozy, candlelit, non-touristy. The menu includes all the Italian favorites, and the garden is a summer delight. ⊛ 151 Mulberry Street at Grand St • Map P4 • 212 343 7000 • $$

Note: Unless otherwise stated, all restaurants accept credit cards and serve vegetarian meals

Left **Orchard Street** Right **Street Scene**

Lower East Side and East Village

THE LOWER EAST SIDE IS ALIVE with memories, a neighborhood still seeming to echo the calls of immigrants crowded into tenements, peddlers hawking wares from pushcarts, and children playing in the streets, the only open spaces to be found. Early churches became synagogues for the Jews who came in record numbers between 1880 and 1920. Some remain, but in recent years, Latinos and Chinese have moved in, adding to the area's rich history. Meanwhile, Orchard Street tempts with bargains, and a hip, young generation is rediscovering the old neighborhood. Nearby, the East Village has its own layers of history, an early Dutch enclave that changed from German to Jewish before becoming a 1960s haven for hippies and the place where punk rock was born. A Ukrainian community has remained through most of these changes, including recent gentrification.

Painting, Ukrainian Museum

Sights

1. Lower East Side Tenement Museum
2. Orchard Street
3. Bialystoker Synagogue
4. Eldridge Street Synagogue
5. Beth Hamedrash Hagadol Synagogue
6. Guss' Pickles
7. St Mark's Place
8. St Mark's-in-the-Bowery Church
9. Renwick Triangle
10. Ukrainian Museum

Street vendor's pushcart, Tenement Museum

Lower East Side Tenement Museum

Guided tours inside a tenement building give an insight into the carefully researched lives of one of three families who lived here; a German-Jewish seamstress in 1874, an orthodox Jewish family from Lithuania in 1918, or a Sicilian Catholic family during the Depression in the 1930s. ◎ *90 Orchard St • Map N5 • 212 431 0233 • Tours: 1–4:30pm Tue–Fri, 11am–4:30pm Sat–Sun (book ahead) • Admission charge*

Orchard Street

The heart of bargain shopping, Orchard Street became a street of shops in 1940, when Mayor Fiorello La Guardia outlawed pushcarts in the city. Many merchants still put some of their wares on the sidewalk on Sundays and lure customers with 20 to 30 percent off brand names. The Lower East Side Visitor Center offers free tours each Sunday between April and December.

◎ *Lower East Side Visitor Center, 261 Broome Street • Map P4 • 212 226 9010 • Open 10am–4pm daily • www.lower-eastsideny.com*

Bialystoker Synagogue

Built in 1826 as a Methodist Episcopal Church, the fieldstone building was acquired in 1905 to house a congregation from the Polish community of Bialystok. A recent two-year restoration has revealed an interior of glowing beauty, painted in bold colors, with Moorish motifs, biblical scenes, and the signs of the zodiac, which are found in some Jewish scriptures. As in all Orthodox synagogues, only men are allowed on the main floor; women are seated in the gallery upstairs. ◎ *7–11 Willett Street • Map P6 • Open during Sat services, or by appointment • Free • www.bialystoker.org*

Eldridge Street Synagogue

A National Historic Landmark. This 1887 Moorish-style synagogue was the first house of worship built in the U.S. by Jewish immigrants from Eastern Europe, from where 80 percent of American Jews come. As many as 1,000 people attended services here at the turn of the century. As congregants left the

Left **Art for sale, Orchard Street** Right **Stained glass, Eldridge Street Synagogue**

neighborhood, attendance waned, and the temple closed in the 1950s. Restoration is now underway and the synagogue has become a vibrant cultural center. 🕾 *12 Eldridge Street • Map P5 • Open 11am–4pm Tue–Thu, Sun • Tours: 11am, noon, 1pm, 2pm, 3pm • Admission charge • www.eldridgestreet.org*

5 Beth Hamedrash Hagadol Synagogue

Artists can often be seen sketching this small, picturesque building. It was constructed in 1850 as the Norfolk Street Baptist Church, but as the neighborhood changed, the membership moved uptown, and in 1885 the structure was converted to a synagogue by America's oldest Russian, Orthodox Jewish congregation. Gothic woodwork and the iron fence from the original church remain. 🕾 *60–64 Norfolk Street • Map P5 • Open by appointment • Free*

6 Guss' Pickles

One of the survivors from the old days of the Jewish Lower East Side, and a fixture for more than 80 years, Guss' was even featured in the movie, *Crossing Delancey*. Fans stand in line on weekends for their fix from the barrels on the sidewalk filled with pickles – sour and half-sour. Guss' also does a thriving

The Changing Scene
Proving that change is the rule in New York, the Lower East Side has emerged as the newest trendy area for clubs, restaurants, and hip boutiques. Some residents are even moving into the tenement buildings their great-grandparents fought to escape from. Ludlow Street is one of the best streets to get a feel for the current scene.

business by mail, shipping all over the U.S. 🕾 *85–87 Orchard Street • Map P5 • Open 9:30am–6pm Sun–Thu, 9:30am–5pm Fri*

7 St. Mark's Place

Once the heart of hippie-dom, this block still has a counter-culture feel and is headquarters for the East Village youth scene. Sidewalks are crowded until late into the night with patrons of funky, punky bars and shops selling music, books, T-shirts, vintage clothing, beads, posters, and black leather everything. The place to get pierced or tattooed. 🕾 *East 8th Street, between 3rd Av & Av A • Map M4*

8 St. Mark's-in-the-Bowery Church

The second-oldest church in New York stands on land where Peter Stuyvesant, governor of Dutch New York in the 1600s, had his

Left **Beth Hamedrash Hagadol Synagogue** Center **Guss' Pickles** Right **Renwick Triangle**

private chapel. Stuyvesant is also buried here. In the 1960s it served as one of the city's most politically committed congregations and continues to be on the avant-garde edge. ◈ *131 East 10th Street • Map M4 • Open 8:30am–4pm Mon–Fri; service 10:30am Sun • Free*

9 Renwick Triangle

This handsome group of townhouses was created in 1861 by James Renwick, Jr., a prominent architect of the day. The houses are on land that was once Peter Stuyvesant's farm, developed by his descendants as a stylish residential area. ◈ *114–128 East 10th Street, 23–25 Stuyvesant Street, between 2nd & 3rd avs • Map M4*

10 Ukrainian Museum

The museum has moved into a plush new facility that showcases a beguiling collection of Ukrainian costumes, lavishly embroidered peasant blouses, colorful sashes, fancy sheepskin and fur vests, wedding wreaths of yarn and ribbons. There are also ceramics, jewelry, and the intricately designed Ukrainian Easter eggs known as *pysanky*. ◈ *226 East 6th St, between 2nd and 3rd avs • Map N4 • Open 1–5pm Wed–Sun • Admission charge*

East Side Exploration

Morning

🕐 From the Delancey Street subway walk south to Grand Street and Kossar's Bialys Bakery, 367 Grand, famous for chewy, onion-flavored rolls, or the Doughnut Plant, 379 Grand, where the oversize cakes achieve gourmet status. Walk east for two historic houses of worship, the **Beth Hamedrash Hagadol Synagogue** and the **Bialystoker Synagogue** (see p91).

Return along East Broadway, passing the Henry Street Settlement at No. 281, in three restored Federal buildings. The gallery at the Educational Alliance, No. 197, has good art and photography exhibits. Walk to Orchard for **Guss' Pickles**, and pick up a bargain at the shops here. If you're hot try one of the 50 flavors of ice cream at Le Laboratorio del Gelato, or continue to East Houston Street, and have lunch at **Katz's Delicatessen** (p95), a New York institution.

Afternoon

After lunch, walk uptown on 2nd Avenue. Turn left on East 6th to visit the **Ukrainian Museum**, a small and hidden gem of costumes and culture. Walk to **St. Mark's Place**, browsing through the funky shops and bars on your way, and then walk east again on Stuyvesant Street, admiring the landmark townhouses of the **Renwick Triangle**. Lastly, stop at **St. Mark's-in-the-Bowery Church**, one of the oldest in the city, where you can pay your respects to Peter Stuyvesant's grave.

Left **Lismore Hosiery Co.** Right **Kleins of Monticello**

TOP10 Bargain Stores

1 Harry Zarin Fabric Warehouse

Since 1936 this mammoth showroom and workshop has provided fabrics and upholstery to the public at wholesale prices. ◈ *318 Grand Street • Map P5*

2 Fishkin Knitwear

Women's knits, clothing, and shoes by American, Italian, and French designers sold at discount. ◈ *314 Grand Street at Allen St • Map P5*

3 Forman's

Whatever your size, you will find it at these adjacent shops stocking brand-name women's fashions at discount prices. ◈ *80–84 Orchard Street • Map P5*

4 Kleins of Monticello

One of the most attractive shops on the block offers well-tailored business and casual wear by American and European designers. ◈ *105 Orchard Street • Map N5*

5 Fine & Klein

Well-known for its wide selection of high quality handbags and accessories, most at a discount. ◈ *119 Orchard Street • Map N5*

6 Giselle

Four floors of designer clothing by European names such as Valentino, Escada, and Ungaro, promising 20 to 30 percent off retail. ◈ *143 Orchard Street • Map N5*

7 Lismore Hosiery Co.

Stored away in boxes stacked floor to ceiling are name brands in underwear and socks for men and women at bargain prices. To take advantage of the savings, know the brand and size you need. ◈ *334 Grand Street • Map P5*

8 Salwen's Umbrellas

Need a really good umbrella, one that won't give in the first gust of wind? This merchant has been selling quality gear to ward off the weather at sunny prices since 1902. ◈ *45 Orchard Street • Map P5*

9 Altman Luggage

From computer cases to carry-ons, brand names like Lark, TravelPro, and American Tourister are sold for less at this well-stocked emporium. ◈ *135 Orchard Street • Map N5*

10 Harris Levy

One of the last survivors of what used to be rows of discount stores selling linens for table, bed, and bath. European linens and home accessories are a specialty at this store. ◈ *278 Grand Street • Map P5*

Price Categories

For a three-course meal for one with a glass of house wine, and all unavoidable charges including tax.

$	under $25
$$	$25–$50
$$$	$50–$80
$$$$	over $80

Katz's Delicatessen

🔟 Restaurants

1 Lansky Lounge & Grill
The only sign that this renovated grill was once a speakeasy is the entrance in a hidden back alley. Serves steak and chops to a hip crowd.
◎ *104 Norfolk St • Map N5 • 212 677 9489 • $$*

2 Katz's Delicatessen
Savor a pastrami sandwich on rye here, and you'll understand why New York delis are famous.
◎ *205 East Houston Street at Ludlow St • Map N5 • 212 254 2246 • $*

3 Sammy's Roumanian
It looks like a Jewish wedding every night. Chopped liver and shmaltz will freak your cholesterol level, but you'll enjoy every minute.
◎ *157 Chrystie Street • Map N4 • 212 673 0330 • No vegetarian options • $$*

4 WD-50
A hip, foodie café famous for the exciting creations of chef Wylie Dufresne. Be prepared to wait. ◎ *50 Clinton Street, between Rivington & Stanton sts • Map N5 • 212 477 2900 • $$$*

5 Le Père Pinard
A fine place to relax with wine and French bistro fare in the heated garden out back. ◎ *175 Ludlow Street, between Houston & Stanton sts • Map N5 • 212 777 4917 • $$*

6 Veselka
A funky Ukrainian diner serving borscht, blintzes, and pierogis for a pittance. Tables at the back are quieter. ◎ *144 2nd Avenue at 9th St • Map M4 • 212 228 9682 • No credit cards • $*

7 Daily Chow
A big Pan-Asian diner offering specialties from all of Asia and potent cocktails in the busy bar. ◎ *2 East 2nd Street at the Bowery • Map N4 • 212 254 7887 • $*

8 La Palapa
Authentic Mexican regional cuisine and great margaritas in a beautifully decorated dining room.
◎ *77 St Mark's Place, between 1st & 2nd avs • Map M4 • 212 777 2537 • $$*

9 Le Tableau
This cozy and candlelit French restaurant uses quality ingredients. Bargains include the *prix fixe* and tasting menus, which can include wine pairings. ◎ *511 West 5th Street, between avs A and B • Map N5 • 212 874 2742 • $$*

10 Teresa's
Polish comfort food, guaranteed to fill you up without emptying your pockets. The pierogis and potato pancakes are perfection. ◎ *103 1st Avenue, between East 6th & 7th sts • Map N5 • 212 228 0604 • No credit cards • $*

Note: *Unless otherwise stated, all restaurants accept credit cards and serve vegetarian meals*

Left **Mural, Greene Street** Right **Haughwout Building**

SoHo and TriBeCa

UNTIL RECENTLY, THE AREA NAMED *for its shape (TRIangle BElow CAnal) consisted mostly of abandoned warehouses. Then Robert De Niro set up his Tribeca Film Center, stylish restaurants began to open, and the big loft spaces started to draw celebrity residents. Now TriBeCa is one of New York's hottest neighborhoods, the center of the city's movie industry with a TriBeCa Film Festival and plenty of nightlife. SoHo (South of Houston) has also come full circle. The empty loft spaces first drew artists, then galleries, then crowds of* browsers and the restaurants to serve them. The new chic image quickly drove up rents and drove out many galleries. Some remain, and the streets are lined with designer clothing and home furnishing boutiques, maintaining SoHo's lure as the city's favorite Sunday brunch-and-browse neighborhood. Both areas boast the cast-iron architecture that is a New York specialty.

Gallery, White Street

🔟 Sights

1. Greene Street
2. New Museum of Contemporary Art
3. Prada
4. New York City Fire Museum
5. Haughwout Building
6. "Little" Singer Building
7. Canal Street
8. Harrison Street
9. White Street
10. TriBeCa Film Center

Preceding pages **New York skyline at night**

Greene Street

1 Cast-iron architecture flourished in New York in the late 19th century, as a way to produce decorative elements such as columns and arches and create impressive buildings inexpensively. Greene Street, between Canal and Grand streets, and between Broome and Spring streets, has 50 of these beauties, rows of columned façades creating a striking streetscape. ✆ *Map N4*

New Museum of Contemporary Art

2 Since its founding in 1977, this provocative museum has mounted shows featuring experimental work that other museums often overlook, particularly new multi-media forms, which sometimes extend into intriguing window displays. The museum is temporarily located in the Chelsea Art Museum, before moving to a new facility at 235 Bowery in late 2007. ✆ *556 West 22nd Street at 11th Ave • Map L2 • Open noon–8pm Thu, noon–6pm Tue, Wed, & Fri–Sat • Admission charge, free Thu after 6pm • www.newmuseum.org*

Prada

3 The sign reads "Guggenheim SoHo" but the new occupant of the building is an extraordinary $40 million flagship store for trend-setting Italian retailer Prada, a sign of SoHo's shift from art to fashion. Dutch architect Rem Kookhaas is responsible for the ultra-hip floating stairs, undulating walls, futuristic elevators and hi-tech dressing rooms. The entire Prada line is sold. ✆ *575 Broadway at Prince St • Map N4 • Open 11am–7pm Mon–Sat, 12–6pm Sun.*

New York City Fire Museum

4 A nostalgic treasure housed in a 1904 firehouse, this splendid collection includes the city's fire-fighting engines, equipment, garb and memorabilia from the 18th century to the present. A moving photo display depicts the World Trade Centre attack and honors the hundreds of firefighters lost there. ✆ *278 Spring Street • Map N3 • Open 10am–5pm Tue–Sat, 10am–4pm Sun • Admission charge • www.nycfiremuseum.org*

Left **New Museum of Contemporary Art** Right **Prada**

5 Haughwout Building

A cast-iron masterpiece, this structure was built in 1857 to house a fashionable china and glassware emporium. The design of colonnaded arches flanked by taller Corinthian columns was adapted from the façade of the Sansovino Library in Venice. This motif is repeated 92 times across the front of the building. A 1995 restoration removed grime and restored the elegant original pale color. This building boasted the first Otis safety elevator, an innovation that made the skyscraper possible. ✆ 488–492 Broadway at Broome St • Map P4

6 "Little" Singer Building

By the early 1900s, cast iron was giving way to steel-framed brick and terra-cotta. One notable example is Ernest Flagg's "Little" Singer Building (to distinguish it from a taller tower also built for Singer). Influenced by Parisian architecture of the period, it has a charming 12-story façade and graceful cast-iron balconies. ✆ 561–3 Broadway, between Prince & Spring sts • Map N4

Haughwout Building

TriBeCa's Movie Business

TriBeCa is known as Hollywood East, and although much of its movie business is behind the scenes, many screenings take place. Big name stars have been sighted heading for the Grand Screen Room at the TriBeCa Grand Hotel (see p177). The TriBeCa Film Festival, begun in May 2002, is a further star-spotting event.

7 Canal Street

The end of SoHo, the beginning of TriBeCa, and a world of its own, no street better shows the contrasts of New York. Canal Street is crowded with peddlers selling fake Rolex watches and Gucci bags, electronics that may or may not be new, and bargain stores offering sneakers, jeans, and flea-market finds. Keep heading east into Chinatown, and the sidewalk goods shift to vegetables and displays of fish. ✆ Map P3–4

8 Harrison Street

This rare group of Federal townhouses, built between 1796 and 1828, did not exist as a row until 1975, when the houses

Left **"Little" Singer Building** Right **Canal Street**

Harrison Street

were moved to this site to be saved from the urban renewal that razed much of the area. At the end of the block (No. 6) is the former New York Mercantile Exchange, a Queen Anne building dating from 1884 and in use until 1977 when the Exchange moved to the World Financial Center (see p45). ❧ Map P3

9 White Street

The best example of cast-iron architecture in TriBeCa is a sampling of several styles. No. 2 has Federal features and a gambrel roof; Nos. 8–10, designed by Henry Fernbach in 1869, sport Tuscan columns and arches and use the Neo-Renaissance device of building shorter upper stories to give an illusion of height. There is a complete change of pace at No. 38, which houses neon artist Rudi Stern's gallery, Let There Be Neon. ❧ Map P3–4

10 TriBeCa Film Center

A turn-of-the-century coffee warehouse has been converted into office space for the film and entertainment industry. The guiding spirit was Robert De Niro, whose TriBeCa Productions was founded in 1988. Miramax has set up offices here and the building is also home to the TriBeCa Grill, owned by De Niro and restaurateur Drew Nieporent. The restaurant has managed to maintain its star appeal for over a decade. ❧ 375 Greenwich Street • Map P3

A Stroll Around SoHo and TriBeCa

Morning

🕐 The Bleecker Street subway stop is a good starting point to explore Soho's shops and galleries. Galleries worth a visit are Deitch Projects, No. 59; Peter Blum, No. 99; and Spencer Brownstone at 39 Wooster St; and David Beitzel at 102 Prince St. **Greene Street** (see p99) has a number of interesting boutiques, such as Plein Sud, Helmut Lang, and Vivienne Tam.

The Drawing Center (see p43) exhibits work from emerging artists and is great for poetry readings. This is also a prime area for photography galleries. The most interesting are Janet Borden, June Bateman, and Staley Wise, all located at 560 Broadway. Afterwards, stop for a pancake lunch at Palacinka, 28 Grand Street, between 6th Avenue and Thompson Street.

Afternoon

Drop in on designer boutiques Miu Miu, 100 Prince Street, and Anna Sui, 113 Greene Street, before proceeding to TriBeCa. Take a stroll along **White** and **Harrison** streets to view the historic architecture and stop for a drink at the **Church Lounge** (see p102).

Spend the rest of the afternoon taking in the exhibits at the Apex Art Gallery, 291 Church Street, and the Ace Gallery, 275 Hudson Street, a cavernous space showing large-scale art. Make your way to **Dylan Prime** (see p102) for an early evening cocktail then head to TriBeCa to a leading restaurant, such as Danube, Nobu, Bouley, or Montrachet (see p103).

Around Town – SoHo & TriBeCa

Around Town – SoHo & TriBeCa

Left **Pravda** Center **Dylan Prime** Right **Temple Bar**

🔟 Nightlife

1 Pravda
Vodkas from across the world are served in this bar featuring Russian mementos, leather chairs, and a low gold ceiling. ⊗ *281 Lafayette Street, between Prince and Houston sts • Map N4 • 212 226 4696*

2 Church Lounge
Almost the entire ground floor of the hotel is devoted to this popular bar with plush seats and a dramatic eight-story atrium. ⊗ *TriBeCa Grand Hotel, 2 Sixth Avenue • Map N3 • 212 519 6600*

3 Dylan Prime
An extensive cocktail menu, and an attractive space with lofty ceilings help make this a current hotspot. ⊗ *62 Laight Street, between Greenwich & Collister sts • Map P3 • 212 334 4783*

4 Liquor Store Bar
The building dates to 1804 and was once a liquor store, but now it's a comfortable, low-key place to have a beer. ⊗ *235 West Broadway at White St • Map P3 • 212 226 7121*

5 The Sporting Club
You'll never miss a game in this popular, memorabilia-filled sports lounge crammed with giant TV screens. ⊗ *99 Hudson Street, between Franklin & Leonard sts • Map P3 • 212 219 0900*

6 Puck Fair
At this cosy multi-level pub you can settle in to enjoy a pint along with tasty Irish snacks. ⊗ *289 Lafayette Street, between Houston & Prince sts • Map N4 • 212 431 1200*

7 Grand Bar
Like its sister TriBeCa Grand, the SoHo Grand is a neighborhood nightlife mecca, comfortable, softly lit, with food if you want it, and filled with beautiful people. ⊗ *SoHo Grand Hotel, 310 West Broadway, between Canal & Grand sts • Map P3 • 212 965 3000*

8 Merc Bar
This trendy SoHo meeting place attracts all manner of sophisticates who dig the mountain lodge decor. ⊗ *151 Mercer Street, between Houston & Prince sts • Map N4 • 212 966 2727*

9 Temple Bar
Dark, swanky, sexy, and pricey, but the martinis are mammoth. A good place to bring a date – or find one. ⊗ *332 Lafayette Street, between Bleecker & East Houston sts • Map N4 • 212 925 4242*

🔟 The Room
The Room is a friendly, candle-lit place with no hard liquor, but 60 kinds of beer and 20 wines. ⊗ *144 Sullivan Street, between Prince & Houston sts • Map N3 • 212 477 2102*

Price Categories

For a three-course meal for one with a glass of house wine, and all unavoidable charges including tax.

$	under $25
$$	$25–$50
$$$	$50–$80
$$$$	over $80

Left **Montrachet** Right **Balthazar**

TOP 10 Restaurants

1 Danube
Light as air "nouveau Austrian" food at David Bouley's warm and wonderful TriBeCa restaurant *(see p68)*. ◈ *30 Hudson Street between Duane & Reade sts • Map P3 • 212 791 3771 • $$$$*

2 Nobu
Nobu Matsuhisa's sublime Japanese/Peruvian fusion fare in a whimsical setting *(see p68)*. ◈ *105 Hudson Street • Map P3 • 212 219 0500 • $$$$*

3 Nobu Next Door
The no-reservations policy at this restaurant means you might get to taste the famous Nobu black cod with miso. ◈ *106 Hudson Street at Franklin St • Map P3 • 212 334 4445 • $$$*

4 Bouley
David Bouley can't go wrong when it comes to food. The room isn't memorable, but the New French cuisine is heavenly. ◈ *120 West Broadway at Duane St • Map P3 • 212 964 2525 • $$$$*

5 Montrachet
The first of Drew Nieporent's restaurant empire still ranks among the city's best, known for its casual decor, modern French cuisine, and exceptional wine list. ◈ *239 West Broadway, nr West Broadway & North Moore sts • Map P3 • 212 219 2777 • $$$$*

6 Le Zinc
The proprietors of the very haute Chanterelle have opened a welcome, more informal bistro. Onion fritters and skate are recommended. ◈ *139 Duane Street, between Church St & West Broadway • Map P3 • 212 513 0001 • $$*

7 Balthazar
As close to a Parisian bistro as you're likely to find in SoHo, Balthazar's only problem is its popularity. A buzzing scene. ◈ *80 Spring Street at Broadway • Map N3 • 212 965 1414 • $$$*

8 Raoul's
Another bit of the Left Bank in SoHo, with an updated French menu and a great garden. ◈ *180 Prince Street, between Sullivan & Thompson sts • Map N4 • 212 966 3518 • $$$*

9 The Odeon
Art Deco decor, consistently good food, and a star-studded crowd keeps the vibe right, even after 20 years. ◈ *145 Broadway at Thomas Street • Map P3 • 212 233 0507 • $$*

10 Hampton Chutney Co.
Perfect for an inexpensive snack of *dosas*: crêpes stuffed with creative combinations. ◈ *68 Prince Street • Map N4 • 212 226 9996 • $*

Left **Washington Square Park** Center **Jefferson Market Courthouse** Right **Bar on Bleecker Street**

Greenwich Village

IT WAS DIFFERENT FROM THE START, *a crazy pattern of streets that broke from the city's grid plan, reflecting the boundaries of a rural village. As a bohemian haven, the leafy lanes of the Village have been home to artists and writers. Jazz musicians, beat poets, performers like the young Bob Dylan found their places here. Later it became popular with gays, and today cafés and funky shops attract the young from all over the city. The village really comes to life at night, when cafés, theaters, and clubs beckon at every turn.*

Sights

1. Washington Square Park
2. MacDougal Alley
3. Washington Mews
4. Grove Court
5. Jefferson Market Courthouse
6. Cherry Lane Theater
7. Bleecker Street
8. New York University
9. Judson Memorial Church
10. 75½ Bedford Street

Balconies, Greenwich Village

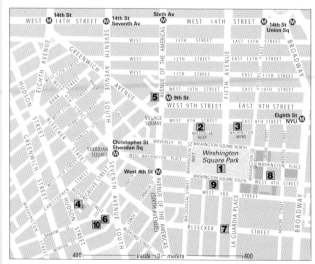

Washington Square Park
In 1826, a marshy area was filled to form this popular park. The newly-restored marble arch by Stanford White went up in 1895, replacing a wooden version that marked the centenary of George Washington's inauguration. Mothers with strollers, chess players, and young lovers now occupy benches where drug dealers once reigned. The fountain in the center is where Bob Dylan sang his first folk songs. ✆ 5th Avenue, between Waverly Pl & 4th St • Map N3

MacDougal Alley
These 19th-century stables for the fine homes on Washington Square North were converted into studios by artists early in the 20th century, causing the street to be known as "Art Alley de Luxe." Among the residents were painter Guy Pene du Bois and sculptor Gertrude Vanderbilt Whitney, who established the first Whitney Museum in 1914 at 8 West 8th Street, adjoining her studio. ✆ East of MacDougal Street, between 8th St & Waverly Pl • Map M3

Washington Mews
Another group of stables turned into houses around 1900, the Mews attracted both writers and artists. No. 14A housed, at various times, author John Dos Passos and artists Edward Hopper, William Glackens, and Rockwell Kent. Writer Sherwood Anderson often stayed at No. 54 with his friend and patron, Mary Emmett. In contrast to the modern buildings in much of Manhattan, this type of quaint enclave is the reason many find the Village so appealing. ✆ University Place to 5th Avenue • Map M3

Grove Court
This group of six townhouses in a bend in the street was developed by grocer Samuel Cocks, who thought that having residents nearby would help his business at No. 18. But while such private courts are prized today, they were not considered respectable in the 1850s, and the disreputable types who moved in earned it the nickname "Mixed Ale Alley." O. Henry used the block as the setting for The Last Leaf. ✆ Grove Street near Bedford St • Map N3

Left **MacDougal Street** Right **Grove Court**

5 Jefferson Market Courthouse

The site was a market in 1833, named after the former president, Thomas Jefferson. The fire lookout tower had a giant bell that alerted volunteer firefighters. When the courthouse was built in 1877, the bell was installed in its clock tower. The building became a treasured Village landmark, and, after the market had moved and court sessions were discontinued, it was eventually saved from demolition after a spirited local campaign and converted into a branch of the New York Public Library *(see p124)* in the 1950s. ◉ *425 6th Avenue, between 9th & 10th sts • Map M3 • Open noon–8pm Mon, Wed, 10am–6pm Tue, noon–6pm Thu, 1pm–6pm Fri, 10am–5pm Sat • Free*

6 Cherry Lane Theatre

In 1924, a warehouse was converted into one of the first Off-Broadway theaters and showcased plays by the likes of Edward Albee, Eugene Ionesco, David Mamet, and Harold Pinter. Today, the "Cherry Lane Alternative" uses established playwrights to mentor talented newcomers. ◉ *38 Commerce Street, between Bedford & Barrow sts • Map N3 • 212 989 2020 • www.cherrylanetheatre.com*

7 Bleecker Street

The present line-up of ordinary shops and restaurants belies the history of this street. James

The Halloween Parade

Anything goes in this wildly gaudy annual parade of cross-dressers and amazing costumes. It draws 25,000 marchers and many times that many spectators. The parade route goes up 6th Avenue, from the Village to 23rd Street, starting at 7pm.

Fenimore Cooper lived at No. 145 in 1833, Theodore Dreiser stayed at No. 160 when he came to New York in 1895, and James Agee lived at No. 172 from 1941 to 1951. The café at No. 189, the corner of Bleecker and MacDougal, was the San Remo bar, the favorite gathering place for William Burroughs, Allen Ginsberg, Gregory Corso, and Jack Kerouac, leading lights of the beat generation. ◉ *Between 6th Avenue & West Broadway • Map N3*

8 New York University

Founded in 1831, N.Y.U. enlarged the scope of early 19th-century study from its previous concentration on Greek and Latin to contemporary subjects: a "rational and practical education" for those aspiring to careers in business, industry, science, and the arts, as well as in law, medicine, and the ministry. It has grown into the largest private university in America and now occupies many blocks around Washington Square. ◉ *Washington Square • Map N4*

Left **Cherry Lane Theater** Right **Bleecker Street**

Judson Memorial Church

9 An elegant work in Romanesque style by Stanford White, with stained glass by John La Farge, the church was built in 1888–93 as a memorial to Adoniram Judson, the first American Baptist missionary in Asia. John D. Rockefeller, Jr. *(see p48)* contributed to the construction. White's use of mottled yellow brick and white terra-cotta trim introduced light coloration into American church architecture.
⊗ *55 Washington Square South • Map N3 • Open for services 11am Sun • Free*

75¹/₂ Bedford Street

10 Ever quirky, New York's narrowest home, just 9.5 ft (3 m) wide, was built in 1893 in a passageway in the Village. Poet Edna St. Vincent Millay lived here, as did actors John Barrymore and, later, Cary Grant. No. 77 Bedford Street is the oldest house in the Village, dating from around 1799, and at No. 103 is the house known as "Twin Peaks," an 1830 structure remodeled in 1925 by Clifford Reed Daily to house artists and writers, who would presumably be inspired by the whimsical architecture. ⊗ *Between Morton & Barrow sts • Map N3*

A Village Stroll

Morning

Begin at **Washington Square** *(p108)* and the elegant townhouse row where Edith Wharton and Henry James once lived. Find the charming houses of **Washington Mews** and **MacDougal Alley** *(p105)*, then follow 6th Avenue, past the **Jefferson Market Courthouse**, to West 10th Street.

Stroll down the passageway at the front of the Alexander Onassis Center for Hellenic Studies. This walkway once led up to the Tile Club, a gathering place for the artists of the Tenth Street Studio, where Augustus Saint-Gaudens, John La Farge, and Winslow Homer lived and worked. Continue along Waverly Place, Grove Steet, and Bedford Street, each with its share of prize townhouse architecture. Have lunch at a typical Village bistro like **Café Loup** *(see p109)*.

Afternoon

After lunch, why not while away a few hours browsing in the local shops? Vintage clothing can be admired at specialty shops such as Cheap Jack's, 841 Broadway between 13th and 14th streets, while just across the street at No. 840 you'll find Forbidden Planet, a nirvana for comic book fanatics.

West 8th Street and West 4th Street are also crammed with shops, and several coffeehouses are great for people-watching. Try Caffe Reggio, 119 MacDougal Street, where the literary lights of the beat generation used to read their poetry.

Left **Washington Mews** Center **Chumley's** Right **White Horse Tavern**

Literary Landmarks

1 Washington Square
Prominent figures who lived here include Edith Wharton at No. 7 in 1882. Henry James was born at No. 21 in 1843. ✎ *Map N3*

2 St. Luke's Place
Poet Marianne Moore lived here, and Theodore Dreiser wrote *An American Tragedy* at No. 16. ✎ *Between Hudson Street & 7th Avenue South • Map N3*

3 Patchin Place
A charming pocket of 19th-century houses that later attracted ee cummings, John Masefield, and Eugene O'Neill, among others. ✎ *West 10th Street • Map N3*

4 Chumley's
Book covers of Steinbeck, Hemingway, Faulkner, and others who drank here adorn the walls of this prohibition-era speakeasy. ✎ *86 Bedford Street • Map N3*

5 White Horse Tavern
Favorite hangout of Norman Mailer and Dylan Thomas, who announced one night in 1953, "I've had 18 straight whiskeys," and passed out. He died the next day. ✎ *567 Hudson Street at 11th St • Map N3*

6 Willa Cather Residence
Willa Cather wrote six novels here and her Friday "at homes" were attended by the likes of D. H. Lawrence. ✎ *5 Bank Street, between West & Greenwich sts • Map N3 • Closed to public*

7 Mark Twain Residence
A plaque marks the home (1904–08) of Mark Twain, designed by James Renwick, Jr., architect of St. Patrick's Cathedral. Twain received guests while propped up in a huge carved bed. ✎ *21 Fifth Avenue at 9th St • Map M3 • Closed to public*

8 William Styron Residence
This was Styron's first "tiny but rather nice" apartment after writing *Lie Down in Darkness* aged 23. ✎ *43 Greenwich Avenue • Map M3 • Closed to public*

9 Edward Albee Residence
Albee wrote *The Zoo Story* here. He first saw the words "Who's Afraid of Virginia Woolf?" written in soap on a saloon mirror nearby. ✎ *238 West 4th Street • Map N3 • Closed to public*

10 West 10th Street
Mark Twain lived at No. 14 in 1900–1, Hart Crane at No. 54 in 1917, and Edward Albee lived in the carriage house at No. 50 during the 1960s. ✎ *Map M3 • Closed to public*

 Around Town – Greenwich Village

For more on figures in New York history See pp48–9

Price Categories

For a three-course meal for one with a glass of house wine, and all unavoidable charges including tax.	**$** under $25
	$$ $25–$50
	$$$ $50–$80
	$$$$ over $80

Left **Babbo** Right **Blue Ribbon Bakery**

Restaurants

1 Babbo
An attractive setting and the inventive Italian fare created by TV chef Mario Batali make this a very popular spot. Reserve in advance to ensure a table. ◎ *110 Waverly Place • Map N3 • 212 777 0303 • $$$*

2 Il Mulino
Another top Italian. Quality is consistent, portions are large, and the brick-walled room is inviting. Try the homemade ravioli with black truffles in creamy champagne sauce. ◎ *86 West 3rd Street, between Sullivan & Thompson sts • Map N3 • 212 673 3783 • $$$*

3 Blue Hill
Highly praised New American fare that uses local, seasonal ingredients, served in intimate, elegant surroundings. ◎ *75 Washington Place at MacDougal St • Map N3 • 212 539 1776 • $$$*

4 Blue Ribbon Bakery
A casual Village favorite with an enormous, eclectic menu that includes everything from croissants and caviar to the signature fried chicken. ◎ *33 Downing Street at Bedford St • Map N3 • 212 337 0404 • $$*

5 Café de Bruxelles
Mussels and frites can't be beat at this comfortable restaurant. Don't miss the impressive selection of Belgian beers either. ◎ *118 Greenwich Avenue at West 13th St • Map M3 • 212 206 1830 • $$*

6 Café Loup
An agreeable French bistro, where favorite dishes include tuna carpaccio, steak, and roast chicken. The setting is romantic, but there's also a funky bar. ◎ *105 West 13th Street • Map M3 • 212 255 4746 • $$*

7 Da Silvano
Watch the celebrities come and go from a table outside. The northern Italian fare here is consistent, and the buzz even better. ◎ *260 Sixth Avenue, between Bleecker & West Houston sts • Map N3 • 212 982 2343 • $$$*

8 Home
Food like Mom used to make (provided she was a terrific cook) keeps this narrow café crowded. The patio provides a breath of fresh air. ◎ *20 Cornelia Street, between Bleeker St & 6th Avenue • Map N3 • 212 243 9579 • $$*

9 Pastis
Hot, hot, hot is this straight-out-of-Paris café; order steak frites or escargots, and get into the spirit of things. ◎ *9 9th Avenue at Little West 12th St • Map M2 • 212 929 4844 • $$$*

10 Sushi Samba
The Japanese/Brazilian fusion cuisine and cocktails are inspired, but the trendy crowd comes here for the rooftop deck and live music on sunny days. ◎ *87 Seventh Ave South at Bleecker St • Map N3 • 212 691 7885 • $$*

Around Town – Greenwich Village

 Note: *Unless otherwise stated, all restaurants accept credit cards and serve vegetarian meals*

Left **Gramercy Park** Center foreground **Metropolitan Life Tower** Right **Rooftops on Broadway**

Union Square, Gramercy Park, and Flatiron

CHANGE IS IN THE AIR *in this flourishing section of Manhattan. Union Square, once a hangout for drug dealers and scene of protest rallies, has been renovated and transformed. A Greenmarket fills the square with fresh produce four times a week, drawing patrons from all over the city, and the neighborhood around the square is attracting an increasing number of new apartments, shops, and restaurants. The shops and lively eating places now extend up Fifth Avenue into the once-neglected Flatiron District, named for the building at the intersection of Fifth Avenue and Broadway at 23rd Street. Quiet Madison Square, opposite the Flatiron Building, recently became the site of two of the city's hottest restaurants and is receiving its own restoration. No change was needed in Gramercy Park, the most European of the city's neighborhoods.*

Fantasy Fountain, Greg Wyatt, Gramercy Park

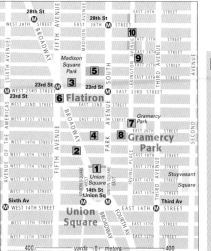

🔟 Sights

1. Union Square Greenmarket
2. ABC Carpet & Home
3. Madison Square
4. Theodore Roosevelt Birthplace
5. Metropolitan Life Tower
6. Flatiron Building
7. Gramercy Park
8. National Arts Club
9. 69th Regiment Armory
10. "Curry Hill"

Union Square Greenmarket

Herbs and berries, miniature vegetables, fresh flowers and homebaked pastries, newly woven yarns, hams, honey – all of these and more can be found at the bountiful Greenmarket that fills Union Square each Monday, Wednesday, Friday, and Saturday. More than 200 regional farmers take part in the market, each offering only goods that they have grown or made. A colorful New York scene not to be missed. ⊗ *At Broadway & 14th Street • Map M4 • Open 8am–6pm*

ABC Carpet & Home

The city's most eclectic emporium, two landmark buildings that are part flea market, part antiques fair, and part Middle Eastern bazaar. Offerings include fancy French or rugged Mexican furniture, antiques and reproductions, fabrics and accessories, linens, bedding, flowers, foods, and a whole building for rugs. There are two dining places: Lucy and Pipa. ⊗ *881 & 888 Broadway at East 19th St • Map L4*

Madison Square

The square opened in 1847 at the center of a fine residential area where politician Theodore Roosevelt and writer Edith Wharton were born. The original Madison Square Garden was here, at Madison Avenue and 26th Street. Later office development brought distinguished sites such as the Flatiron and Metropolitan Life buildings. Today the statue-filled park is being renovated and the area rediscovered. ⊗ *23rd to 26th sts, between Broadway & Madison Av • Map L3*

Theodore Roosevelt Birthplace

The boyhood home where the colorful 26th President was born in 1858 has been reconstructed. Exhibits trace his political career as well as his explorations, displaying everything from toys to campaign buttons, and emblems of the trademark "Rough Rider" hat Roosevelt wore in the Spanish-American war. The house offers a rare glimpse of a privileged 19th-century New York lifestyle. ⊗ *28 East 20th Street, between Broadway & Park Av South • Map L4 • Open 9am–5pm Tue–Sat • Admission charge*

Left **Madison Square** Right **Theodore Roosevelt Birthplace**

5 Metropolitan Life Tower

This 54-story tower, built along the east side of Madison Square in 1909, was the world's tallest building at that time, an appropriate corporate symbol for the world's largest insurance company. Designed by Napoleon Le Brun and Sons, the tower follows the form of the campanile in the Piazza San Marco in Venice. Although it was altered in the 1960s, when the entire structure was renovated, the ornate four-faced clock and crowning cupola remain, a familiar landmark on the New York skyline. ✪ *1 Madison Avenue, near 24th St • Map L4 • Open during office hours • Free*

6 Flatiron Building

Though dwarfed by countless taller structures today, this unusual building – its shape conforming to a triangular plot of land – remains striking, a symbol of the beginning of the skyscraper era. Its slim, rounded façade is as proud as a ship's prow sailing up the avenue. Completed in 1902, it anchored the north end of the prestigious Ladies' Mile shopping district, located between Union and Madison squares. The designer, famous Chicago architect Daniel Burnham, included detailed Italian Renaissance decoration on the building from top to bottom, much of it in terra-cotta. ✪ *175 Fifth Avenue at Broadway & 23rd St • Map L3 • Open office hours • Free*

The City's Squares

Manhattan has only four London-style squares, Union, Madison, Stuyvesant and Gramercy Park, all formed in the 1800s by real estate speculators hoping to profit by selling surrounding lots to the wealthy. The squares provide welcome breaks among the city's dense, tall buildings, but only Gramercy Park has remained residential.

7 Gramercy Park

Samuel Ruggles laid out this neighborhood around a private park in the 1830s. It remains the city's only private park and a desirable place to live. Stanford White remodeled No. 16 in 1888 for Edwin Booth, who founded the Players Club here. His statue stands in the park *(see pp114)*. ✪ *Lexington Avenue, between 20th & 21st sts • Map L4 • Closed to public*

8 National Arts Club

Originally the home of Samuel Tilden, a governor of New York and opponent of the notorious Boss Tweed *(see pp48–9)*. The Gothic Revival brownstone was designed by Calvert Vaux, of Central Park fame. The National Arts Club, whose members have included leading American artists since the 1800s, bought the building in 1906. Each member is asked to donate a work to the club. Its galleries are open to the public. ✪ *15 Gramercy Park South • Map L4*

Flatiron Building

Writers' faces, National Arts Club

9. 69th Regiment Armory

This Beaux Arts building was used as the drill hall and offices of a military unit privately formed in 1848. In 1913, the controversial exhibition of modern art known as the Armory Show was held here, including works by Van Gogh, Duchamp, and Brancusi. The show was widely panned in the press, but it brought modern art to New York on a large scale and had a profound and lasting effect on American art. ✎ *Lexington Avenue, between 25th & 26th sts • Map L4 • Closed to public*

10. "Curry Hill"

Despite changes around it, this three-block corridor just south of Murray Hill remains filled with Indian shops selling saris and gifts, and is lined with restaurants that are a boon for diners (particularly vegetarians) in search of interesting food at reasonable prices. Kalustyan's, 123 Lexington Avenue, is a treasure trove of fragrant spices and grains and features some 31 different kinds of rice. ✎ *Lexington Avenue, between 26th & 29th sts • Map L4*

Exploring Gramercy Park and Flatiron

Morning

Book-lovers should start on 12th Street, where the city's biggest used bookstore, the Strand, is located at No. 828. From here, head north up Broadway to Union Square, visiting the **Greenmarket** *(see p111)*. Continuing up Broadway brings you to the Paragon Sports superstore, 867 Broadway at 18th Street, and Fishs Eddy, 889 Broadway at 19th, selling all but indestructible vintage and new china. The fascinating **ABC Carpet & Home** awaits at No. 888 *(see p111)*.

At the **Flatiron Building**, turn east to **Madison Square** *(p111)*, then have lunch at **Tabla** or the gourmet **11 Madison Park** *(p115)*. Several restaurants on **"Curry Hill"** also offer inexpensive lunches, including Pongal, No. 110, and Cardamomm at 100 Lexington Ave.

Afternoon

While you are in the neighborhood, check out the intriguing spices at Kalustyan's, 123 Lexington Avenue.

More shops can be found on Fifth Avenue between 14th and 23rd streets, including Emporio Armani, No. 110, between 16th & 17th and Daffy's, No. 111, a discount store offering designer finds.

End your day in the civilized oasis of the **Gramercy Park** neighborhood. Be sure to stroll East 19th Street, known as the "Block Beautiful," for its handsome 1920s houses.

Left **Farragut Monument** Center **George Washington** Right **Marquis de Lafayette**

Statues and Monuments

1 George Washington
The city's first major outdoor statue was created in 1856 by Henry Kirke Brown. The statue is a 14-foot (4.26-metre) equestrian figure on a granite pedestal. ⊗ *Union Square facing 14th St • Map M4*

2 Abraham Lincoln
This pensive figure by Henry Kirke Brown was commissioned shortly after the president's assassination in 1865. ⊗ *North end of Union Square near 16th St • Map M4*

3 Marquis de Lafayette
A larger-than-life 1873 statue of Lafayette pledging his heart to the American Revolution by Frédéric-Auguste Bartholdi, creator of the Statue of Liberty. ⊗ *Madison Square • Map L3–4*

4 Mohandas K (Mahatma) Gandhi
The site for this 1986 statue of the hero of Indian independence was chosen because the park was frequently the site of protest gatherings. ⊗ *Union Square • Map M4*

5 Edwin Booth as Hamlet
The founder of the Players Club is shown in his most famous role, about to give Hamlet's soliloquy. The 1917 statue faces his former house. ⊗ *Gramercy Park • Map L4*

6 Fantasy Fountain
Greg Wyatt's 1983 smiling sun and moon flanked by dancing giraffes, from whose mouths water flows in warm weather. ⊗ *Southeast corner of Gramercy Park • Map L4*

7 Worth Monument
An 1850s obelisk marks the grave of the only public figure buried under the streets of Manhattan, General Worth, hero of the Mexican Wars. ⊗ *Traffic Island, 23rd Street & Broadway • Map L3*

8 Farragut Monument
This 1880 memorial to a naval hero established Augustus Saint-Gaudens as the nation's foremost sculptor; Stanford White designed the base. ⊗ *Madison Square • Map L3–4*

9 Chester Alan Arthur
Arthur became the 21st President when James Garfield was assassinated. George Edwin Bissell sculpted him in 1898, standing in front of an elaborate chair. ⊗ *Madison Square • Map L3–4*

10 William Seward
In 1876 Randolph Rogers immortalized the secretary of state under Lincoln, best remembered for his much-criticized purchase of Alaska in 1867. ⊗ *Madison Square • Map L3–4*

For more on figures in New York's history **See pp48–9**

Tabla, Madison Avenue

🔟 Restaurants

1 Union Square Café
One of New York's most popular restaurants uses ingredients from the neighboring Union Square Greenmarket *(see p68)*. ◈ *21 East 16th Street at Union Square West • Map M4 • 212 243 4020 • $$$*

2 Gramercy Tavern
Unpretentious fine dining where the inventive American cuisine is universally praised. Great desserts *(see p69)*. ◈ *42 East 20th Street at Broadway • Map L4 • 212 477 0777 • $$$*

3 11 Madison Park
Danny Meyer has made 11 Madison Square chic with his imaginative New American cuisine in an elegant Art Deco setting. ◈ *Madison Avenue at East 24th St • Map L4 • 212 889 0905 • $$$*

4 Tocqueville
The chef prepares French cuisine with Japanese touches in this hidden gem. ◈ *15 East 15th St, between Union Square West & 5th Ave • Map M4 • 212 647 1515 • $$$*

5 Tabla and Tabla Bread Bar
Another Danny Meyer success on Madison Square; New American with Indian seasonings, served in colorful surroundings. ◈ *11 Madison Avenue at East 25th St • Map L4 • 212 889 0667 • Tabla $$$, Bread Bar $$*

6 Fleur de Sel
An intimate modern French restaurant with a small menu that shows meticulous dedication. ◈ *5 East 20th Street, between 5th Ave & Broadway • Map L4 • 212 460 9100 • $$$*

7 Olives
Popular restaurant for the beautiful set in the W Hotel. The menu features modern Mediterranean dishes, and they serve afternoon tea. ◈ *201 Park Ave South at 17th St • Map M4 • 212 353 8345 • $$$*

8 Veritas
An amazing wine list is the big draw, but the New American cuisine is also outstanding. Reserve ahead. ◈ *43 East 20th Street, between Broadway & Park Av South • Map L4 • 212 353 3700 • $$$$*

9 Kitchen 22
Top chef Charlie Palmer delivers a bargain prix-fixe menu in a stylish venue that draws a hip crowd. ◈ *36 E 22nd St • Map L4 • 212 228 4399 • $$*

10 Craftbar
Tom Collichio's scaled-down version of Craft next door still gives diners the chance to create their own menus but at cheaper prices. ◈ *47 E 19th Street at Park Ave Sth • Map M4 • 212 780 0880 • $$*

Left **Macy's façade** Center **Ornamental clock, Herald Square** Right **Chelsea Piers**

Chelsea and Herald Square

A NEIGHBORHOOD *that has seen a great deal of recent change, Chelsea was a quiet enclave of 19th-century brownstones that never made it as a fashionable address. Now it is a hub for gay New Yorkers and center for the city's avant-garde art galleries. Buildings along 6th Avenue are now occupied by superstores and discount outlets, and to the west, Chelsea Piers has transformed the waterfront. Uptown, the Garment District begins around 27th Street, with Herald Square and Macy's at the heart of the city's busiest shopping area.*

🔟 Sights

1. 6th Avenue Shopping
2. Annex Antiques and Flea Market
3. Flower District
4. Chelsea Hotel
5. Chelsea Historic District
6. General Theological Seminary
7. Chelsea Piers
8. Fashion Institute of Technology (F.I.T.)
9. Herald Square
10. Macy's

Cheerleaders at Macy's

1 6th Avenue Shopping

Anchored by Macy's, which opened in 1858, this was once a popular district known as "Fashion Row". The 1876 cast-iron façade of the Hugh O'Neill Dry Goods Store at Nos. 655–71 exemplifies the era, when the arrival of the 6th Avenue elevated line provided easy access to the area. As Manhattan's commercial center moved northward, these cast-iron palaces were left deserted until recently, when they found new life as bargain fashion outlets and superstores. ⬡ *6th Avenue, 18th to 23rd sts • Map L3*

2 Annex Antiques and Flea Market

On weekends, year-round, an empty parking lot becomes one of the city's most popular outdoor markets. A tradition for more than 30 years, some 600 dealers, from Maine to Maryland, set up booths selling clothing, silver, jewelry, furniture, art, and "junktiques" from old tools to vintage eyeglasses. Many prize antiques can be discovered at The Amex, an indoor market just around the corner at 112 West 25th Street, and at The Showplace, 40 West 26th Street, with 135 dealers on three floors. ⬡ *6th Avenue at 26th St • Map L3 • Open sunrise to sunset • Admission charge*

Façade, Chelsea Hotel

3 Flower District

Here, at the heart of the city's wholesale flower district, you can hardly see the sidewalk for the masses of greenery, shrubs, and flowers. Manhattan's largest concentration of shops selling house plants, trees, blooming plants, and all manner of flowers, fresh, dried, and artificial can be found here; if you can't find what you want, it probably doesn't exist. The district extends along 6th Avenue roughly from 25th to 30th streets. ⬡ *6th Avenue at 27th St • Map L3*

4 Chelsea Hotel

Seedy it is, yet there's a definite mystique to this 1884 building bedecked with wrought-iron balconies. Once a fancy apartment, it became a hotel favored by musicians, artists, and writers. Former guests, commemorated on brass plaques outside, include Tennessee Williams, Mark Twain, Jack Kerouac, and Brendan Behan. Dylan Thomas spent his last years here. Notoriously, it was also the place where punk rocker Sid Vicious killed his girlfriend Nancy Spungeon in 1978. Step into the lobby and take a look at the wild artwork, and soak up the ambience at the bar. ⬡ *212 West 23rd Street, between 7th & 8th avs • Map L3*

Left **The Flower District** Right **Chelsea Hotel, cast-iron stairwell**

5 Chelsea Historic District

Clement Moore, author of *A Visit from St. Nicholas*, developed this land in the 1830s. The finest of the town houses built here are the seven known as "Cushman Row," Nos. 406–18 West 20th Street, which are among the city's best examples of Greek Revival architecture. Houses at Nos. 446–50 West 20th are in the Italianate style, for which Chelsea is also known. ✎ *Between 9th & 10th avenues, 20th & 21st sts • Map L2*

6 General Theological Seminary

America's oldest Episcopal seminary was founded in 1819. This campus was built around two quadrangles in the 1830s, on a site donated by Clement Moore, who taught at the seminary. The main building, added in 1960, includes a library with the largest collection of Latin Bibles in the world. There are lovely inner gardens (9th Avenue entrance). ✎ *20th to 21st streets • Map L2 • Open noon–3pm Mon–Fri, 11am–3pm Sat • Free*

7 Chelsea Piers

Four neglected piers have been turned into a 30-acre sports and recreation complex, and Manhattan's largest venue for film and TV production. Sports facilities include ice skating, inline skating and skateboarding, batting cages, playing fields, a basketball court, bowling alley, golf driving ranges, and a marina offering harbor cruises and sailing instruction. Pier Park is a place to relax with a water view. ✎ *23rd Street at the Hudson River • Map L2 • Open 6am–midnight daily • Admission charge • www.chelseapiers.com*

8 Fashion Institute of Technology (F.I.T.)

Founded in 1944 and now a branch of the State University of New York, the Fashion Institute of Technology is a prestigious school teaching art, fashion design, and marketing, and boasts famous alumni, including Calvin Klein, Norma Kamali, and David Chu. Students benefit from internships with New York's

---

The World's Largest Store

Macy's is more than a store to most New Yorkers. It is a major part of the city, sponsoring the famous Thanksgiving Day Parade, the city's Fourth of July fireworks and everything from an annual spring flower show filling the main floor, to Tap-O-Mania, when thousands of tap dancers converge on Herald Square.

Left **Chelsea Piers** Center **"Cushman Row", Chelsea Historic District** Right **Herald Square**

34th Street entrance, Macy's

leading stores and designers. Of greatest interest to the public is the gallery, which has changing exhibits, often from their collection of clothing and textiles. ✪ *7th Avenue at West 27th St • Map L3 • Open noon–8pm Tue-Fri, 10am–5pm Sat • Free*

9 Herald Square

The center of a rowdy theater district known as the Tenderloin in the 1870s and 80s, until it was reformed. The Manhattan Opera House was razed in 1901 to make way for Macy's, and other stores soon followed. The clock on the island where Broadway meets 6th Avenue is all that is left of the building occupied by the *New York Herald* until 1921. ✪ *Broadway at 6th Av • Map K3*

10 Macy's

Former whaler R. H. Macy founded the store in 1858 on 6th Avenue and 14th Street; the red star logo was from his tattoo, a souvenir of sailing days. Innovations included pricing goods a few cents below a full dollar and offering a money-back guarantee. The store was sold in 1888 and moved to the present building *(see p64)*. ✪ *151 West 34th Street at 6th Av • Map K3 • www.macys.com*

A Day Around Chelsea

Morning

🕐 Wind your way through Chelsea, starting with the megastores now occupying former "Fashion Row," on **6th Avenue** *(p117)* between 18th and 23rd streets. Walk west on 16th Street to 9th Avenue and Chelsea Market, a one-time Nabisco factory where the first Oreo cookies were made, now a block-long line of stalls offering all manner of food. The Food Network tapes its TV shows in a street-level studio here.

Continue up 9th Avenue to 20th Street, for the **Chelsea Historic District** and **General Theological Seminary**. Then head for the ever-expanding "Gallery Row," from 21st to 24th streets, 10th to 11th avenues. A good lunch bet in the neighborhood is **The Red Cat**, offering Mediterranean fare *(see p121)*.

Afternoon

Walk east on 23rd Street to the **Chelsea Hotel** *(see p117)*, and when you get to 6th Avenue, turn uptown for the big antiques market and the colorful **Flower District** *(see p117)*. A stroll for one block further west on 27th brings you to the **Fashion Institute of Technology**, where the gallery usually has interesting displays.

Head for one of the great hidden treasures in this area, St. John the Baptist Church, at 210 East 31st Street, whose dingy façade belies a glowing Gothic interior. Continue to 34th Street for **Herald Square** and **Macy's**.

Left **Dia Center for the Arts** Right **Marlborough**

🔟 Chelsea Galleries

1 Dia Center for the Arts
The spacious galleries here reopen in late 2006, but Dia has another museum in Beacon, NY. ⌖ *548 West 22nd Street at 10th Av • Map L2 • **Beacon museum:** 3 Beckman St, Beacon • Open 11am–6pm Thu–Mon (mid-Oct–mid-Apr: 11am–4pm)*

2 Matthew Marks
Of the two galleries, the original shows large-scale works, while the second specializes in new work *(see p43)*. ⌖ *522 West 22nd Street at 10th Av • Open noon–6pm Tues–Sat; 523 West 24th Street at 10th Av • Map L2 • Open 10am–6pm Tue–Sat • Free*

3 Paula Cooper
The lofty setting itself is worth a visit. Many of Cooper's shows are controversial *(see p43)*. ⌖ *534 West 21st Street at 10th Av • Map L2 • Open 11am–6pm Tue–Sat • Free*

4 Paul Kasmin
Son of a British art dealer, Kasmin has nurtured many newcomers *(see p43)*. ⌖ *293 10th Avenue at 27th St • Map M2 • Open 10am–6pm Tue–Fri, 11am–6pm Sat • Free*

5 Barbara Gladstone
A dramatic backdrop for large-scale pieces, video pioneers, and photography. ⌖ *515 West 24th Street at 10th Av • Map L2 • Open 10am–6pm Tue–Sat • Free*

6 Andrea Rosen
Since moving from SoHo to Chelsea, Rosen's eclectic exhibitions have made this one of the most visited galleries in the area. ⌖ *525 West 24th Street at 10th Av • Map L2 • Open 10am–6pm Tue–Sat • Free*

7 Marlborough, Chelsea
The 57th Street gallery shows established luminaries, while this downtown satellite has new sculpture and painting *(see p42)*. ⌖ *211 West 19th Street at 7th Av • Map L3 • Open 10am–5:30pm Tue–Sat • Free*

8 Robert Miller
This gallery shows big names like Diane Arbus, Walker Evans, Andy Warhol, and Jacob Epstein. ⌖ *526 West 26th Street at 10th Av • Map L2 • Open 10am–6pm Tue–Sat • Free*

9 Sonnabend
A power in the art world, representing early pop artists, and still on the lookout for new trends. ⌖ *536 West 22nd Street at 10th Av • Map L2 • Open 10am–6pm Tue–Sat • Free*

10 303 Gallery
Featuring artists of critical acclaim in several media. ⌖ *525 West 22nd Street at 10th Av • Map L2 • Open 10am–6pm Tue–Sat • Free*

Price Categories

For a three-course meal for one with a glass of house wine, and all unavoidable charges including tax.

$	under $25
$$	$25–$50
$$$	$50–$80
$$$$	over $80

Left **Rocking Horse Café Mexicano** Right **Empire Diner**

TOP 10 Places to Eat

1 Da Umberto
Popular over the years for sophisticated Tuscan fare and a long list of daily specials. ◈ *107 West 17th Street, between 6th & 7th avs • Map M3 • 212 989 0303 • $$$*

2 Periyali
A billowing canopy and white walls set the scene for classy Greek dining; creative dishes put the food in gourmet territory. ◈ *35 West 20th Street, between 5th & 6th avs • Map L3 • 212 463 7890 • $$$*

3 The Red Cat
This warm neighborhood place serves first-rate American fare; don't miss the Parmesan frites with mustard aioli. ◈ *227 10th Avenue, between 23rd & 24th sts • Map L2 • 212 242 1122 • $$*

4 Chelsea Bistro & Bar
A romantic bit of Paris in Chelsea, with a candlelit terrace and sophisticated bistro menu. ◈ *358 West 23rd Street, between 8th & 9th avs • Map L2 • 212 727 2026 • $$*

5 Le Madri
Northern Italian cooking attracts a well-heeled crowd who enjoy the *osso buco* and extensive wine list. ◈ *168 West 18th Street at 7th Av • Map M3 • 212 727 8022 • $$$*

6 Rocking Horse Café Mexicano
Always packed with diners who come for the great margaritas and excellent Mexican food at reasonable prices.
◈ *182 Eighth Avenue, between 19th & 20th sts • Map L2 • 212 463 9511 • $$*

7 El Cid
Tapas, paella, sangria, and all the other Spanish favorites are on hand at this friendly restaurant. ◈ *322 West 15th Street, between 8th & 9th avs • Map M2 • 212 929 9332 • $$*

8 Monster Sushi
As the name implies, enormous rolls of sushi are provided at very reasonable prices. ◈ *158 West 23rd St • Map L3 • 212 620 9131 • $$*

9 Bottino
Thanks to the booming gallery scene, this attracts a stylish crowd for good northern Italian fare and a lovely garden. ◈ *246 10th Avenue, between 24th & 25th sts • Map L2 • 212 206 6766 • $$*

10 Empire Diner
The door is always open at this rail car converted to a 24-hour Art Deco diner. The best people-watching comes after midnight. ◈ *210 10th Avenue at 22nd St • Map L2 • 212 243 2736 • $*

Left **Prometheus, Rockefeller Center** Center **Grand Central Terminal** Right **Chrysler Building**

Midtown

THE LIGHTS OF TIMES SQUARE, THE SPIRES *of the Empire State and Chrysler buildings, Rockefeller Center, the United Nations Headquarters, stores on 5th Avenue, museums, theaters, and grand buildings galore – all are found in the midtown area between 34th and 59th streets, extending from the East River as far as Broadway. The concentration of attractions makes this the most important area of the city for* visitors, and many a day can be spent taking in the sights. Fifth Avenue, the dividing line between the East and West sides, is in many ways the Main Street of Manhattan, and in itself offers a generous sampling of the city's riches, from architecture to commerce. Midtown also reflects the city's characteristic diversity, with attractions that range from the bustling retail of the Diamond District, to the stately halls of the New York Public Library.

St. Patrick's Cathedral

Sights

1. Times Square
2. Empire State Building
3. Rockefeller Center
4. Chrysler Building
5. Grand Central Terminal
6. New York Public Library
7. St. Patrick's Cathedral
8. United Nations Headquarters
9. Diamond District
10. Carnegie Hall

1 Times Square
The city's most famous intersection, and symbol of the lively surrounding theater district *(see pp22-5).*

2 Empire State Building
New York's most famous, and tallest, skyscraper is an Art Deco classic. Since the structure was completed in 1931 more than 120 million visitors have looked down on the city from its observatories *(see pp8–9).*

3 Rockefeller Center
Rockefeller Center is the hub of midtown New York, alive with activity day and night, integrating shops, gardens, dining and office space, and countless works of art *(see pp12–15).*

4 Chrysler Building
The unmistakable shimmering spire of the Chrysler Building is one of New York's great landmarks. The grand Art Deco lobby, once used as a showroom for Chrysler cars, has been restored to show off its lavish marbles and granite, and a vast painted ceiling depicts transportation scenes of the late 1920s *(see p44).* ⊗ *405 Lexington Avenue at 42nd St • Map K4 • Open (lobby only) 7am–6pm Mon–Fri • Free*

5 Grand Central Terminal
One of the world's great rail terminals, the outstanding Beaux Arts building *(see p47)* is New York's most visited, with 500,000 people passing through it daily. Since restoration work was completed, its admirers are no longer limited to travelers. Grand Central has become an attraction in its own right, with 15 restaurants, over 40 shops, the New York City Transit Museum and a gourmet food market. ⊗ *42nd Street, between Park & Lexington avs • Map J–K4 • Open 5:30am–1:30am daily • Free • www.grandcentralterminal.com*

Left **Empire State Building** Center **Rockefeller Center** Right **Chrysler Building**

6 New York Public Library

Carrère and Hastings won a competition for the design of this great Beaux Arts building. Their genius reached its height in the Main Reading Room, a paneled space as majestic as a cathedral, extending almost two city blocks, with enormous arched windows, 18 grand chandeliers, and an elaborately decorated, vaulted ceiling *(see p47)*. ⊗ *5th Avenue at 42nd St • Map K3 • Open 10am–6pm Thu–Sat, 11am–7:30pm Tue & Wed, 1–6pm Sun • Free • www.nypl.org*

7 St. Patrick's Cathedral

America's largest Catholic cathedral is a place more than 5,000 people worship every Sunday. When Archbishop John Hughes decided to build a cathedral here in 1850, many criticized the choice of a site so far from the city's center at the time. Today his foresight has given the church one of the best locations in Manhattan *(see p46)*. ⊗ *5th Avenue, between 50th & 51 sts • Map J3 • Open 7:30am–8:30pm daily • Free*

William O. Partridge's Pieta, St. Patrick's Cathedral

Time for Tea

Taking tea is an increasingly popular custom in New York. Among the top places are the elegant Palm Court at the Plaza Hotel, 59th and 5th, the Tea Box Café at Takashimaya *(see p126)*, the tea room at the St. Regis Hotel *(see p172)*, and the *salon de thé* at Fauchon, 442 Park Avenue at 56th.

8 United Nations Headquarters

John D. Rockefeller, Jr. donated $8.5 million to purchase the 18-acre East River site, and American Wallace Harrison worked with international consultants to create this striking headquarters. The United Nations was formed in 1945, to work for peace and economic and social well-being around the globe. Currently, 189 members meet in the General Assembly, the closest thing to a world parliament. Guided tours allow visitors to see the various council chambers, the General

Left **New York Public Library** Right **St. Patrick's Cathedral**

Assembly Hall, and many of the works by prominent artists, including Marc Chagall and Henry Moore. ◉ *First Avenue at 46th St • Map J5 • Open (for tours) 9:30am–4:45pm Mon–Fri, 10am–4:30pm Sat–Sun (Jan–Feb: Mon–Fri only) • Admission charge • www.un.org*

9 Diamond District

Jewels glisten in every window of this block, the center of the city's retail and wholesale trade. It handles 80 percent of the diamonds coming into the U.S. Developed largely by Orthodox Jews, the district grew in importance during the World War II when thousands fled the diamond centers of Antwerp and Amsterdam to settle in New York. Above the shops are offices and workshops where the stones are cut and set.
◉ *47th Street, between 5th & 6th avs • Map J3*

10 Carnegie Hall

New York almost lost its most famous concert hall when the New York Philharmonic moved to the newly built Lincoln Center in the 1950s. However, a coalition, led by violinist Isaac Stern, successfully fought to save the building from demolition. It was bought by the city in 1960 and became a National Historic Landmark in 1964. A major 1986 renovation restored much of the original appearance while updating technical facilities and preserving the hall's famous acoustics. Musical memorabilia fills the halls and the Rose Museum *(see p46)*. ◉ *West 57th Street at 7th Av • Map H3 • Open 11am–4:30pm daily • Free • www.carnegiehall.org*

A Day Exploring Midtown

Morning

Start at the **Morgan Library** *(see p41)*, and see Morgan's opulent study, then proceed to 42nd Street and turn east for a tour through **Grand Central Terminal** *(see p123)*. Continue east on 42nd Street, stopping to look at the outstanding lobbies of the **Chrysler Building** *(see p123)*, the **Daily News Building**, and the **Ford Foundation**, and climbing the stairs to see the **Tudor City** complex *(see p127)*.

End the morning with a tour of the **United Nations HQ**. If you reserve ahead, you can have lunch in the very special U.N. delegate's dining room (212 963 7625).

Afternoon

Take the 42nd Street crosstown bus back to Fifth Avenue and visit the **New York Public Library**. Walk uptown to 47th Street and turn west for the **Diamond District**, then pay a quick visit to the **Museum of Television and Radio** *(see p128)* on 52nd Street between Fifth and Sixth avenues. Pop in to the new home of the **American Museum of Folk Art** *(see p139)* and stop for a coffee in the museum's café before taking in the exhibits of traditional art.

Return to 5th Avenue where the uptown shops include **Tiffany and Company**'s *(see p10)* windows of jewels, **Bergdorf Goodman**'s *(see p10)* stylish displays, and F.A.O. Schwarz. Round the day off at the Plaza Hotel at 59th Street, perfect for a refreshing cocktail in a landmark setting.

Left **H&M** Center **Henri Bendel** Right **Niketown**

TOP 10 Places to Shop

1 Department Stores
Bountiful stocks of beautiful clothing await at Bergdorf Goodman, Saks Fifth Avenue, Lord & Taylor, and Bloomingdales. ⊗ *5th Avenue, between 38th & 58th sts • Map K3–H3*

2 H&M
Flagship store of the Swedish retailer known for great young fashion with small price tags *(see p65).* ⊗ *5th Avenue at 51st St • Map J3*

3 Henri Bendel
This is one of the most attractive stores in the city, featuring designer fashions and a notable selection of cosmetics *(see p64).* ⊗ *712 5th Avenue at 55th St • Map H3*

4 Takashimaya
Tasteful New York home of a leading Japanese department store, filled with the finest clothing, home accessories, and art *(see p64).* ⊗ *693 5th Avenue, between 54th & 55th sts • Map H3*

5 Felissimo
A five-story, Japanese-owned townhouse filled with unusual and tasteful jewelry, clothing, home furnishings and accessories. ⊗ *10 West 56th Street, between 5th & 6th avs • Map H3*

6 Museum of Modern Art Design Shop
Lamps, furniture, toys, jewelry, posters – whatever the item here, you can be sure it will be the epitome of good design. ⊗ *44 West 53rd Street, between 5th & 6th avs • Map J3*

7 Designer Boutiques
Many designers have moved north, but 57th Street between 5th and Madison remains impressive, with Burberry, Hermes, Chanel, and Dior. Prada is at No. 724 5th Avenue. ⊗ *57th Street, between 5th & Madison avs • Map H4*

8 Fortunoff's
If Tiffany is out of your league, try this retailer specializing in fine jewelry at more reasonable prices. ⊗ *681 5th Avenue at 54th St • Map H3*

9 Niketown
Commercial, high-tech shopping fun, all to entice you to buy sneakers and sportswear. ⊗ *6 East 57th Street, between 5th & Madison avs • Map H4*

10 Trump Tower
An over-the-top mall of expensive boutiques, the Trump Tower is worth visiting for the pink marble-with-waterfall surroundings even if you don't buy. ⊗ *725 5th Avenue at 56th St • Map H3*

For more on shopping See p165

Left **Ford Foundation Building** Center **Lever House** Right **Tudor City**

🔟 Midtown Architecture

1 Lever House
This 24-story building of glass and steel by Gordon Bunshaft was the first "glass box" in New York (see p44). ◈ *390 Park Avenue • Map H4 • Lobby open during office hours*

2 General Electric Building
This 1931 Art Deco building has a clock whose arms grasp at lightning bolts. ◈ *570 Lexington Avenue • Map H4 • Closed to public*

3 Chanin Building
One of the great early Art Deco skyscrapers (c.1929) notable for its terra-cotta frieze and bronze band illustrating the theory of evolution. ◈ *122 East 42nd Street • Map K4 • Lobby open during office hours*

4 Daily News Building
The *Daily News* has moved on, but this fine 1930 building is still an Art Deco classic. Step inside and marvel at the revolving globe. ◈ *220 East 42nd Street at 2nd Av • Map K4 • Lobby open during office hours*

5 Ford Foundation
Considered one of the city's best modern designs (1967). Every office opens onto a skylit, 12-story atrium with lush landscaping and a pond. ◈ *320 East 43rd Street at 1st Av • Map J4 • Lobby open during office hours*

6 Fred F. French Building
Built for the best-known real estate firm of its day, this 1927 building is opulent inside and out. Don't miss the lobby. ◈ *521 5th Av • Map J3 • Lobby open during office hours*

7 Tudor City
Fred R. French created this mock-Tudor enclave, designed to prove that middle-class housing could succeed in Midtown. ◈ *1st to 2nd Avenues, 40th to 43rd sts • Map J4–K4 • Lobby open during office hours*

8 NY Yacht Club
The window bays of this 1899 private club are the carved sterns of ships, sailing on a sea of sculpted waves. ◈ *37 West 44th Street at 5th Av • Map J3 • Closed to public*

9 American Standard Building
Raymond Hood's first New York skyscraper is an ornate black tower built in 1924, now a hotel. ◈ *40 West 40th Street • Map K3 • Lobby open during office hours*

10 Condé Nast Building
The 48-story tower, built in 1999, is striking and environmentally friendly, with photovoltaic cells on the façade and integrated recycling chutes. ◈ *4 Times Square • Map J3 • Lobby open during office hours*

For more on architecture **See pp46–7**

Left **Morgan Library** Center **Museum of Television and Radio** Right **New York Public Library**

🔟 Midtown Museums

1 Morgan Library
The library reopened in 2006 after a major expansion to hold this private collection of rare books, prints, and manuscripts *(see p41)*. 🏛 *29 East 36th Street at Madison Av • Map K4 • www. morganlibrary.com • Admission charge*

2 Museum of Modern Art
Reopened in 2005 following a massive renovation program, the new building is worthy of this outstanding collection *(see p40)*. 🏛 *11 West 53rd Street at 5th Av • Map H3*

3 American Museum of Folk Art
The new museum quadruples the space for this extensive collection of folk art. 🏛 *45 West 53rd Street • Map H3 • Open 10:30am–5:30pm Tue–Sun (to 7:30pm Fri) • Admission charge*

4 Museum of Arts and Design
The permanent collection, which dates from 1900, includes 2000 craft exhibits. 🏛 *40 West 53rd St at 5th Av • Map H3 • Open 10am–6pm Fri–Wed (10am–8pm Thu) • Admission charge*

5 International Center of Photography
Two floors of retrospectives and changing exhibits. 🏛 *1133 6th Avenue • Map J3 • Open 10am–5pm Tue–Thu, 10am–8pm Fri, 10am–6pm Sat & Sun • Admission charge*

6 Museum of Television and Radio
Watch your favorites from over 60,000 radio and TV programs, plus special exhibits and classic screenings. 🏛 *25 West 52nd Street between 5th & 6th avs • Map J3 • Open noon–6pm Tue, Wed & Fri–Sun; noon–8pm Thu • www.mtr.org • Admission charge*

7 Whitney Museum at Philip Morris
A midtown branch of the museum used for small shows from its contemporary collection. 🏛 *120 Park Avenue at 42nd St • Map K4 • Open during office hours • Free*

8 New York Public Library Galleries
Rare prints, paintings, and changing exhibitions. 🏛 *5th Avenue at 42nd St • Map K3 • Open 11am-6pm Tue-Wed, 10am–6pm Thu–Sat • Free*

9 Dahesh Museum of Art
A private collection of 2,000 works of 19th- and 20th-century art. 🏛 *580 Madison Avenue at 57th St • Map J3 • Open 11am–6pm Tue–Sun*

10 Municipal Art Society Galleries
Changing exhibits covering the city's architecture and neighborhoods. 🏛 *457 Madison Avenue • Map J4 • Open 11am–5pm Mon–Wed, Fri & Sat • Free*

For more New York museums See pp40–41

Price Categories

For a three-course
meal for one with a   **$** under $25
glass of house wine,   **$$** $25–$50
and all unavoidable   **$$$** $50–$80
charges including tax.   **$$$$** over $80

Left **Grand Central Oyster Bar and Restaurant** Right **Le Colonial**

Restaurants

1 Four Seasons
An award-winning New York institution with landmark decor and great celebrity spotting opportunities *(see p69)*. ◈ *99 East 52nd Street at Park Av • Map J4 • 212 754 9494 • $$$*

2 Le Bernardin
Impeccable fish served in every imaginable way. Seafood doesn't come any better than this *(see p69)*. ◈ *155 West 51st Street at 6th Av • Map J3 • 212 489 1515 • $$$$*

3 Blue Fin
One of the coolest places in the area, this restaurant is dedicated to serving seafood dishes including sushi. ◈ *1567 Broadway at 47th Street • Map J3 • 212 918 1400 • $$$*

4 Alain Ducasse at the Essex House
The celebrated French chef offers outstanding delicacies in an upscale and intimate dining room. The sumptuous food comes at a price. ◈ *155 West 58th Street, between 6th & 7th avs • Map H3 • 212 265 7300 • $$$$*

5 Le Colonial
Sultry decor straight out of 1930s Saigon sets the scene for a Vietnamese/French menu full of delicate contrasts and combinations. Relax with an after-dinner drink in the lounge upstairs. ◈ *149 East 57th Street at Lexington Av • Map H4 • 212 752 0808 • $$$*

6 Osteria del Circo
The sons of Le Cirque's owner have created their own whimsical circus, serving traditional Tuscan fare. ◈ *120 West 55th Street at 6th Av • Map H3 • 212 265 3636 • $$$*

7 Grand Central Oyster Bar and Restaurant
A New York classic, this bustling and ever-popular restaurant serves only the freshest seafood. ◈ *Grand Central Terminal, lower level, 42nd Street at Lexington Av • Map K4 • 212 490 6650 • $$*

8 Brasserie
Newly remodeled with sleek, high-tech decor. The updated bistro menu features modern French/American Pacific dishes but still includes a few classics. ◈ *100 East 53rd Street at Lexington Av • Map J4 • 212 751 4840 • $$*

9 L'Impero
High-end Italian food served in a cozy dining room tucked away in Tudor City. Excellent prix-fixe menu, crowd-pleasing desserts, and outstanding service. ◈ *45 Tudor City Place • Map J5 • 212 559 5045 • $$$*

10 La Bonne Soupe
A midtown haven for the thrifty, with comfortable, old-fashioned, French bistro charm. This theater district favorite is a great place to eat after a show. Three-course meals starting at $14. ◈ *48 West 55th Street, between 5th & 6th avs • Map H3 • 212 586 7650 • $$*

Note: *Unless otherwise stated, all restaurants accept credit cards and serve vegetarian meals*

Left **Toward Roosevelt Island** *(see p134)* Right **River promenade, Carl Schurz Park** *(see p135)*

Upper East Side

WHEN NEW YORK'S UPPER CRUST *moved uptown a century ago*, their destination was the Upper East Side, and it is still the address of choice for many wealthy families. Most of the older Beaux Arts mansions around 5th Avenue are now occupied by embassies or museums; today's elite live in the solid apartment buildings that went up on 5th and Park Avenues, convenient for patronizing the boutiques on Madison, the city's most exclusive shopping street. Only churches and a few restaurants remain of German Yorkville or the Hungarian and Czech neighborhoods that used to fill the blocks east of Lexington. Young families now occupy the newer buildings in this area. For visitors, the Upper East Side is home to many of the city's best museums.

Mount Vernon *(see p135)*

Sights

1 Central Park

2 Metropolitan Museum of Art

3 Solomon R. Guggenheim Museum

4 Museum Mile

5 Bridgemarket

6 Roosevelt Island

7 Seventh Regiment Armory

8 Henderson Place Historic District

9 Gracie Mansion and Carl Schurz Park

10 Mount Vernon Hotel Museum and Gardens

Preceding pages **Central Park skaters**

Central Park
The 843-acre swathe of green that provides recreation and beauty for more than two million visitors each year *(see pp26–7)*.

Metropolitan Museum of Art
More a collection of museums, spanning 5,000 years of global culture *(see pp28–31)*.

Solomon R. Guggenheim Museum
A notable collection of modern art set in Frank Lloyd Wright's only New York building *(see pp32–3)*.

Museum Mile
Nine museums are situated within one convenient mile. They unite for a free open house day in June. Participants include the Metropolitan Museum of Art, National Academy of Fine Arts, Cooper-Hewitt National Design Museum, Soloman R. Guggenheim Museum, Jewish Museum, Neue Gallery for German and Austrian Art, Museum of the City of New York *(see p41)*, and El Museo del Barrio. ⊗ • *5th Avenue from 82nd to 104th sts • Map F4–D • Opening times vary*

Bridgemarket
Britain's Sir Terence Conran was a major player in the development of this cathedral-like space beneath the 59th Street bridge. The vaults are among the most dramatic works by Rafael Guastavino, a Spanish architect noted for his use of Catalan-style tiling. Beneath the grand ceilings are Guastavino's restaurant *(see p137)* and a Food Emporium market. The complex, which is responsible for the rapid revitalization of the neighborhood, also includes the Conran Shop for high-end home decor, and a public plaza. ⊗ *59th Street, between 1st & York avs • Map H5*

For New York's Top 10 museums **See pp40–41**

6 Roosevelt Island

A four-minute tram ride is the route to this East River enclave. Once known as "Welfare Island," when it was home to a prison, poor house, and hospital for the insane, the 147-acre island was renamed and redeveloped in the 1970s according to a master plan drawn up by Philip Johnson and John Burgee, intended to create a quiet, almost traffic-free residential community. The plan has not been fully developed, although more than 3,000 apartments have been built, and while there is a subway stop from Manhattan, the only auto access is via a bridge in Queens. *Trams every 15 mins from TramPlaza, 2nd Avenue at 59th St • Map H5*

7 Seventh Regiment Armory

The socially prominent members of the Seventh Regiment, formed in 1806, had the wherewithal to construct a remarkable armory in 1877–89, with a drill room 200 by 300 feet (60 by 90 m) and 100 feet (30 m) high, and an administration building in the form of a medieval fortress. Interior decoration was by Louis Comfort Tiffany, Stanford White, and others, and the result is opulent rooms with lavish Victorian furnishings. The drill room is used for the prestigious

St. Nicholas Russian Orthodox Cathedral
An unexpected bit of Russia, this building was constructed in 1902 in Muscovite Baroque style with a façade of red brick, white stone, and blue and yellow tiles. The incense-filled interior has marble columns and an altar enclosed by wooden screens trimmed with gold. Mass is still said in Russian. It is located at 15 East 97th Street.

Winter Antiques Show every January, as well as for many society charity balls. *643 Park Avenue at 66th St • Map G4 • 212 452 3067 • Open by appointment only*

8 Henderson Place Historic District

Built in 1881 by the developer John C. Henderson for "persons of moderate means," these winning Queen Anne houses made of brick and stone are embellished with towers, bays, gables, dormers, and slate roofs. They were an investment and remained in Henderson's family until the 20th century. Today they are unique in the city and rank among the most desirable places to live. Each block front was composed as a unit, with small towers at the end. Twenty-four of the original 32 units remain. *East End Avenue, between 86th & 87th sts • Map F5*

Left **Seventh Regiment Armory** Right **Henderson Place Historic District**

9 Gracie Mansion and Carl Schurz Park

The balconied, wooden, country home built by merchant Archibald Gracie in 1799 was the original home of the Museum of the City of New York and became the official residence of Mayor under Fiorello LaGuardia in 1942. It is located at the northern end of a park laid out in 1891, with a wide promenade that stretches along the East River. The park was named for a prominent statesman and newspaper editor who lived in the neighborhood. ⓢ East End Avenue at 88th St • Map E5 • 212 570 4751 • Open Apr–mid Nov, tours at 10am, 11am, 1pm, 2pm; Wed for pre-booked tours • Admission charge

10 Mount Vernon Hotel Museum and Gardens

A rare bit of old New York, this was the stone carriage house of a 1799 estate. When the house burned in 1826, the carriage house was converted into an inn and became a fashionable resort for New Yorkers who wanted to escape to what was then still countryside. The building and garden have been restored by the Colonial Dames of America and furnished with historic objects. Guides are on hand to explain the unique history of the attraction. ⓢ 421 East 61st Street • Map H5 • Open 11am–4pm Tue–Sun, closed August, public holidays • Admission charge • www.mvhm.org

A Day Exploring the Upper East Side

Morning

Start at the **Guggenheim** (see pp32–3) and admire Frank Lloyd Wright's great architectural achievement before seeing the fine modern art collection. "Must sees" include Chagall's *Paris Through the Window*, Modigliani's *Nude*, and Picasso's *Woman Ironing*. Stop for coffee at the café on the main floor of the museum before leaving.

Head east along 92nd Street to see two rare remaining wooden houses, No. 120, built in 1859, and No. 122, in 1871. Continue east for **Gracie Mansion** and **Henderson Place** and rest on a bench with a river view in **Carl Schurz Park**. One block west on York Avenue, a 31 bus will take you to the spectacular **Bridgemarket** (see p133). Have lunch at **Guastavino's** (see p137), and admire the great ceilings.

Afternoon

Take the 57th Street crosstown bus back to Madison Avenue and head uptown, browsing the designer boutiques. Detour on any of the side streets in the upper 60s and 70s to see the townhouses of affluent New Yorkers. Pay a quick visit to the **Frick Collection** (see p41) then stop for coffee at one of the cafés on Madison Avenue.

Spend the rest of the afternoon at the **Metropolitan Museum of Art** (see pp28–31), a New York "must," and see Rembrandt's *Self-portrait*, *Cypresses* by Van Gogh, and Michelangelo's Sistine Chapel studies. End the day with a candlelit meal at **Erminia** (see p137).

Left **Giorgio Armani** Right **Yves Saint Laurent**

Madison Avenue Boutiques

 Around Town – Upper East Side

1 Bottega Veneta
The first in the uptown Madison Avenue boutique line-up, known for luxury leather goods, shoes, and fashion. *635 Madison Avenue, between 59th & 60th sts • Map H4*

2 Shanghai Tang
The colorful townhouse home of a well-known Hong Kong retailer, selling luxury fashions and home furnishings. *714 Madison Avenue, between 63rd & 64th sts • Map H4*

3 Valentino
If you can afford it, join the rich and famous; many of his gowns are worn at the Oscars. *747 Madison Avenue at 65th St • Map G4*

4 Giorgio Armani
The New York flagship of the Italian master, known for his superb tailoring, offers a good range from his collection. *760 Madison Avenue at 65th St • Map G4*

5 BCBG Max Azria
"*Bon chic, bon genre,*" (good style, good attitude), is the motto of this hot designer. Fans of his sexy fashions include many young Hollywood stars. *770 Madison Avenue at 66th St • Map G4*

6 Moschino
An other-worldly setting provides the backdrop for whimsical, with-it clothing, continuing the legacy of the late Italian designer. *803 Madison Avenue, between 67th & 68th sts • Map G4*

7 Dolce & Gabbana
Spot the celebrities at this chic Italian outpost – one of the hot labels of the moment. *825 Madison Avenue, between 67th & 68th sts • Map G4*

8 DKNY
Donna Karan designs wearable fashions for every lifestyle and occasion. *655 Madison Avenue at 60th St • Map H4*

9 Yves Saint Laurent
The legacy of the legendary French *couturier* lingers, with a particular appeal to the young. *855-59 Madison Avenue, between 70th & 71st sts • Map G4*

10 Polo Ralph Lauren
The 1898 Rhinelander Mansion is the back-drop for the king of preppy fashion, who spent $14 million renovating the old mansion. Sportswear is in a separate shop across the street. *867 Madison Avenue at 72nd St • Map G4*

For more on shopping in New York See p165

Price Categories

For a three-course meal for one with a glass of house wine, and all unavoidable charges including tax.	**$** under $25
	$$ $25–$50
	$$$ $50–$80
	$$$$ over $80

Left **Guastavino's** Right **Orsay**

🔟 Restaurants

1 Daniel

A flower-filled dining room provides the setting for Daniel Boulud's award-winning seasonal French menus *(see p68)*. ❧ *60 East 65th Street at Park Av • Map G4 • 212 288 0033 • $$$$*

2 Guastavino's

A great setting, beneath the 59th Street bridge, with formal French dining in the upstairs club and a huge brasserie downstairs. ❧ *409 East 59th Street at 1st Av • Map H5 • 212 980 2455 • $$$*

3 Payard Bistro

Although the French food is superb, the drawcard is François Payard's exquisite desserts, such as "New York, New York." Open for morning pastries, afternoon tea, light snacks, and dinner. ❧ *1032 Lexington Avenue at 77th St • Map F4 • 212 717 5252 • $$$*

4 Café Boulud

Since Daniel *(above)* opened, Boulud's original restaurant here has become more casual, but the menu and tab are serious. In summer, the terrace tables are a fine dining spot convenient for Museum Mile. ❧ *20 East 76th Street at 5th Av • Map G4 • 212 772 2600 • $$$*

5 davidburke & donatella

Creative New American cuisine served in a stunning space – a series of rooms filled with high-rolling clientele. ❧ *133 East 61st St, between Lexington & Park avs • Map H4 • 212 813 2121 • $$$*

6 Erminia

They don't come more romantic than this tiny, candlelit Italian with beamed ceilings and a menu of well-prepared classics. A popular choice on Valentine's Day. ❧ *250 East 83rd Street, between 2nd & 3rd avs • Map F4 • 212 879 4284 • $$$*

7 Etats-Unis

Despite the French name, the inventive cuisine is New American and draws a loyal following. The menu changes daily. ❧ *242 East 81st Street, between 2nd & 3rd avs • Map F4 • 212 517 8826 • $$$*

8 Orsay

Replacing society hangout Mortimer's isn't easy, but this chic French café has succeeded, serving authentic bistro fare. ❧ *1057–59 Lexington Avenue at 75th St • Map G4 • 212 517 6400 • $$$*

9 Taste

Self-serve commissary by day, sophisticated ambience by night. The simple style allows the flavors to speak for themselves. The wine list provides some bargains to accompany the new American cuisine. ❧ *1413 3rd Avenue at 80th St • Map F4 • 212 717 9798 • $$*

10 E.J.'s Luncheonette

A family-friendly diner that serves large portions of well-prepared American breakfasts. Great pancakes are served all day, along with granola and fresh fruit. ❧ *1271 3rd Avenue at 73rd St • Map G4 • 212 472 0600 • No credit cards • $*

Left **Monument, Riverside Park** Center **Riverside Gardens** Right **Apartment buildings**

Upper West Side

THIS AREA DID NOT BEGIN TO DEVELOP *until the 1870s, when the 9th Avenue El went up, making it possible to commute to midtown. When the Dakota, New York's first luxury apartment building, was completed in 1884, it was followed by others on Central Park West and Broadway, while side streets were filled with handsome brownstones. The West Side remains a desirable neighborhood with a reputation for attracting intellectuals, and much of the city's best residential architecture. The creation of Lincoln Center in the 1950s was a great boost, and the American Museum of Natural History is also a draw.*

Mask, Natural History Museum

🔟 Sights

1. **American Museum of Natural History**
2. **Lincoln Center for the Performing Arts**
3. **New York Historical Society**
4. **Columbus Circle**
5. **Pomander Walk**
6. **Riverside Park**
7. **Riverside Drive/West End Historic District**
8. **Children's Museum of Manhattan**
9. **Zabar's**
10. **Green Flea Market/ 77th Street Flea Market**

American Museum of Natural History

The mammoth museum whose holdings include 32 million artifacts *(see pp34–7)*.

Lincoln Center for the Performing Arts

Built on 15 acres in the 1950s, transforming slums into a giant cultural complex, the Lincoln Center houses an array of venues: the Metropolitan Opera; the New York City Opera and Ballet; the New York Philharmonic; the Lincoln Center and Walter Reade theaters; Avery Fisher and Alice Tully halls; and the Julliard School *(see p50)*. In the summer, popular Mostly Mozart concerts take place, and free concerts are held in the adjacent park. In October 2004, Jazz at the Lincoln Center moved to its new headquarters in the Time Warner building at Columbus Circle. ✎
Columbus to Amsterdam avs, between 62nd & 66th sts • Map G2 • Tours 10:30am, 12:30pm, 2:30pm, & 4:30pm daily • Admission charge

New-York Historical Society

New York's oldest museum, founded in 1804, has organized much of its vast collection into the 4th floor Henry Luce III Center, which displays 40,000 objects divided into areas such as paintings, sculpture, furniture, silver, tools, and, notably, Tiffany lamps. Other galleries are used for changing exhibits. The society also maintains a research library.
✎ *2 West 77th Street at Central Park West • Map G2 • Open 10am–6pm Tue–Sun; Library 10am–5pm Tue–Sat (Tue–Fri in summer) • www.nyhistory.org • Admission charge*

Columbus Circle

One of the largest building projects in New York's history is transforming this neglected urban plaza into an important public site. The redevelopment has attracted national and international businesses, such as giant media company Time Warner, which now has its headquarters in an 80-storey skyscraper. The new building contains shops, entertainment, restaurants, and the Mandarin Oriental hotel. It is also the new home of Jazz at the Lincoln Center, the world's first performing arts facility dedicated to jazz. Other buildings in Columbus Circle include Hearst House, Trump International Hotel, and the Maine Monument. ✎ *Columbus Circle • Map H2*

Lincoln Center for the Performing Arts

5 Pomander Walk

This double row of small brick and stucco, timbered, Tudoresque townhouses, hidden on a private street, is one of the many delightful surprises to be discovered in Manhattan. The developer, a restaurateur named Thomas Healy, took his inspiration in 1921 from the sets used for a popular play by Lewis Parker called *Pomander Walk*, hoping to recreate the village atmosphere depicted in the play. Gloria Swanson, Rosalind Russell, and Humphrey Bogart are among the players who have lived here.
◎ *261–7 West 94th Street, between Broadway & West End Av • Map E2*

6 Riverside Park

Another example of the landscape genius of Frederick Law Olmsted, a woodsy, hilly band of green planned in 1873, following curving Riverside Drive for 70 blocks and hiding the abandoned railroad tracks below. Playgrounds, sports fields, a promenade, and monuments were added later. The impressive 1902 marble Soldiers' and Sailors' monument at 89th Street, a memorial to those who died in the Civil War, was modeled after the Monument of Lysicrates in Athens.
◎ *Riverside Drive, 72nd to 155th sts • Map C1 • Open 6am–1am daily • Free*

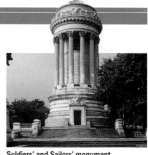

Soldiers' and Sailors' monument

7 Riverside Drive/ West End Historic District

A walk through this area shows the late 19th-century townhouses that characterize the Upper West Side. West 88th Street is a good example. The earliest, Nos. 267–71, were built in 1884. Nos. 302–38, from the early 1890s, have stepped gables and Roman brick, while Nos. 315–23, circa 1896, have bow fronts in brown or white stone. The Yeshiva Ketana School, at 346 West 89th Street, begun in 1901 by Herts and Tallant, occupies one of only two survivors of the mansions that once lined Riverside Drive. ◎ *Between Riverside Drive & West End Av, 85th & 95th sts • Map E1*

8 Children's Museum of Manhattan

Founded in 1973, in a former school building, this is a museum dedicated to the principal that children learn best through

---

Upper West Side Architecture

The Upper West Side's side streets are lined with fine rows of the brownstones favored by New York's 19th-century middle classes. Built of inexpensive, local, brown sandstone, the narrow buildings are typically three or four stories high, and have a flight of steps called a "stoop" leading to the living floors.

Left **House façade, Pomander Walk**

self-discovery. It uses a variety of participatory activities and fantasy world environments to engage its young visitors in learning that is fun. The Tisch Building, as the museum is known, has been renovated in a $6.5 million expansion headed by the museum chairman, Laurie Tisch Sussman. The museum's many activities include exhibits to intrigue older children, while Word Play is an enticing environment for newborns to four year olds *(see p66)*. ✪ *212 West 83rd Street at Broadway • Map F2 • Open Sep–Jun: 10am–5pm Wed–Sun; Jul–Aug: 10am–5pm Tue–Sun • Admission charge*

Zabar's
9 A monument to New York's mania for finding the best foods and a landmark since 1934, this always-crowded market sells smoked salmon, sturgeon, and other Jewish delicacies, wonderful bread, desserts, coffee, and cheeses, and big selections of oils, vinegars, and gourmet gift baskets. The second floor is filled with cooking equipment, and a coffee counter at the 80th Street corner lets you taste the delicious baked goods. ✪ *2245 Broadway at 80th St • Map F2*

Green Flea Market/ 77th Street Flea Market
10 Flea market junkies throng this school yard every Sunday, hoping for finds from among the piles of vintage clothing, crafts, books, jewelry, prints, and all manner of memorabilia. Less glamorous, new merchandise, from socks to T-shirts, is also sold here. On a good day as many as 300 booths crowd the premises. A weekly green market shares the same space. ✪ *I.S.44, 77th Street at Columbus Av • Map F2*

Walk on the West Side

Morning

Begin at **Lincoln Center** *(see p139)* and admire the plaza, the Chagall windows at the Metropolitan Opera, and the Henry Moore statue in front of Lincoln Center Theater. The New York Public Library for the Performing Arts on Amsterdam Avenue, behind the theater, is notable for its enormous collection of books on the performing arts.

Make your way up Broadway, window shopping and noting some of the landmark buildings such as the **Apthorp Apartments** *(see p142)* and the **Ansonia Hotel** *(p142)*, and the West Side's gastronomic palaces, such as Fairway, at 75th Street, and **Zabar's**. Almost any of the side streets will reveal examples of the area's great line-up of brownstone townhouses. Finally, head east to Columbus Avenue and **Calle Ocho** *(p143)* for a Cuban lunch.

Afternoon

The **American Museum of Natural History** *(see pp34–7)* can easily fill an entire afternoon, and the **New-York Historical Society** *(p139)* has an amazing collection on show.

Stroll down Central Park West and admire the landmark **apartment buildings** *(p142)* that can be seen here, and then head for **Central Park** *(pp26-7)*, the city's vast "backyard". Take a boat out on the lake, or enjoy a gondola ride around it, followed by refreshments at the Loeb Boathouse, the perfect end to an afternoon.

Left **Detail, Dakota** Center left **Balcony, Dorilton** Center right **San Remo** Right **Hotel des Artistes**

🔟 Apartment Buildings

1 Dakota
Famous as the site where John Lennon was shot, the block was thought so far west in 1884, it might as well be in Dakota. ✪ 1 West 72nd Street at Central Park West • Map G2 • Closed to public

2 Dorilton
One of the most flamboyant examples of the Beaux Arts era, this 1902 apartment house has an iron gate fit for a palace. ✪ 171 West 71st Street at Broadway • Map G2 • Closed to public

3 Ansonia Hotel
This 1908 apartment-hotel included soundproof partitions, a feature that has attracted many distinguished musicians. ✪ 2109 Broadway, between 73rd & 74th sts • Map G2

4 Apthorp Apartments
Modeled after an Italian Renaissance palazzo, this luxury 1908 building includes a huge interior courtyard.
✪ Broadway, between 78th & 79th sts • Map F2

5 Belnord
Even larger than the Apthorp, this 1908 Renaissance Revival structure is where Nobel Prize-winning author Isaac Bashevis Singer lived and wrote. ✪ 225 West 86th Street, at Amsterdam Av • Map F2 • Closed to public

6 Majestic
The first of Irwin Chanin's two 1931 landmarks, one of the original four twin towers that dominate the West Side skyline. ✪ 115 Central Park West, between 71st & 72nd sts • Map G2 • Closed to public

7 Century
Irwin Chanin's second twin tower, the tallest on the block, and an Art Deco icon. ✪ 25 Central Park West, between 62nd & 63rd sts • Map H2 • Closed to public

8 San Remo
Emery Roth's 1930 Art Deco masterpiece is a sophisticated adaptation of Renaissance forms. The twin towers hide water tanks. ✪ 145–6 Central Park West, between 74th & 75th sts • Map G2 • Closed to public

9 Eldorado
Another Art Deco Roth design. Groucho Marx and Marilyn Monroe were once tenants. ✪ 300 Central Park West, between 90th & 91st sts • Map E2

🔟 Hotel des Artistes
Built in 1918 to serve as artists' studios and apartments, the lofty spaces are much coveted. Residents have included Noel Coward, Isadora Duncan, and Joel Grey. ✪ West 67th Street, between Central Park West & Columbus Av • Map G2

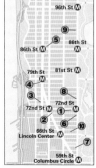

For more historic New York buildings **See pp46–7**

SHUN LEE CAFE

Left **Shun Lee Cafe** Right **Rosa Mexicano**

🔟 Restaurants

1 Jean Georges
Jean-Georges Vongerichten's namesake restaurant is among the best in New York *(see p68)*.
◈ 1 Central Park West, Trump International Hotel • Map H2 • 212 299 3900 • $$$$

2 Per Se
Book well in advance for this critically-acclaimed restaurant owned by Thomas Keller.
◈ Time Warner Center, Columbus Circle • Map H2 • 212 823 9335 • $$$$

3 Shun Lee Café
This clean-lined, black-and-white dim sum café is arguably the best north of Chinatown.
◈ 43 West 65th Street at Columbus Av • Map G2 • 212 769 3888 • $$

4 Fiorello's Café
The bountiful antipasto bar is good enough reason to visit, but the thin-crust pizzas and Italian menu are equally tempting. ◈ 1900 Broadway, between 63rd & 64th sts • Map H2 • 212 595 5330 • $$

5 Tavern On The Green
Eclectic contemporary American cuisine is served at this grand restaurant overlooking Central Park. Dine al fresco in the private garden in summer.
◈ Central Park West at 67th Street • Map G2 • 212 873 3200 • $$

6 Gabriel's
Sophisticated Tuscan food keeps this stylish room filled with Lincoln Center-goers at night.
◈ 11 West 60th Street at Columbus Av • Map H2 • 212 956 4600 • $$$

7 Rosa Mexicano
A branch of New York's top Mexican restaurant, famous for its guacamole made to order and power-packed margaritas.
◈ 61 Columbus Avenue at 62nd St • Map H2 • 212 977 7700 • $$$

8 Café Luxembourg
A classic Parisian bistro with a zinc-topped bar and a hip clientele. The steak frites can't be beat.
◈ 200 West 70th Street at Amsterdam Av • Map G2 • 212 873 7411 • $$$

9 Calle Ocho
Every night feels like a Latin party here; modern dishes from the Cuban chef are inspired by cuisine from Peru to Puerto Rico.
◈ 446 Columbus Avenue, between 81st & 82nd sts • Map F2 • 212 873 5025 • $$$

10 Gennaro
Fans say this tiny café serves the best Italian food on the Upper West Side, at the most reasonable prices, which explains the constant lines.
◈ 665 Amsterdam Avenue, between 92nd & 93rd sts • Map E2 • 212 665 5348 • No credit cards • $$

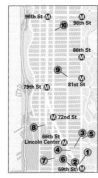

Note: Unless otherwise stated, all restaurants accept credit cards and serve vegetarian meals

143

Left **Columbia University** Center **Rose Window, St. John the Divine** Right **Streetside Musicians**

Morningside Heights and Harlem

THE AREA BETWEEN MORNINGSIDE PARK *and the Hudson River, from 110th–125th streets, is dominated by Columbia University and two important churches. Further west and extending north is Harlem, America's best-known African-American community. In the 1880s, when rail connected the neighborhood to Midtown, the large townhouses were occupied by Irish, Italian, and Jewish families, but by the 1920s black families predominated. The Harlem Renaissance, when nightclubs with black entertainers were frequented by whites, ended with the Depression. Nevertheless, recent development is reviving the area, causing some to declare a second Renaissance.*

🔟 Sights

1 Columbia University

2 Cathedral Church of St. John the Divine

3 Riverside Church

4 Hamilton Heights Historic District

5 St. Nicholas Historic District (Strivers' Row)

6 Abyssinian Baptist Church

7 Marcus Garvey Park

8 Studio Museum in Harlem

9 Schomburg Center for Research in Black Culture

10 Malcolm Shabazz Mosque/Harlem Market

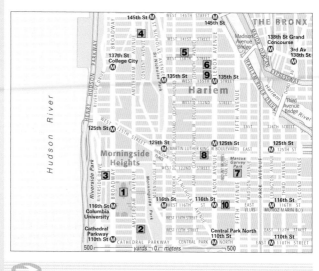

Columbia University

1 One of America's oldest universities, noted for its law, medicine, and journalism schools, Columbia was founded in 1754 as King's College. It moved in 1897 to its present campus, designed by Charles McKim with lawns and plazas on a serene terrace set apart from the street. Notable buildings include McKim's 1898 Low Library, and St. Paul's Chapel with three windows by La Farge. ⊗ *West 116th Street at Broadway • Map C3 • www.columbia.edu*

Cathedral Church of St. John the Divine

2 The mother church of the Episcopal Diocese of New York, begun in 1892 and still incomplete, is the largest cathedral in the world. Over 600 feet (180m) long and 146 feet (45m) wide, the church is a mix of Romanesque and Gothic styles. Its most impressive features include the west entrance, the rose window, bay altars, and the Peace Fountain on the south lawn. The medieval stone carving techniques used on the building are taught in workshops for disadvantaged youths (*see p46*).

(*see p46*)

⊗ *1047 Amsterdam Avenue at 112th St • Map C3 • Open 7am–6pm Mon–Sat, 1–7pm Sun (to 6pm Jul–Aug) • Free • www.stjohndivine.org*

Riverside Church

3 This skyscraper Gothic church modeled on Chartres cathedral and financed by John D. Rockefeller Jr. in 1930, has a 21-story tower with wonderful Hudson River views. Inside the tower is the largest carillon in the world, dedicated to Rockefeller's mother. The brilliant stained-glass windows are copies of those at Chartres with four notable exceptions – the early 16th-century Flemish windows on the east wall. The congregation has long been active in liberal social causes. ⊗ *490 Riverside Drive at 122nd St • Map C1 • Open 10:30am–5pm Tue–Sun • Admission charge • www.theriversidechurchny.org*

Hamilton Heights Historic District

4 Once part of the country estates of the wealthy, like Alexander Hamilton whose 1802 home, Hamilton Grange, is here, this location on a hill above Harlem became desirable in the 1880s when an elevated rail line was built. Fine residences went up between 1886 and 1906, and in the 1920s and 30s they attracted Harlem's elite, when the area was dubbed Sugar Hill. Chief Justice Thurgood Marshall and musicians Count Basie, Duke Ellington, and Cab Calloway were among those who lived here. ⊗ *West 141st to West 145th streets • Map A2*

Riverside Church

5 St. Nicholas Historic District (Strivers' Row)

These fine houses, originally known as the King Model Houses, went up in 1891 when Harlem was a neighborhood for the gentry. Three architects, including McKim, Mead, and White, managed to blend Renaissance, Georgian, and Victorian styles and create a harmonious whole. Successful African-Americans moved here in the 1920s and 30s, giving rise to the nickname Strivers' Row. ⊗ *202–250 West 138th Street, between 7th & 8th avs • Map A3*

6 Abyssinian Baptist Church

One of the oldest and most influential African-American churches in the U.S. was organized in 1808 by a group protesting segregation within the Baptist church. The congregation became politically active under such leaders as congressman Adam Clayton Powell, Jr. Today the church is widely attended on Sundays by many who come to hear the wonderful gospel choir. ⊗ *132 West 138th Street, between 7th Lenox avs • Map A3 • Sunday services 9am & 11am • www.abyssinian.org*

7 Marcus Garvey Park

A black nationalist who encouraged emigration to Africa, Garvey became a hero of the Black Pride movement, and the park's name was changed from Mount Morris in 1973 to honor him. It adjoins the Mount Morris Historical District of handsome houses and churches from an earlier, affluent, German-Jewish era. In the 1920s, as Harlem became mostly African-American, the synagogues became churches, and the houses were divided up. ⊗ *West 120th to West 124th streets, between Lenox & 5th avs • Map B3*

8 Studio Museum in Harlem

Opened in 1967 as an artists' studio, the organization expanded to become an important center for work by black artists. A local bank donated space for the present building, which opened in 1982 and has undergone a major expansion that will add more gallery space, an enlarged sculpture garden, an auditorium, and a café. ⊗ *144 West 125th Street, between 7th & Lenox avs • Map B3 • Open noon–6pm Wed–Fri, Sun, 10am–6pm Sat • Donations • www.studiomuseum.org*

Studio Museum, Harlem

Harlem Market

9 Schomburg Center for Research in Black Culture

A complex opened in 1991 houses the largest research center for African and African-American culture in the U.S. The immense collection was assembled by the late Arthur Schomburg, who became curator when the collection was given to the New York Public Library. The original building was the unofficial meeting place for writers in the black literary renaissance of the 1920s, and the present building includes a theater and two art galleries. ⊗ *515 Lenox Ave at 135th St • Map A3 • Open noon–8pm Tue–Wed, noon–6pm Thu–Fri, 10am–6pm Sat • Free*

10 Malcolm Shabazz Mosque/Harlem Market

The mosque, Masjid Malcolm Shabazz, was the ministry of the late Malcolm X, and the area around it has become the center of an active Muslim community. Local shops sell books, tapes, and Muslim clothing, and restaurants serve Sengalese cuisine. Street vendors who used to crowd the sidewalks of 125th Street have been moved into an organized complex of market stalls selling African art, dolls, drums, masks, dashiki shirts, and fabrics in African prints. ⊗ *Mosque, 102 West 116th Street at Lenox Av • Map C3 • Open 9am–5pm daily • Free • Harlem Market, 52–60 West 116th Street, between 5th & Lenox avs • Map C3 • Open 10am–6pm daily • Free*

A Day in Harlem and Morningside Heights

Morning

Begin late Sunday morning and take the No. 2 or No. 3 subway uptown to 135th Street and Lenox Avenue. Walk to 138th Street and turn west to hear the fabulous choir at the **Abyssinian Baptist Church**.

Continue west along 138th Street to see the fine 1890s homes of the **St. Nicholas Historic District** and stop on 8th Avenue to enjoy a gospel brunch at **Londel's Supper Club** *(see p148)*.

Afternoon

Retrace your steps to Lenox Avenue and head downtown to 125th Street to peruse the shops. Turn west for the famous **Apollo Theater** *(see p148)* and excellent displays of African-American art at the **Studio Museum in Harlem**. Afterwards, stop for coffee at the Starbucks on Lenox Avenue at 125th Street.

Take the M60 bus to West 120th Street and Broadway. Walk down to **Riverside Church** *(see p145)* for fine views over the Hudson River from the bell tower. Across the street is the monument honoring the 18th U.S. president, Ulysses S. Grant. At 116th Street, head east two blocks to Broadway and the entrance to **Columbia University** *(see p145)*. One block east on Amsterdam Avenue is the **Cathedral Church of St. John the Divine** *(see p145)* with its immense interior. End the day with some good southern cooking at **Miss Mamie's** *(see p149)* and return to Broadway for the No. 1 or No. 9 subway back downtown.

Around Town – Morningside Heights & Harlem

Left **Gospel at Sylvia's** Right **Apollo Theater**

TOP 10 Places for Music

1 Lenox Lounge
A standby for 50 years, the lounge has a new retro look and features the latest sounds in jazz as well as more traditional numbers. ✪ 288 Malcolm X Blvd, between 124th & 125th sts • Map B3

2 Showman's
Live jazz is the lure on Monday, Thursday, and Saturday nights at this club, where the vibes and people are as cool as the music. ✪ 375 West 125th Street, between St. Nicholas & Morningside Dr • Map B2

3 Londel's Supper Club
Part of the new Harlem, with upscale ambience, waiters in tuxedos, delicious Southern fare, and good live jazz on weekends. ✪ 2620 Frederick Douglass Blvd, between 139th & 140th sts • Map A3

4 St. Nick's Pub
Savion Glover and Ray Charles have been known to drop by at this popular venue. Live jazz can be heard six nights a week. ✪ 773 St. Nicholas Avenue at 149th St • Subway line A, B, C, or D to 145th Street

5 Sylvia's
The place is jammed for Saturday and Sunday gospel brunches, and always fun despite the tour groups. ✪ 328 Lenox Avenue, between 126th & 127th sts • Map B3

6 Cotton Club
Duke Ellington and Cab Calloway are long gone, and the location has changed, but the famous club of the 1920s is currently making a comeback. ✪ 656 West 125th St nr West 125th and Dr Martin Luther King Jr Blvd • Map B2

7 Apollo Theater
This theater is Harlem's famous showcase, where Ella Fitzgerald and James Brown launched their careers. ✪ 253 West 125th Street, between 7th & 8th avs • Map B3

8 Aaron Davis Hall
Home to jazz series, as well as ballet, opera, and the Harlem Film Festival. ✪ City College campus, West 135th St & Convent Av • Map A2

9 Miller Theatre
Columbia's main performance venue runs the musical gamut, with jazz an important part. ✪ Columbia University, 2960 Broadway at 116th Street • Map C2

10 Smoke
Columbia students and jazz lovers of all ages congregate at this intimate club to hear top notch jazz groups every weekend. ✪ 2751 Broadway at 106th St • Map D2

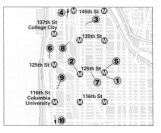

Price Categories		
For a three-course meal for one with a glass of house wine, and all unavoidable charges including tax.	**$**	under $25
	$$	$25–$50
	$$$	$50–$80
	$$$$	over $80

Left **Charles' Southern Style Kitchen** Right **Terrace in the Sky**

TOP 10 Restaurants

1 Charles' Southern Style Kitchen

Famous fried chicken, ribs, and collard greens can't be beat at this tiny no-frills and very popular spot. ◈ *2841 Frederick Douglass Blvd, between 151st & 152nd sts • Subway line C or E to 155th Street • 212 926 4313 • $*

2 Sugar Shack

Top-rated Southern soul food is served in a comfortable setting. ◈ *2611 Frederick Douglass Blvd at 139th St • Map A3 • 212 491 4422 • $*

3 Miss Maude's/Miss Mamie's

Down-home, cheerful cafés run by Norma Jean Darden, who knows her Southern cooking. ◈ *Miss Maude's, 547 Lenox Avenue at 137th St • 212 690 3100 • Miss Mamie's, 366 Cathedral Pkwy, between Manhattan Av and Columbus Av • 212 865 6744 • Map A3, D2 • Both $*

4 Copeland's

Take your pick of Southern classics at this popular spot; don't miss the Sunday gospel brunch. ◈ *547 West 145th Street at Broadway • Map A2 • 212 234 2357 • $*

5 Bayou

Cajun is a specialty of Steve Manning, who spent 10 years in New Orleans perfecting crawfish *étouffé*. ◈ *308 Lenox Avenue at 125th St • Map B3 • 212 426 3800 • No disabled access • $$*

6 Mo Bay

A lively Jamaican restaurant serving ribs, catfish, and jerk chicken with nightly jazz. ◈ *17 West 125th Street, between Lenox & 5th avs • 212 876 9300 • Map B3 • $$*

7 Amy Ruth's

A cheerful café with an updated slant on Southern classics. Waffles are a house specialty. ◈ *113 West 116th Street, between Powell & Lenox avs • Map C3 • 212 280 8779 • $$*

8 Le Baobab

The Senegalese cooking and the tab are both agreeable here. ◈ *120 West 116th Street at Lenox Av • Map C3 • 212 864 4700 • No credit cards • $$*

9 Toast

Sandwiches are the forte of this informal café, and the home-fries unmissable. ◈ *3157 Broadway, between Tiemann Pl & LaSalle St • Map B2 • 212 662 1144 • $*

10 Terrace in the Sky

This elegant, rooftop restaurant is so romantic, weddings are held here. The continental fare lives up to the setting. ◈ *400 West 119th Street at Amsterdam Av • Map C2 • 212 666 9490 • $$$*

Note: *Unless otherwise stated, all restaurants accept credit cards and serve vegetarian meals*

Left **New York Botanical Garden** Center **Bronx Zoo** Right **Park Slope Historic District**

The Outer Boroughs

MANHATTAN IS JUST ONE *of New York's five boroughs, each of which has its own unique attractions. Brooklyn alone, with its fine brownstone neighborhoods and numerous top-class sights, would be one of the largest cities in the U.S. The Bronx, to the north, boasts one of New York's finest zoos, plus the New York Botanical Garden and Yankee Stadium, while Queens, a veritable melting pot of nationalities, is famous for its museums, ethnic dining, and numerous sports events. The ferry to Staten Island leads to New York's only restored historic village.*

TOP 10 Sights

1. Bronx Zoo
2. New York Botanical Garden
3. Brooklyn Botanic Garden
4. Brooklyn Heights Historic District
5. Prospect Park
6. Park Slope Historic District
7. Flushing Meadow-Corona Park
8. Yankee Stadium
9. Historic Richmond Town
10. City Island/North Wind Institute Museum

Brooklyn Bridge

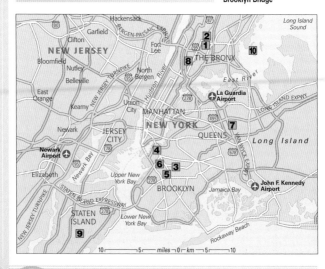

Bronx Zoo

1 Well past its 100th birthday, this sprawling zoo on 265 acres gets better all the time. The newest exhibits are a Butterfly Garden and Tiger Mountain, while the 6.5-acre Congo Gorilla Forest, an African rainforest habitat, brings visitors nose to nose with the inhabitants. The unusual World of Darkness shows nocturnal animals like bats in action *(see p64)*. ❧ *Bronx River Parkway & Boston Rd, Bronx • Subway Pelham Pkwy • Open Apr–Oct: 10am–5pm Mon–Fri, 10am–5:30pm Sat, Sun, & hols; Nov–Mar: 10am–4:30pm daily • Admission charge • www.bronxzoo.com*

New York Botanical Garden

2 One of the oldest and largest botanical gardens in the world, this National Historic Landmark covers 250 acres and includes 48 gardens and plant collections and 50 acres of forest, the only remains of woods that once covered New York. The Enid A. Haupt Conservatory, a restored Victorian glass house, is home to tropical rain forest and arid desert plants. A tram makes it easy to see the highlights, and guided tours are offered. The new Leon Levy Visitor Center has a visitor orientation area, a shop, and a cafe. ❧ *Bronx River Parkway & Kazimiroff Blvd, Bronx • Subway Bedford Park Blvd • Open Apr–Oct: 10am–6pm Tue–Sun; Nov–Mar: 10am–5pm Tue–Sun • Admission charge (free Wed & Sat am)*

Brooklyn Botanic Garden

3 A small but magnificent oasis, this 52-acre garden designed by the Olmsted brothers in 1910 is home to more than 12,000 plantings. It is best known for the Cranford Rose Gardens where thousands of roses cascade down arches and climb lattices, and the authentic Japanese Hill-and-Pond Garden, planted in 1915. It is also known for its Cherry Esplanade and Cherry Walk, one of the foremost cherry-blossom sites outside Japan. The Steinhardt Conservatory houses tropical and desert plants and one of America's largest bonsai collections.
❧ *900 Washington Avenue, Brooklyn • Subway Eastern Pkwy • Open Apr–Sep: 8am–6pm Tue–Fri, 10am–6pm Sat, Sun, & hols; Oct–Mar: 8am–4:30pm Tue–Fri, 10am–4:30pm Sat, Sun, & hols • Admission charge (free Tue & Sat am) • www.bbg.org*

Brooklyn Botanic Garden

4 Brooklyn Heights Historic District

Overlooking the East River and lower Manhattan skyline, the Brooklyn Heights Historic District is an enclave of old-world charm. Along its quaint streets are pre-served, Federal, wooden and brick townhouses of the 1820s and even grander Greek Revival homes of the following decades. ◈ *Court Street to Furman Street, between Fulton & State sts • Subway Clark St*

5 Prospect Park

Frederic Olmsted and Calvert Vaux considered this park, opened in 1867, to be their masterpiece. The 90-acre Long Meadow is the longest unbroken green space in the city. The pools and weeping willows of the Vale of Cashmere are particularly fine, along with Vaux's Oriental Pavilion and Concert Grove. ◈ *Between Eastern Parkway & Park-side Avenue, Brooklyn • Subway Grand Army Plaza*

Carousel horse, Prospect Park

6 Park Slope Historic District

These blocks on the western edge of Prospect Park became desirable places to live after the opening of the Brooklyn Bridge in 1883. The Victorian brownstones from the late 19th and early 20th centuries are outstanding U.S. Romanesque Revival and Queen Anne residences. ◈ *Prospect Park*

Train to Queens

This subway route, dubbed the International Express, serves New York's most varied ethnic communities. Take 61st Street, Woodside for Irish pubs, 46th Street for the Middle East, 69th Street for the Philippines. A $1 guide is available from Queens Council on the Arts, 79-01 Park Lane South, Woodhaven, NY 11421.

West to 8th Avenue, between 14th St & St. John's Pl, Brooklyn • Subway 7th Av

7 Flushing Meadow-Corona Park

The site of two World Fairs, this is now a spacious park with pic-nic areas, fields for cricket and soccer, paths for bik-ers and skaters, boating lakes, and many other attractions. The New York Mets' Shea Stadium, the U.S. Tennis Center, the New York Hall of Science, and the Queens Museum of Art are also here. The Unisphere, the symbol of the 1964 World Fair, still stands. ◈ *Queens • Subway 111th St, Willets Pt–Shea Stadium*

8 Yankee Stadium

A sports shrine, completed in 1923 and known as "The House that Ruth Built" for the legions of fans who came to see superhero Babe Ruth. Other legendary

Left **World's Fair Unisphere, Flushing Meadow-Corona Park** Right **Yankee Stadium**

Historic Richmond Town

heroes of America's most winning baseball team include Joe DiMaggio and Mickey Mantle. The legendary 54,000-seat stadium was updated in the 1970s, but a new modern complex may appear in the future. ✪ *East 161st St and River Avenue, Bronx* • *Subway 161st St–River Avenue* • *Opening times vary* • *Admission charge*

9 Historic Richmond Town

This restored village has 29 buildings from the town of Richmond, Staten Island's seat of government from 1729. Other historic buildings were moved here from other sites. The Dutch-style Voorlezer's House (1695) is the island's oldest home on its original site. ✪ *441 Clarke Avenue, Staten Island* • *Bus S74 from ferry* • *Open Sep–Jun: 1–5pm Wed–Sun; Jul–Aug: 10am–5pm Wed–Sat, 1–5pm Sun* • *Admission charge* • *www.historicrichmondtown.org*

10 City Island/North Wind Institute Museum

This tiny Bronx outpost on Long Island Sound was founded in 1685. The boatyards are a forest of masts, and the main street is lined with seafood restaurants and nautical bars. The North Wind Institute Museum is full of nautical lore. ✪ *North Wind Institute Museum, 190 Fordham St, City Island, Bronx* • *Subway Pelham Bay Park & Bx29 bus to City Island* • *Open 1–5pm Sun* • *Admission charge* • *www.cityislandmuseum.org*

A Day Out in Brooklyn

Morning

🕐 Take the No. 2 or 3 subway train to Eastern Parkway – Brooklyn Museum, for the world-class **Brooklyn Museum** *(see p41)*. The museum is part of a civic complex that includes the stately Grand Army Plaza, the **Brooklyn Botanic Garden** *(see p151)*, with its well-known Japanese garden, and neighboring **Prospect Park**.

Along the western edge of Prospect Park is the beautiful **Park Slope Historic District**. Stop for coffee at Ozzie's, 57 7th Avenue, before taking in the area's historic residences. Browse the hip line-up of small shops along 7th Avenue, and stop for lunch at one of the many cafés here.

Afternoon

Return by train to Borough Hall and head for the **Brooklyn Heights Historic District**. Walk along Pierrepont, Willow, and Cranberry streets to see some 19th century houses; Truman Capote wrote *Breakfast at Tiffany's* in the basement of No. 70 Willow, and Arthur Miller once owned the property at No. 155.

A short walk east brings you to **Atlantic Avenue** *(see p156)*. Look in on the spice shops here, and stop for refreshments at the Waterfront Ale House, 155 Atlantic Avenue. Head back to the Brooklyn Bridge, stopping at the Brooklyn Heights Promenade for dramatic vistas of Lower Manhattan's towers. End the day with dinner at the romantic **River Café** *(see p157)*.

Left **Brooklyn Museum** Center **Hall of Science** Right **Museum of the Moving Image**

🔟 Museums

1 Brooklyn Museum
The permanent collection has objects from ancient Egyptian to contemporary art *(see p41)*. ◈ *200 Eastern Parkway, Brooklyn • Subway Eastern Pkwy • Open 10am–5pm Wed–Fri, 11am–6pm Sat & Sun; 11am–11pm first Sat of month • Admission charge*

2 Isamu Noguchi Garden Museum
Thirteen galleries and a serene Japanese sculpture garden. ◈ *9–101 33rd Rd at Vernon Blvd, Queens • Bus 103 to Vernon Blvd • Open 10am–5pm Wed–Fri, 11am–6pm Sat & Sun • Admission charge*

3 Museum of the Moving Image
Artifacts and screenings show the history and techniques of film and TV. ◈ *35th Avenue at 36th St, Queens • Subway Steinway St • Open noon–5pm Wed, Thu, noon–8pm Fri, 11am–6:30pm Sat, Sun • Admission charge*

4 New York Hall of Science
A science and technology museum with hands-on exhibits and outdoor play area. ◈ *4701 111th Street, Queens • Subway 111th St • Open Jul & Aug: 9:30am–5pm Mon–Fri, 10am–6pm Sat & Sun; Sep–Jun: 9:30am–2pm Mon–Thu, 9:30am–5pm Fri, 10am–6pm Sat & Sun • Admission charge*

5 Queens Museum of Art
The New York Panorama scale model has 800,000 buildings. ◈ *New York City Building, Queens • Subway 111th St • Open Sep–Jun: 10am–5pm Wed–Fri, noon–5pm Sat & Sun; Jul–Aug: 1–8pm Wed–Sun • Admission charge*

6 P.S. 1 MoMA
Since 1976 this center has displayed contemporary art and provided studio space for artists. ◈ *22–25 Jackson Avenue at 46th Av, Queens • Subway 23rd St-Ely Ave • Open noon–6pm Thu–Mon • Admission charge*

7 Van Cortlandt House Museum
This restored 1748 Georgian house is the Bronx's oldest building. ◈ *Van Cortlandt Park, Bronx • Subway 242nd St • Open 10am–3pm Tue–Fri, 11am–4pm Sat & Sun; last tickets 30 mins before closing • Admission charge • www.vancortlandthouse.org*

8 Jacques Marchais Museum of Tibetan Art
A collection of Tibetan art in a Himalayan-style building with a garden. ◈ *338 Lighthouse Ave, Staten Island • Bus S74 from ferry • Open 1–5pm Wed–Sun • Admission charge*

9 Staten Island Historical Society Museum
In historic Richmondtown is a museum housed in the County Clerk's office, built in 1848. ◈ *441 Clarke Street, Staten Island • Bus S74 from ferry • Opening times vary • Admission charge*

10 Snug Harbor Cultural Center
Chinese garden, performance spaces, art center, children's museum, and a maritime collection. ◈ *1000 Richmond Terrace, Staten Island • Bus S40 from ferry • Opening times vary • Admission charge*

Around Town – The Outer Boroughs

For more on New York's museums See pp40–41

Left **New York Aquarium** Center **Staten Island Ferry** Right **Staten Island Children's Museum**

🔟 Family Adventures

1 New York Aquarium
Walk through a swamp and stay dry beneath a waterfall *(see p67).* ⊗ *Surf Ave and West 8th St, Brooklyn • Subway W 8th St • Open Apr–May, Sep–Oct: 10am–5pm Mon–Fri (5:30pm Sat, Sun & hols); Jun–Aug: 10am–6pm Mon–Fri (7pm Sat, Sun & hols); Nov–Mar: 10am–4:30pm daily • Admission charge*

2 Brooklyn Children's Museum
Permanent collections and changing exhibits. ⊗ *145 Brooklyn Av at St. Marks Pl, Brooklyn • Subway Kingston • Open 1–6pm Wed–Fri (Jul–Aug: Tue–Fri), 11am–6pm Sat & Sun • Admission charge*

3 Prospect Park Zoo
Tunnel through a prairie dog town, master baboon language, leapfrog across lily pads. ⊗ *450 Flat-bush Avenue, Brooklyn • Subway Prospect Park • Open 10am–4:30pm daily; Apr–Oct: 10am–5pm Mon–Fri, 10am–5:30pm Sat, Sun & hols • Admission charge*

4 Prospect Park Carousel
This 1912 carousel with hand-carved animals was moved here from Coney Island in 1950. ⊗ *Prospect Park, Brooklyn • Subway Prospect Park • Open Apr–Oct: noon–5pm Sat, Sun & hols (6pm Jul–Aug) • Rides $1*

5 Lefferts Homestead Children's House Museum
A rare 18th-century Dutch Colonial farmhouse shows early farm life. ⊗ *Prospect Park, Brooklyn • Subway Prospect Park • Open Apr–Nov: noon–5pm Thu–Sun & hols • Free*

6 Puppetworks
Hand-carved marionettes are used to present children's classics. ⊗ *338 6th Avenue at 4th St, Brooklyn • Subway 7th Avenue (Brooklyn) • Performances 12:30pm, 2:30pm Sat & Sun • Admission charge, reservations required.*

7 Sheepshead Bay Fishing Boats
A fishing fleet takes passengers for day and evening excursions. ⊗ *Eamons Avenue, Brooklyn • Subway to Sheepshead Bay • Boats leave 6:30–9am, 1pm, & 7pm, or can be chartered • Charge*

8 Staten Island Children's Museum
A 6-ft (2-m) kinetic porpoise welcomes you to this interactive playground exploring water, insects, and visual and performing arts. ⊗ *1000 Richmond Terrace, Staten Island • Bus S40 from ferry • Open summer: 11am–5pm Tue–Sun; winter: noon–5pm Tue–Sun • Admission charge*

9 Staten Island Zoo
The African Savannah at Twilight is a highlight. Other top sights include the Tropical Forest and Serpentarium. ⊗ *614 Broadway, Staten Island • Bus S48 from ferry • Open 10am–4:45pm daily • Admission charge*

10 Staten Island Ferry
A free ride with fabulous views of Manhattan. St. George Terminal buses go to Staten Island's sights *(see p59).* ⊗ *Bus to St. George Terminal, Staten Island • Boats every 15 mins–1 hr, 24 hours daily from Whitehall and South sts • Free*

Around Town – The Outer Boroughs

⮞ *For more family days out in New York* **See pp66–7**

🔟 Family Adventures

1 New York Aquarium
Walk through a swamp and stay dry beneath a waterfall *(see p67).* ⊗ *Surf Ave and West 8th St, Brooklyn • Subway W 8th St • Open Apr–May, Sep–Oct: 10am–5pm Mon–Fri (5:30pm Sat, Sun & hols); Jun–Aug: 10am–6pm Mon–Fri (7pm Sat, Sun & hols); Nov–Mar: 10am–4:30pm daily • Admission charge*

2 Brooklyn Children's Museum
Permanent collections and changing exhibits. ⊗ *145 Brooklyn Av at St. Marks Pl, Brooklyn • Subway Kingston • Open 1–6pm Wed–Fri (Jul–Aug: Tue–Fri), 11am–6pm Sat & Sun • Admission charge*

3 Prospect Park Zoo
Tunnel through a prairie dog town, master baboon language, leapfrog across lily pads. ⊗ *450 Flat-bush Avenue, Brooklyn • Subway Prospect Park • Open 10am–4:30pm daily; Apr–Oct: 10am–5pm Mon–Fri, 10am–5:30pm Sat, Sun & hols • Admission charge*

4 Prospect Park Carousel
This 1912 carousel with hand-carved animals was moved here from Coney Island in 1950. ⊗ *Prospect Park, Brooklyn • Subway Prospect Park • Open Apr–Oct: noon–5pm Sat, Sun & hols (6pm Jul–Aug) • Rides $1*

5 Lefferts Homestead Children's House Museum
A rare 18th-century Dutch Colonial farmhouse shows early farm life. ⊗ *Prospect Park, Brooklyn • Subway Prospect Park • Open Apr–Nov: noon–5pm Thu–Sun & hols • Free*

6 Puppetworks
Hand-carved marionettes are used to present children's classics. ⊗ *338 6th Avenue at 4th St, Brooklyn • Subway 7th Avenue (Brooklyn) • Performances 12:30pm, 2:30pm Sat & Sun • Admission charge, reservations required.*

7 Sheepshead Bay Fishing Boats
A fishing fleet takes passengers for day and evening excursions. ⊗ *Eamons Avenue, Brooklyn • Subway to Sheepshead Bay • Boats leave 6:30–9am, 1pm, & 7pm, or can be chartered • Charge*

8 Staten Island Children's Museum
A 6-ft (2-m) kinetic porpoise welcomes you to this interactive playground exploring water, insects, and visual and performing arts. ⊗ *1000 Richmond Terrace, Staten Island • Bus S40 from ferry • Open summer: 11am–5pm Tue–Sun; winter: noon–5pm Tue–Sun • Admission charge*

9 Staten Island Zoo
The African Savannah at Twilight is a highlight. Other top sights include the Tropical Forest and Serpentarium. ⊗ *614 Broadway, Staten Island • Bus S48 from ferry • Open 10am–4:45pm daily • Admission charge*

10 Staten Island Ferry
A free ride with fabulous views of Manhattan. St. George Terminal buses go to Staten Island's sights *(see p59).* ⊗ *Bus to St. George Terminal, Staten Island • Boats every 15 mins–1 hr, 24 hours daily from Whitehall and South sts • Free*

Around Town – The Outer Boroughs

⮞ *For more family days out in New York* **See pp66–7**

Left **Designer shoes, Madison Avenue** Right **Household goods on display**

🔟 Ethnic Shopping

1 Broadway, Astoria
Astoria has the largest Greek community outside Greece, with restaurants, coffee shops, and bakeries on Broadway. ◈ *Broadway, Astoria, Queens • Subway Broadway*

2 Main Street, Flushing
Flushing's Chinatown offers bakeries, food, gifts, restaurants, herbal remedies, and acupuncture. Queensborough Library has material in 40 languages. ◈ *Main Street, Flushing, Queens • Subway Main St*

3 74th Street, Jackson Heights
New York's Indian community's shop windows are filled with ornate gold jewelry and rich saris. Food stores are redolent with spices. ◈ *74th Street, Jackson Heights, Queens • Subway Roosevelt Av*

4 Roosevelt Avenue, Jackson Heights
Around the corner from Indian 74th Street, loudspeakers play Latin American rhythms, street vendors sell hot *churros* (fried dough), and shops offer music, foods, gaucho boots, hats, and piñatas. ◈ *Roosevelt Avenue, Jackson Heights, Queens • Subway Roosevelt Av*

5 Arthur Avenue, Bronx
In this Italian neighborhood, dozens of small, family-run stores sell everything from Italian wines, handmade pastas, and sausages to rosaries and votive candles. ◈ *Arthur Avenue, Bronx • Subway Fordham Rd*

6 Nassau Avenue, Greenpoint
Shops in America's largest Polish community are laden with home made *kielbasas* and *babkas*, statues of saints, Polish books, music, and cosmetics. ◈ *Nassau Avenue, Greenpoint, Brooklyn • Train to Nassau Av*

7 Brighton Beach Avenue, Brooklyn
Known as "Little Odessa," Russian is the first language on this busy street selling everything from smoked fish to Russian dolls. A boardwalk stroll by the sea is a bonus. ◈ *Brighton Beach Avenue, Brooklyn • Subway 55th St*

8 13th Avenue, Borough Park
The main street of Borough Park, home to America's largest Orthodox Jewish community, bustles with shops filled with religious articles, tempting baked goods, children's clothing, and linens. ◈ *13th Avenue, Borough Park, Brooklyn • Subway 55th St*

9 18th Avenue, Bensonhurst
Headquarters of an old-world Italian community, the street is lined with coffee shops, bakeries, and delis. ◈ *18th Avenue, Bensonhurst, Brooklyn • Subway 18th Av*

10 Atlantic Avenue, Brooklyn
New York's Middle-Eastern shopping center offers baklava, varieties of olives, dried fruits, spices, and traditional clothing. ◈ *Atlantic Avenue, Brooklyn • Subway Court St*

For more on shopping in New York **See p165**

River Café

Price Categories

For a three-course meal for one with a glass of house wine, and all unavoidable charges including tax.

$	under $25
$$	$25–$50
$$$	$50–$80
$$$$	over $80

TOP 10 Restaurants

1 River Café
Lobster, duck, and seafood are among many specialties. The Chocolate Duo dessert includes a mini chocolate Brooklyn Bridge (see p58). ☏ 1 Water Street, Brooklyn • Subway (A, C) High St • 718 522 5200 • Men require jackets after 5pm • $$$$

2 The Grocery
With its New American menu and fresh produce, The Grocery has been drawing Manhattanites to Brooklyn since 1999. The restaurant boasts a lovely garden. ☏ 288 Smith Street, Brooklyn • Subway (F) Carroll St • 718 596 3335 • $$

3 Peter Luger Steak House
Beef lovers flock to Peter Luger's gritty, beer hall-style location for what has long been considered New York's best steaks. Reservations are necessary. ☏ 178 Broadway, Brooklyn • Subway (J, M, Z) Marcy Av • 718 387 7400 • $$$

4 Al Di La Trattoria
This cozy, northern Italian trattoria serves regional dishes like hanger steak, mussels in tomato sauce, and wonderful pastas. ☏ 248 5th Avenue, Brooklyn • Subway Union St • 718 636 8888 • $$

5 Dominick's Restaurant
Stand in line, join a table, and feast on homemade Southern Italian food at its best. There's no menu; order your favorite or trust the waiter's choice. ☏ 2335 Arthur Avenue, Bronx • Subway Fordham Road • 718 733 2807 • No credit cards • $$

6 S'Agapo
Greek for "I love you," the name is apt for this cheerful, unpretentious spot with wonderful Greek food, weekend music, and a summer terrace. ☏ 3421 34th Avenue, Queens • Subway (N) Broadway • 718 626 0303 • $$

7 Kum Gang San
The place to sample Korean stews, noodle dishes, or do-it-yourself Korean barbecue cooked at the table. Meals begin with Panchan, small dishes of hot and cold, sweet and sour foods. ☏ 138–28 Northern Boulvard, Queens • Subway (7) Main St • 718 461 0909 • $$

8 Joe's Shanghai
The original of this Chinese café chain is popular for its pork or crab soup dumplings, or "steamed buns." There's also a menu of Shanghai specialties. ☏ 136–21 37th Avenue, Queens• Subway (7) Main St • 718 539 3838 • No credit cards • $

9 Jackson Diner
No ambience, but one of New York's best Indian restaurants, with an all-you-can eat buffet lunch. ☏ 37–47 74th Street, Queens • Subway (E, F, G, R) Roosevelt Avenue • 718 672 1232 • No credit cards • $

10 Denino's
A family pizzeria with all the favorites and some adventurous alternatives at the right price. ☏ 524 Port Richmond Avenue, Staten Island • Bus 44 from ferry • 718 442 9401 • No credit cards • $

Note: Unless otherwise stated, all restaurants accept credit cards and serve vegetarian meals

STREETSMART

NEW YORK'S TOP 10

Left **Umbrella** Center left **Comfortable shoes** Center Right **Sunglasses** Right **Seasonal clothing**

TOP 10 Planning Your Trip

1 Seasonal Clothing

New York has distinct seasons with average temperatures ranging from 26–38° F (-3–3° C) in the winter to 67–84° F (19–29° C) in the summer Despite the averages New York weather is predictably unpredictable. Layers are the solution – a short-sleeved knitted shirt, long-sleeved cotton shirt, and sweater will see you through most changes, plus a warm coat for winter.

2 Umbrella and a Raincoat

The months of March and August have the heaviest rainfall, but an umbrella and raincoat are useful all year round.

3 Walking Shoes

Midtown streets are often clogged with traffic, meaning that walking is not only the most pleasant, but often the fastest, way to get around. Invest in a pair of sturdy walking shoes, and break them in before you leave home to avoid developing blisters.

4 Dark Colors

Dry cleaning is expensive in New York, and laundromats are scarce in midtown where most visitors stay. The practical solution is to pack dark clothing, preferably in fast-drying, drip-dry fabrics that can be rinsed out overnight.

5 Hat and Sun-Glasses

Most visitors are more than likely to undertake a lot of walking in New York. Don't make the mistake of thinking that those tall buildings shut out the sun; if anything, it seems intensified in the city. So come prepared with a hat and sunglasses, and don't forget to pack the suntan lotion.

6 Electric Current Adapter

The U.S. uses a 115–120V current, rather than the 220V current used in Europe and elsewhere. Some hair dryers are equipped with an automatic conversion switch, but most 220V appliances will need an adapter, available in airport shops and some department stores. The U.S also uses two-pin plugs, and you will therefore need a two-pin plug adapter.

7 Metric Conversion Chart

Unlike much of the world, the U.S. does not use the metric system. A conversion chart or electronic pocket converter makes it simple to convert miles into kilometers for distances, ounces into litres for capacity measurements, kilograms to pounds for weight, and celcius into fahrenheit for the weather.

8 Student or Senior ID

Subways and buses, movie houses, most major attractions, and many hotels offer discounted rates for seniors over the age of 65. But proof of age is sometimes requested, so bring along a valid photo identification to take advantage of the discounts. Most museums and sightseeing attractions also offer discounted rates for students, again on presentation of the relevant ID. The minimum age for entry into bars and clubs in the U.S is 21 and proof of age will be required on entry.

9 Pocket Calculator

To save having to do laborious calculations in your head to convert the price of goods from dollars into pounds or euros when out shopping, bring a pocket calculator with you. Some are almost as small as a credit card, and fit easily into a wallet or pocket.

10 Driving Licence

If you plan on any out-of-New York trips with a rented car, be sure to bring a valid driving licence with you. You will also need to show official identification with a photograph and signature, such as a passport. A credit card will also be required when renting a car.

Left **Arriving by air** Center **Arriving by ship** Right **Arriving by bus**

🔟 Arriving in New York

1 Arriving by air
Most international flights land at John F. Kennedy Airport and some at Newark. La Guardia Airport serves domestic flights. Cab fares to the city are a fixed $45 from Kennedy Airport, $34–$50 from Newark, and $20–$30 from LaGuardia, plus $3.50 toll and tips.

2 Limousine service
Several limousine companies offer private door-to-door services by appointment, to or from the airports, rail, or ship terminals, at pre-arranged rates averaging $5-$10 more than taxi fares. Reputable services include Carmel and Tel Aviv. ✆ *Carmel: 212 666 6666 • Tel Aviv: 212 777 7777*

3 Supershuttle
Supershuttle vans operate door-to-door and are less than limousines or taxis. They pick up several passengers so allow plenty of time. Prices are $15–22 according to zip code. ✆ *Supershuttle: 800 358 5826*

4 Coach companies
Coaches from the airports to central midtown points cost $8–$13. Shared minibuses with hotel drop-offs cost $13–$19. Transportation information is available at the baggage checkout areas in all airports. ✆ *Advance information: 800 247 7433 • NY–NJ Port Authority: www.panynj.gov*

5 Arriving by train
Amtrak trains from all parts of the U.S. arrive at Penn Station, 7th Avenue and 33rd Street. Long Island Railroad and New Jersey Transit commuter trains also use Penn station, and MetroNorth regional trains use Grand Central Terminal, at Lexington Avenue and 42nd Street. Cabs are widely available at all terminal entrances. ✆ *Amtrak trains: 800 872 7245 • Long Island Railroad: 718 217 5477 • New Jersey Transit: 973 762 5100 • MetroNorth: 212 532 4900*

6 Arriving by bus
Buses are the least expensive way to travel in the U.S. Intercity bus and commuter lines arrive at the Port Authority Bus Terminal. Cabs wait at the 8th Avenue entrance. ✆ *Port Authority Bus Terminal: 8th Avenue at 42nd Street • 212 564 8484*

7 Arriving by ship
Cruise ships arrive in New York at the spacious, modern NYC Passenger Ship Terminal. Customs and immigration officials are on duty to process passengers on overseas cruises. Cabs are found outside the terminal. ✆ *NYC Passenger Ship Terminal: 711 10th Avenue • 212 246 5450*

8 Arriving by car
Cars are a liability in midtown, where parking spaces are nonexistent and parking expenses can run to more than $30 a day. Check in advance with your hotel over the availability and cost of parking, and, if necessary, consider using a suburban motel located near convenient transportation into Manhattan.

9 Customs allowances
$100 worth of gifts ($400 for U.S. citizens), one carton of 200 cigarettes, 100 cigars, and one litre of liquor may be brought into the U.S. without incurring customs fees. No meat, seeds, growing plants, or fresh fruit may be brought in. Prescription drugs should be clearly marked. A receipt for any cameras or laptops will pre-empt any queries when you leave. ✆ *U.S. Customs Service: 800 697 3662. For general information: 877 CUSTOMS*

10 Immigration
Landing cards and customs declaration forms are usually distributed on the plane, to be filled out ready for U.S. customs and immigration. Foreign nationals will have to join a separate (and usually long) line to have their passport inspected at immigration. Most UK and Canadian passport holders do not need visas if staying in the U.S. for 90 days or less; always check with your embassy.

The new JFK Airtrain connects to the subway system; and the Newark Airtrain connects with New Jersey trains to Penn Station

Left **The Visitors Bureau** Center **New York taxi** Right **Student Card**

TOP 10 Useful Information

1 Tourist Information

NYC & Company, the New York Convention & Visitors Bureau, operates a Visitor Information Center with multilingual counselors and free information. ✪ *Visitor Information Center: 810 Seventh Avenue at 53rd St • Map J3 • www. nycvisit.com • 8am–8pm daily*

2 New York Newspapers

The *New York Times* is read nationally and internationally for its extensive foreign coverage. The city's tabloids, the *New York Post* and *New York Daily News*, are known for their attention-grabbing headlines and a number of pages of sports coverage. Many young New Yorkers read the free weekly *Village Voice* and rival *New York Press*.

3 Out-of-Town Newspapers

Foreign and out-of-town newspapers may be found at branches of Barnes & Noble bookstore, and many Sunday papers are carried at the Universal News Stand. If you can't find what you want, Hotalings News Agency, a wholesaler, may be able to help. ✪ *Universal News Stand: 234 West 42nd Street. Map K3 • Hotalings News Agency: 212 974 9419*

4 Entertainment Listings

The Friday *New York Times* arts section, *Time Out New York*, the *New Yorker,* and *New York Magazine* are all comprehensive weekly sources of current happenings in the city, readily available at any newsstand.

5 Museum/ Gallery Guides

Besides listings in the entertainment magazines, *Museums New York* is a quarterly publication ($4.95) available at most newsstands, with write-ups of current museum and gallery exhibitions. The *Art Now Gallery Guide*, free in most galleries, details current offerings around the city. ✪ *Museums New York: 212 604 0877*

6 Opening Hours

Most stores and sightseeing attractions are open daily (*see p165*); banks close on weekends, although ATMs are always available (*see p169*); post offices close on Sundays with the exception of the General Post Office (*see p169*). Many museums close on Mondays and major holidays – check with individual venues for their specific times.

7 Tipping

A tip of at least 15 percent is usual for meals, taxis, and personal services such as haircuts or massages. Bellboys at hotels usually receive $1 per bag, and bartenders $1 per drink. Many diners find it easiest to calculate a tip by simply doubling the tax (8.625 percent) on a restaurant bill.

8 Taxes

Be sure to factor in taxes when you calculate costs in New York. Sales tax is an extra 8.625 percent on every purchase. Hotel taxes add 17.845 percent to the bill, plus an extra $2 per night occupancy tax.

9 Big Apple Greeters

Visitors might like to try an afternoon with a Big Apple Greeter. A volunteer New York guide from this not-for-profit organisation will take small groups or couples on a 2–4 hour tour of any New York neighborhood of your choice or give you an insider's view of the city. ✪ *Big Apple Greeter: 212 669 8159 • www. bigapplegreeter.org*

10 Restrooms

Hotels (*see pp172-9*) and department stores (*see p64*) are the best places for restrooms. Most fast-food restaurants, such as McDonald's, and coffee shops such as Starbucks, also have restrooms and although intended for patrons, these are usually available if you ask for the key.

Left **Traffic control** Center **Staten Island Ferry** Right **Traffic signs**

⑩ Getting Around

1 The Street Plan

Above Greenwich Village, Manhattan is laid out on a straight grid plan, with the avenues running to the north and south, and the streets crossing east to west. All are one-way, alternating the direction with each block, except for Park Avenue, which runs both ways. 5th Avenue is the dividing line between the East and West sides.

2 Finding an Address

To locate the nearest cross street for avenue addresses in Manhattan, drop the last digit of the street number, divide by 2 and add these key numbers:

1st Avenue	3
2nd Avenue	3
3rd Avenue	10
8th Avenue	9
Lexington Avenue	22
Madison Avenue	27

For further address formulas, check the Yellow Pages.

3 Traffic Signs

Traffic lights show red for stop, yellow for caution, and green for go for vehicles, and spell out "walk" and "don't walk" for pedestrians. The "don't walk" sign blinks when the lights are about to change; given the aggressive traffic, it's wise not to attempt to beat the light.

4 Subway Routes

Subways run north and south up and down the city on Lexington Avenue, 6th Avenue, 7th Avenue/ Broadway, and 8th Avenue. The N, R, E, F and W trains to Queens run east to west, crossing Manhattan. A free copy of the current subway map is available at any station booth. ◉ Passenger information: *718 330 1234 • www.mta.info*

5 Bus Routes

Manhattan buses run on every north-south artery except on Park and West End avenues. The most useful crosstown buses run on 96th, 86th, 79th, 67th, 57th, 49/50th, 42nd, 34th, 23rd, and 14th streets. Route numbers are posted on a lighted strip above the front windshield. Free maps are available on most buses.

6 The Metrocard

Metrocards are sold in subways and in shops displaying the sign and are good for subways and buses. Each ride deducts one $2 fare from the card; transfers within two hours are free on buses or subways. Weekly passes for unlimited travel cost $21.

7 Taxi Know-how

Manhattan yellow taxis can be hailed anywhere you spy one. Lights atop the cab go on when the car is available, or to show that the driver is off-duty. Hotel cab stands are good places to look for a cab. ◉ *For taxi complaints: 311*

8 Car rentals

Rentals offices are found throughout the city; drivers must be over 25, and have a valid license and major credit card. Weekends are heavily booked, so phone in advance. ◉ *Hertz: 800 654 3131 • Avis: 800 331 1212 • National: 800 227 7368 • Budget: 800 527 0700*

9 Parking Rules and Penalties

Street parking is not available midtown and is scarce elsewhere. Some avenues have curb meters allowing 15- to 60-minute stays; overstaying means a ticket or having your car towed away, both of which are extremely expensive. Side streets have "alternate side" regulations banning cars, during certain hours and on alternate days, from parking on alternate sides of the street.

10 Ferries and Water Taxis

New York Waterways ferries connect Manhattan with New Jersey and provide transportation to New York Yankee and Mets baseball games. Water taxis run from East 90th Street Pier to Pier 84. ◉ *For ferry schedules: 800 533 3779 • Staten Island ferry information: see p59 • Water taxi information: www.nywatertaxi.com*

Left **Circle Line boat** Center **Touring by bus** Right **Carriage in Central Park**

⁝⁰⁄₁₀ Guided Tours

1 Neighborhood Walking Tours

The best way to see New York is on foot with a knowledgeable guide. Top leaders include: Big Onion Walking Tours (history oriented), Joyce Gold History Tours, and the 92nd Street Y (Jewish oriented). ◈ *Big Onion Walking Tours: 212 439 1090 • Joyce Gold History Tours: 212 242 5762 • 92nd Street Y: 212 415 5500*

2 Architectural Tours

The Municipal Art Society, dedicated to preservation and excellence in urban design, offers enlightening "Discover New York" tours highlighting the city's buildings and neighborhoods, led by architectural historians. ◈ *Municipal Art Society: 212 935 3960*

3 Boat Tours

Circle Line offers two- or three-hour cruises around Manhattan, as well as Harbor Lights evening cruises and one-hour sails from South Street Seaport. New York Waterways has 90-minute harbor trips. ◈ *South Street Seaport: Pier 16 & Pier 83, 212 563 3200 • New York Waterways: 800 533 FERRY*

4 Bus Tours

Gray Line offers two- to ten-hour double-decker and motorcoach Manhattan sightseeing trips with multilingual guides, plus Brooklyn tours and Harlem gospel tours. An all-day tour costs $60 including a bonus Statue of Liberty boat ticket and one-day subway/bus pass. ◈ *Gray Line Bus Tours: 212 397 2620.*

5 Backstage Tours

Among the insider's offerings are Lincoln Center *(see p139)*, the Metropolitan Opera, Radio City Music Hall *(see p13)*, NBC Studios *(see p13)*, Carnegie Hall *(see p125)*, Madison Square Garden, Grand Central Terminal *(see p123)*, Gracie Mansion *(see p135)*, and the New York Public Library *(see p124)*. ◈ *Lincoln Center: 212 875 5350 • Metropolitan Opera: 212 769 7020 • Radio City Music Hall: 212 307 7171 • NBC Studios: 212 664 3700 • Carnegie Hall: 212 906 9765 • Madison Square Garden: 212 465 6080 • Grand Central Terminal: 212 340 2347 • Gracie Mansion: 212 570 4751 • New York Public Library: 212 340 0849*

6 Park Tours

See the glories of Central Park with Urban Park Rangers or volunteer guides from the Park Conservancy. Free programs are held most weekends and some Wednesdays. ◈ *Park Conservancy schedules, 212-310-6600 • Urban Park Rangers, 311*

7 Bicycle Tours

A leisurely, two-hour spin around Central Park takes in all the important sights, with a break for refreshments. Tours cost $35 with bike rental. ◈ *2 Columbus Circle, 59th St & Broadway • Map H2 • 212 541 8759*

8 Garden Tours

The New York Botanical Garden (718 817 8700) holds various tours. ◈ *Tours at 1pm Tue–Sun to either Forest, Conservatory, Rock Garden or highlights. Occasional tours at 2 & 3pm on Tue & Thu • Tickets are free with garden admission • Tram tours run every 20 minutes ($2 adults, $1 children, see p151)*

9 Museum Tours

The Metropolitan Museum of Art *(see p133)* offers 20 different guided tours daily in several languages, covering the highlights of the museum as well as specific galleries; tours are included with the price of admission. The Guggenheim Museum *(see p133)* offers family tours of museum highlights, also free with the price of admission.

10 Carriage Tours

Horse-drawn cabs take passengers on a short, old-fashioned ride through Central Park *(see p26–7)*. Rides cost $34–54. ◈ *Central Park South at 59th St • Map H3*

Left **Givenchy** Center **Gourmet shopping** Center **Barnes & Noble bookstore**

TOP10 Shopping Tips

1 Store Hours
Most stores operate 10am–7pm Mon–Sat, until 8pm Thu, and 11am or noon to 6pm or 7pm Sun. Many stay open on holidays but all close for Christmas and Easter.

2 Credit Cards
MasterCard and Visa are accepted everywhere; American Express and Discover in most places.

3 Women's Clothing
Department stores have the widest selections (see p64), Madison Avenue has the designer names (p136), and SoHo the best trendy fashions (see p65). For discounts, try Orchard Street (p91), Century 21, and Daffy's. Ⓢ Century 21: 22 Cortlandt Street, Map Q4 • Daffy's: 125 East 57th Street & 111 5th Avenue, Map H4 & L3

4 Men's Clothing
For designer fashion go to Barneys, traditional styles Brooks Brothers or Paul Stuart, and Thomas Pink for hipper designs; John Varvatos is sporty. Ⓢ Barneys: 660 Madison Avenue, Map K4 • Brooks Brothers: 346 Madison Avenue, Map L4 • Paul Stuart: 350 Madison Avenue at 45th St, Map J4 • Thomas Pink: 520 Madison Avenue, Map H4 • John Varvatos: 149 Mercer Street, Map N3

5 Books
Barnes & Noble carries a huge range; Murder, Ink specializes in mysteries; Books of Wonder is the place to go for children's books; and the Strand has a wide range of used books. Ⓢ Barnes & Noble: 1960 Broadway, Map G2 • Murder, Ink: 2486 Broadway, Map E2 • Books of Wonder: 16 West 18th St, Map M3 • Strand Book Store: 828 Broadway, Map M4

6 Gourmet Food
Among the city's gastronomic palaces, Zabar's is the best known (see p141), but Dean & DeLuca, the Gourmet Garage, Citarella, and Agata & Valentina have their devotees. Ⓢ Dean & DeLuca: 560 Broadway, Map M4 • Gourmet Garage: 2567 Broadway, Map E2 • Citarella: 2135 Broadway, Map G2 • Agata & Valentina: 1505 1st Avenue, Map F5

7 Crafts and Antiques
Manhattan Art & Antiques and Chelsea Antiques carry a little of everything. For American folk, try Susan Parrish or Kelter–Malce, for Stickley furniture Gallery 352, and for antique-looking furniture, try Uproar Home. Ⓢ Manhattan Art & Antiques: 1050 2nd Avenue, Map G4 • Chelsea Antiques: 110 West 25th St, Map L2 • Susan Parrish: 390 Bleecker St, Map N3 • Kelter–Malce: 74 Jane St, Map M2 • Gallery 352: 142 Duane St, Map Q3 • Uproar Home: 121 Greene St, Map N4

8 Toys and Children's Clothes
F. A. O. Schwarz (see p66) and Toys 'R' Us are amazing but less overwhelming is the Children's General Store. Beautiful clothes are at Bonpoint, cool choices at Space Kiddets, and affordable outfits at Children's Place. Ⓢ Toys 'R' Us: 1514 Broadway, Map J3 • Children's General Store: Grand Central Terminal, Map J4 • Bonpoint: 1269 Madison Ave, Map K4 • Space Kiddets: 46 East 21st St, Map L4 • Children's Place: 1460 Broadway, Map K3

9 Music
Megastores Tower and Virgin will satisfy all tastes. Opera lovers should head for the Metropolitan Opera, vintage collectors the House of Oldies, and for house music Vinylmania. Ⓢ Tower Records: 692 Broadway, Map N4 • Virgin Megastore: 1540 Broadway, Map J3 • Metropolitan Opera Shop: 136 West 65 Street, Map G2 • House of Oldies: 35 Carmine St, Map N3 • Vinylmania: 60 Carmine St, Map N3

10 Perfumes and Cosmetics
Fresh is a Boston firm specializing in perfumes and bodycare. Kiehl's has quality skin products. Aveda features natural products made from plant extracts. Ⓢ Fresh: 57 Spring St, Map N4 • Kiehl's: 109 3rd Ave, Map L4 • Aveda: 233 Spring St, Map N3

For New York stores See pp64–5

Left **TKTS booth** Right **Gotham Bar and Grill**

New York on a Budget

1 TKTS Booths
Tickets for Broadway and off-Broadway shows are sold at a 25 to 50 percent discount (plus a small service charge) on the day of the show at TKTS booths. Payment is in cash or travelers' checks only. Queues get very long very quickly so it is advisable to arrive early. ✆ *47th St & Broadway • Map J3 • Open 3–8pm daily, 10am–2pm for Wed & Sat matinees, 11am–3pm Sun*

2 Free TV Shows
Watch your favorite show for free – if you can get in a request early enough. For more information, call the individual networks. Same-day tickets are sometimes available at the Tourist Information Center *(see p162)* or from the NBC lobby desk. ✆ *ABC: 212 456 3054 • CBS: 212 975 2476 • NBC: 212 664 7174, www.shopnbc.com*

3 Free Events
There are regular free drama performances and concerts in Central Park in July and August. Contact Summerstage (212 360 2777). Free masterclasses and excellent concerts are also held by faculty and talented students at the Juilliard School (212 799 5000).

4 Free Summer Venues
Metropolitan Opera performances, New York Philharmonic concerts, Shakespeare in the Park at the Delacorte Theater in Central Park, and outdoor performances at Lincoln Center's Damrosch Park – all free – are among the reasons why New Yorkers love summer. Contact NYC & Company (212 484 1222) for a current schedule.

5 Saving on Transit
The best transit deal is the $7 Fun Pass, a Metrocard that allows unlimited subway and bus rides from the first ride until 3am the next morning. If you are staying in the city longer, a $20 Metrocard includes two free rides, and a $21 card will buy you unlimited rides for one full week.

6 Cheap Eats
Pre-theater prix fixe dinners are good value, but lunch menus are usually even better. During Restaurant Week, for two weeks in January and again in June, New York's best restaurants offer three-course lunches priced according to the year: $20.02, $20.03, and dinners for $35. The promotion is very popular, so book ahead through www.opentable.com

7 Changing Money
You can save money by using your bank card at ATMs (Automated Teller Machines). Many accept Plus or Cirrus network cards and will debit your account and pay you in dollars. The transaction fees are less than those at Currency Exchanges, and you get the wholesale exchange rate used between banks *(see p169)*.

8 Bargain Buys
CityPass will buy you admission to six top attractions for $53 ($41 for ages 6–17), half the price. You can buy it at participating sites, including the Empire State Building, the Guggenheim Museum, the American Museum of Natural History, the Museum of Modern Art, Circle Line sightseeing cruises, and the Intrepid Sea Air Space Museum.

9 Sale Periods
White sales on linens are held in January and August, coat sales are featured during the November Veteran's Day and February George Washington's Birthday holidays. Bathing suits go on sale after the 4th of July and everything is on sale after Christmas.

10 Discount Malls
Round trips are available seven times a day to Woodbury Common Premium Outlets, a one-hour drive to a mall of 220 discount outlets carrying top name brands such as Armani, Gucci, and Burberry. Tickets cost $35. ✆ *Short Line Bus Tours: Port Authority Bus Terminal, 800 631 8405*

New York Subway

Top 10 Things to Avoid

1 Unlicensed Cabs
Unregulated cars whose drivers solicit passengers at airports or in front of hotels have no safety regulations and no metered limits on what they can charge you. Be patient, and stand in line for a licensed yellow cab instead. (For tips on taxi know-how see p163.)

2 "Going Out of Business" Signs
The "lost our lease" or "going out of business" signs you might see in shops – particularly along 5th Avenue or on Broadway – have been up there for years. The signs are intended to lure unwary customers into stores with, typically, overpriced electronics.

3 Pickpockets
Just as in most large cities around the world, New York has its share of pickpockets hoping to take advantage of distracted visitors. Be especially alert in crowds and when getting on and off crowded buses and subway trains. Even better, use hidden travel wallets to keep your money secure at all times. Leave your valuable jewelry at home or back at the hotel, and never stop to count your money on the street.

4 Ticket Scalpers
You may be more than happy to pay the extra price for tickets to sold-out sporting events or shows, but be aware of the risk you run; sometimes the tickets peddled by scalpers turn out to be counterfeit, and you could wind up with no money and no seat.

5 Three-card Monte Games
You'll see these card games on the street, especially around Broadway. Sometimes it seems as though a player has won big, but be warned – the winner is usually an assistant. You will only win these games if the dealer wants you to.

6 Rush Hour on the Subway
Most workers have no choice and have to ride the subway at its busiest hours. But you do not need to get caught in the crush; avoid the rush hours between 7am and 9am, and between 4.30pm and 6.30pm, and you'll have a much pleasanter ride. (For information on subway routes see p163.)

7 Hotel Phone Charges
Unfortunately there is no regulation on what hotels can charge for telephone calls made by their guests. Read carefully the card that explains your hotel's phone surcharges, since they can be hefty, even if you use a credit card. You can save money by patronizing the telephone booth in the lobby or sometimes by buying a phone card (see p169).

8 Hotel Breakfasts
Hotels notoriously overcharge for their breakfasts, counting on the fact that their guests will find it easier and pleasanter to stay in. But you can save more than half – and often have a better breakfast – just by seeking out a coffee shop down the block.

9 Luggage Hassles
One tip that might help you to avoid luggage hassles: Discourage break-ins by making it harder for thieves; use tape to seal your bags shut and make any tampering obvious. You can also put your travel itinerary inside any bags, so that if they go astray, the airline will be able to track you down. Ⓢ Lost and Found for bus and subway services: 212 712 4500 • Lost and Found for taxis: 311

10 Jaywalking
It may seem tempting to save a few minutes by cutting across traffic in the middle of the street rather than crossing at the traffic lights on the corner, but it could cost you dearly if a speeding, inattentive New York driver comes along. It is much better to follow the city slogan, "Cross at the green, not in-between."

Left **New York city bus "kneeling" to help the elderly** Center **Wheelchair access** Right **Tour bus**

🔟 Special Needs

1 Information Sources

Hospital Audiences, Inc, publishes Access for All ($5), a guide to available resources at all New York's cultural institutions. The Mayor's Office for People with Disabilities provides services to residents and also has information on city facilities. ◈ *Hospital Audiences, Inc: 212 575 7660 • People with Disabilities: 212 788 2830*

2 Accommodation for the Disabled

New York city law requires that all facilities built after 1987 provide entrances and accessible restroom facilities for the disabled. All city buses now have steps that can be lowered to allow wheelchair access, and most street corners also have curb cuts for wheelchairs.

3 Special Tours

Hands On is an organization devoted to the hearing-impaired, and publishes a calendar of information on museum and backstage tours, performances, films, and other events available with sign language interpretation. ◈ *Hands On: 212 822 8550*

4 Aids for the Hearing-Impaired

All Broadway shows have free amplification devices for the hearing-impaired, and sign language interpretation can be arranged with the Theater Access Project or Hands On.

◈ *Theater Access Project: 212 221 1103 • Hands On: 212 822 8550*

5 Aids for the Sight-impaired

Lighthouse International is an organization devoted to enabling the vision-impaired to cope through rehabilitation and education. It offers tips for travelers, and also lends receivers so that you can hear the new talking traffic signs at 59th Street and Lexington Avenue. ◈ *Lighthouse International: 111 East 59th Street, between Park & Lexington avs • Map H4 • 800 829 0500*

6 Facilities for Infants and Toddlers

Department stores are equipped with diaper changing stations (*see p64*); because space is so tight in New York, other facilities tend to be scarce. Most restaurants do have highchairs these days, but it is always wise to call and check what facilities they have for children before you set out.

7 Babysitting

The Babysitter's Guild, established over 60 years ago, is a reliable source for babysitting. Staff can accommodate 16 different languages and rates are $15 per hour, for a four-hour minimum, plus $4.50 for transportation ($7 after midnight). ◈ *The Babysitter's Guild: 212 682 0227*

8 Legal Assistance

The Legal Aid Society offers free advice and referrals; Legal Services for New York City, a non-profit referral service, also offers assistance to those with legal problems. ◈ *The Legal Aid Society: 212 577 3300 • Legal Services for New York City: 212 431 7200*

9 Other Useful Numbers

Help is at hand in the city for various eventualities. ◈ *Clothing repairs: Ramon's Tailor Shop 212 226 0747.* All-night drugstores: *Duane Reade 212 541 9708, Genovese 212 772 0104. Emergency car repairs: Citywide Towing 212 924 8104.* Lost and found for buses and subways: *212 712 4500.* Lost and found for taxis: *311.*

10 Student Identification

Foreign students will benefit from having an International Student Identity Card (ISIC) which can help to secure discounts on transportation, rental cars, hotels, and various attractions in New York and across the U.S. The cards cost $22 and are available from the Council on International Educational Exchange (CIEE). ◈ *CIEE: 633 3rd Avenue • Map J4 • 800 407 8839*

For New York's Top 10 places for children See pp66–7

Left **Standard mailbox** Center **Automated teller machine** Right **Currency exchange counter**

🔟 Banking and Communications

1 Banking Hours
Most New York banks are open from Monday through Friday, 9am–4pm, though individual branches may have longer opening hours. Only larger banks are equipped to exchange foreign currency. Be prepared to show a passport or other photo identification when changing currency.

2 Currency Exchange Locations
People's Foreign Exchange offers currency exchange with no commission charge. Travelex Currency Services charge a fee.
❦ *People's Foreign Exchange: 575 5th Avenue at 47th St. Map K3. 212 883 0550 • Travelex Currency Services: 1590 Broadway at 48th St. Map J3. 212 265 6063*

3 Automated Teller Machines (ATMs)
ATM machines can be found at almost all banks and are open 24 hours a day. They accept most common bank cards and credit cards, although they usually charge a small service fee. ❦ *For banks accepting Cirrus bank cards: 800 424 7787 • Plus cards: 800 843 7587.*

4 Credit Cards
Cash advances can be obtained from ATM machines using Master-Card and Visa cards; Banks accepting Cirrus (see ATM section) take MasterCard; Plus card banks (see ATM section) accept Visa. American Express members can also withdraw cash with their credit card at American Express offices.

5 Cashing Checks
Travelers' checks in dollars issued by well-known organizations such as American Express or Travelex are widely accepted in the U.S. in restaurants, banks, and stores, although personal checks on a foreign bank are not. American Express offices will also cash checks for their cardholders.

6 Telephones
Public telephones are found on many street corners, in hotel lobbies, and in restaurants and department stores. You will need 25 cents in coins to make a local three-minute call, and more if you talk longer. You can buy prepaid telephone cards at many newsstands, which conveniently eliminate the need for coins.

7 Internet Access
Many hotels now have free dataport connections for laptop Internet access. In addition, free access to the Internet is available for members of the public at the Science and Business branch of the New York Public Library.

❦ *188 Madison Avenue at 34th St • Map K4 • 212 592 7000.*

8 Sending Mail
Postage for letters sent within the U.S. costs 37 cents for the first ounce, and 23 cents for additional ounces; stamps for postcards cost 21 cents. To send mail internationally, post-cards cost 70 cents, and letters start at 80 cents for the first half-ounce.

9 Post Office Hours
All city post offices are open from 9am to 5pm Monday to Saturday; the General Post Office stays open 24 hours a day. Most hotels sell stamps and will mail letters for their guests.
❦ *General Post Office: 421 Eighth Avenue at 33rd St. Map K2. 212 967 8585 • For branch locations: 800 275 8777*

10 Express and Courier Delivery
The U.S. Post Office Express Mail next-day delivery service starts at $12.25 for up to 8 ounces; global 2- to 3-day delivery costs from $24. Next-day delivery is also available from Federal Express, DHL, and United Parcel Service; all include pick-up services in their charges. ❦ *Federal Express: 800 GO FEDEX • DHL: 800 CALL DHL • UPS: 800 742 5877*

Left **Sign for public payphones** Center **Kaufman's Pharmacy** Right **New York ambulance**

TOP10 Security and Health

1 Discouraging Thieves

Pickpockets are on the lookout for tourists, who usually have substantial amounts of cash on them. Don't flaunt jewelry or advertise your status by wearing a waistpack and sporting your camera around your neck. A local grocery store bag is a good, inconspicuous place for cameras.

2 Avoiding Scams

Beware of distractions in front of you when boarding buses or subways; a pickpocket's accomplice behind you may be after your wallet.

If you buy electronics from street peddlers for next to nothing, you may find next to nothing of value inside the box when you open it.

3 Locations to Avoid

New York's crime rate is way down, but it makes little sense to take chances. Most city parks are delightful during the day, but after dark are not safe places to explore; nor are low-income neighborhoods very safe places for visitors to roam late at night.

4 Hotel Room Safety

Don't advertise your empty hotel room by putting out the "please make up this room" sign. Leave the lights on if you think you will be returning late. Other than the maids, don't admit strangers to your room; if necessary, phone the desk to verify someone who claims to be an employee of the hotel.

5 Walk-in Medical Clinics

The D.O.C.S clinics, affiliated with the Beth Israel Medical Center, offer convenient by appointment or walk-in services for adults and children. ✆ *55 East 34th Street, between Madison & Park avs. Map K4. 212 252 6000. Open 8am–8pm Mon–Thu; 8am–7pm Fri; 9am–3pm Sat; 9am–2pm Sun • 1555 3rd Avenue at 88th St. Map E4. 212 828 2300 • 202 West 23rd Street at 7th Av. Map L3. 212 352 2600*

6 Hospital Emergency Rooms

Emergency treatment is available 24 hours a day; if you are able, call the number on your policy first, and check which hospitals your insurance company deals with. ✆ *Roosevelt Hospital: 428 West 59th Street at 9th Av. Map H2. 212 523 6800 • St. Vincent's Hospital: 153 West 11th Street at 7th Av. Map M3. 212 604 7998*

7 Dental Emergencies

For dental crises, D.O.C.S has walk-in clinics. You can also contact N.Y.U. Dental Care for urgent treatment. ✆ *N.Y.U. Dental Care: 345 East 24th Street, between 1st & 2nd avs • Map L4 • 212 998 9800, 212 998 9828 weekend & out of hours*

8 Travel Insurance

Most U.S. insurance is effective throughout the country, but those with foreign insurance coverage should take out comprehensive medical travel insurance before arriving in the U.S. Should you need any treatment, you will be expected to pay for it at the time of service and the bill can be an extremely steep one.

9 Smoking

Smoking is illegal in almost all public places in New York, including subways, movie theaters, restaurants and bars. The fines are stiff, $100 and up.

10 Telephone Helplines

Various helplines are available to call in a crisis. ✆ *Suicide Help Line: 212 532 2400 • Sex Crimes Report Line: 212 267 7273 • Victim Services Agency: 212 577 7777 • Travelers' Aid: 212 944 0013*

Emergency Numbers

Police, fire, and Medical Emergencies
911
N.Y. Hotel Urgent Medical Services
212 737 1212

Sunbathers basking at Jones Beach

TOP 10 Excursions from New York

1 Jones Beach State Park

Miles of ocean beaches, pools, a boardwalk with games, miniature golf, and entertainment are all part of this exceptional recreational center on Long Island's south shore. A great day's outing from the city. ✪ *Long Island Railroad connects with buses • LIRR: 718 217 5477 • 90 mins from Manhattan*

2 Fire Island

An escapist's dream. No cars are allowed on this tranquil island off Long Island, rimmed with 26 miles (42 km) of beach. Visitors get around on foot or bike, and shop or dine in tiny, village centers. ✪ *Long Island Railroad to Bayshore ferry boats • LIRR: 718 217 5477 • 2 hrs, 30 mins from Manhattan*

3 The Hamptons

Celebrity-watching is a favorite sport in the sophisticated Hamptons on eastern Long Island, where society and entertainment names gather to enjoy the miles of beach and beautiful old colonial towns such as Southampton and Easthampton. ✪ *Long Island Railroad • LIRR: 718 217 5477 • 2 hrs, 30 mins from Manhattan*

4 New Jersey Shore

With the Atlantic Ocean beaches stretching the length of the state, the New Jersey shore is ideal for families. It offers lively boardwalks, laidback beach escapes, and Victorian towns like Spring Lake and Cape May, filled with romantic inns. ✪ *New Jersey Transit trains: 973 762 5100 • 90 mins from Manhattan*

5 Hyde Park

F. D. Roosevelt's estate and presidential library, the lavish Vanderbilt mansion, a chance to preview the work of future great chefs at the Culinary Institute of America, and scenic river views are among the lures of this Hudson River valley town. By car, Rhinebeck, 10 miles (16 km) away, is a good overnight base. ✪ *Metro North trains: 212 532 4900 • Short Line buses: 800 631 8405 • 2 hrs from Manhattan*

6 Buck's County, PA

This bucolic enclave of hills, streams, covered bridges, and mellow stone farmhouses offers visitors cozy, country inns, fine dining, choice antiquing, and gallery hopping. New Hope, a charming art colony, is the place to stay. ✪ *Trans-Bridge Line buses: 800 962 9135 • 2 hrs from Manhattan*

7 Princeton, NJ

Home to one of the oldest and most elite universities in America, Princeton is also a lovely town filled with fine 18th-century homes. On campus are Nassau Hall, the 1783 U.S. Capitol, and a museum of sculpture.
✪ *New Jersey Transit trains to Princeton: 973 762 5100 • 90 mins from Manhattan*

8 Philadelphia, PA

Boasting Independence Hall, colonial neighborhoods, a lively riverfront, and more than 100 museums, including some noted collections of Impressionist art, Philadelphia is a great addition to a visit to New York. ✪ *Amtrak trains: 800 USA RAIL • 1 hr, 45 mins from Manhattan*

9 Caramoor, Katonah

The 100-acre Caramoor estate, in northern Westchester County, includes a museum of room settings brought from European palaces, and a Venetian theater that hosts an outdoor summer music festival. ✪ *Metro North "Caramoor Specials": 212 532 4900 • 75 mins from Manhattan*

10 Tarrytown Mansions

Kykuit, the Rockefeller mansion overlooking the Hudson River, is the major draw, but Tarrytown also offers Philipsburg Manor, a restored Dutch farm estate. A little farther south in Irvington is Sunnyside, home of author Washington Irving, and Lyndhurst, palace of financier Jay Gould. ✪ *Metro North trains: 212 532 4900. 1 hr from Manhattan • New York Waterway river cruises to Kykuit: 800 533 3779*

Left **The Four Seasons** Center **The Carlyle** Right **The Pierre**

🔟 Best Hotels in New York

1 Four Seasons
For luxury in a modern mode, this dramatic, pale-hued tower by I.M. Pei is the ultimate, with rooms among the city's largest, and every amenity. The bar and restaurant draws the city's elite. 🔊 *57 East 57th Street, New York, NY 10022 • Map H4 • 212 758 5700 • www.fourseasons. com • $$$$$*

2 Carlyle
Antiques set the stage for an uptown, luxury lair, that has long attracted the famous with its hushed European ambience and spacious quarters in understated good taste. Café Carlyle is the city's poshest cabaret. 🔊 *35 East 76th Street, New York, NY 10021 • Map G4 • 212 744 1600 • www. thecarlyle.com • $$$$$*

3 New York Palace
Fresh from lavish refurbishment, the hotel straddles the opulent 1882 Villard Houses and a 55-story tower, with a choice of traditional or contemporary room decor. Room service is from the legendary Le Cirque 2000. 🔊 *455 Madison Avenue at 50th Street, New York, NY 10022 • Map J4 • 212 888 7000 • www. newyorkpalace.com • $$$$$*

4 Trump International Hotel and Towers
High ceilings and tall windows mean fabulous city and Central Park views, and the amenities are equally bountiful – jacuzzis, personal business cards, room service from Jean Georges *(see p68)*, or a chef to cook for you. 🔊 *1 Central Park West, New York, NY 10023 • Map H2 • 212 299 1000 • www. trumpintl.com • $$$$$*

5 Peninsula
The Hong Kong hotel group has done itself proud, turning a 1905 classic into a state-of-the-art luxury lodging. Rooms are contemporary with Art Nouveau accents and bedside controls for the many gadgets. The health club with pool is superb. 🔊 *700 5th Avenue, New York, NY 10019 • Map H3 • 212 956 2888 • www. peninsula.com • $$$$$*

6 Pierre
A landmark opposite Central Park since the 1930s, the Pierre, part of the Four Seasons group, is a bastion of old-world elegance. Personal service is a hallmark that draws many of the elite. 🔊 *2 East 61st Street, New York, NY 10021 • Map H3 • 212 838 8000 • www. fourseasons.com/pierre • $$$$$*

7 St. Regis
Rooms come with Louis XVI furnishings, silk wall coverings, chandeliers, and a butler tending to your every need at this Beaux Arts beauty. French restaurant Lespinasse *(see p129)* is attached. 🔊 *2 East 55th Street, New York, NY 10022 • Map H4 • 212 753 4500 • www. stregis.com • $$$$$*

8 The Mark
Discretely elegant, this member of the prestigious Mandarin group is a contemporary sanctuary. It draws an international clientele who appreciate the Biedemeier furnishings, antique prints, luxury linens, and conveniences such as cordless phones. 🔊 *25 East 77th Street, New York, NY 10021 • Map F3 • 212 744 4300 • www.themarkhotel.com • $$$$$*

9 Hotel Plaza Athénée
An intimate, 152-room Parisian outpost located on a quiet upper East Side street. Modern facilities include a fitness center and staff waiting to attend to your every need. 🔊 *37 East 64th Street, New York, NY 10021 • Map H4 • 212 734 9100 • www.plaza-athenee.com • $$$$$*

10 Regency Hotel
A gilt and mirrored sanctuary favored by show business moguls, the hotel has Regency decor that inspired the name and oversize suites. The restaurant, 540, a power breakfast favorite, turns into Feinstein's club *(see p56)* at night. 🔊 *540 Park Avenue, New York, NY 10021 • Map H4 • 212 759 4100 • www.loewshotels. com/regency • $$$$–$$$$$*

 Note: *Unless otherwise stated, all hotels accept credit cards, and have en-suite bathrooms and air conditioning*

Left **Rihga Royal** Center **Renaissance New York** Right **Le Parker Meridien**

🔟 Deluxe Hotels

1 Stanhope-Park Hyatt

Museum-goers favor this elegant, 185-room hotel, across from the Metropolitan Museum of Art (*see pp28–31*), and recently upgraded by new management with old-world grace and new technology. ✆ *995 5th Avenue, New York, NY 10028 • Map F3 • 212 774 1234 • www.hyatt.com • $$$$–$$$$$*

2 Renaissance New York

An upscale oasis in the Theater District, with an elegant lobby, handsome traditional furnishings, and deep tubs in the bathrooms. The hotel's restaurant offers a dazzling Times Square view. ✆ *714 7th Avenue, New York, NY 10026 • Map J3 • 212 765 7676 • www.renaissance hotels.com • $$$–$$$$*

3 Michelangelo

A handsome, New York outpost of an Italian hotel, with unusually spacious rooms in a choice of Art Deco, French Country, or Neo-Classical styles. ✆ *152 West 51st Street, New York, NY 10019 • Map J3 • 212 765 0505 • www. michelangelohotel.com • $$$$*

4 Rihga Royal

Space is the main attraction of this striking, 54-story skyscraper, recently added to the Marriott chain. Every room is a well appointed suite with a bay-windowed living room. The location is ideal for both theater and shopping. ✆ *151 West 54th Street, New York, NY 10019 • Map H3 • 212 307 5000 • www.rihgaroyalny. com • $$$–$$$$$*

5 Ritz-Carlton New York, Battery Park

Towering 39 stories above the harbor with wide-angle views over Manhattan and Ellis Island (harbor-side rooms are equipped with telescopes), this downtown newcomer offers sleek modern decor and luxury ameneties for business or leisure travel. ✆ *2 West Street, New York, NY 10004 • Map R3 • 212 344 0800 • www.ritzcarlton. com • $$$$$*

6 Le Parker Meridien

The soaring public spaces, fitness facilities, and rooftop pool are assets of this lively hotel. Newly designed, compact guest rooms offer ergonomic chairs, giant TVs, and DVD/CD players. ✆ *118 West 57th Street, New York, NY 10019 • Map H3 • 212 245 5000 • www. parkermeridien.com • $$$$*

7 70 Park Avenue

A small, sophisticated haven, with smart decor of Neo-Classical furnishings and a rich, gold and green color scheme. Other features include guest privileges at the well-equipped nearby fitness center. ✆ *70 Park Avenue, New York, NY 10016 • Map K4 • 212 973 2400 • www. 70parkavenue.com • $$$*

8 The Plaza

The grande dame of New York hotels, this 19-story, French Renaissance building opened in 1907 as a residence for the wealthy and is now a National Historic Landmark. The hotel is closed for renovations and is due to reopen in 2007. ✆ *5th Avenue at Central Park South, New York, NY 10019 • Map H3 • 212 759 3000 • www.fairmont.com • $$$$–$$$$$*

9 Millennium U.N. Plaza Hotel

Kevin Roche's soaring tower attracts an international clientele, who enjoy panoramic views from rooms beginning on the 28th floor, a glass-enclosed swimming pool, and New York's only indoor hotel tennis court. ✆ *U.N. Plaza, 1st Avenue & 44th St, New York, NY 10017 • Map J5 • 212 758 1234 • www.unplaza.com • $$$$*

10 Waldorf-Astoria

An Art Deco landmark with a magnificent lobby, the 1,407-room Waldorf offers a variety of rooms, some grand and some disappointing. ✆ *301 Park Avenue, New York NY 10017 • Map J4 • 212 355 3000 • www.waldorfastoria.com • $$–$$$$$*

Left **The Warwick Hotel** Center **The Mansfield Hotel** Right **Roger Williams Hotel**

Mid-Range Hotels

1 Roger Smith Hotel
An art-filled and artful change of pace, the Roger Smith is owned by sculptor/designer James Knowles who has filled it with art exhibits. Rooms are contemporary with antique accents, and breakfast is included. ⊗ *501 Lexington Avenue, New York, NY 10022 • Map J4 • 212 755 1400 • www. rogersmith.com • $$$*

2 Warwick Hotel
William Randolph Hearst built the hotel in 1927, with large rooms and ample closets, and celebrities have been coming ever since. The lobby is small; rooms have traditional furnishings and mahogany armoires. ⊗ *65 West 54th Street, New York, NY 10019 • Map J3 • 212 247 2700 • www. warwickhotels.com • $$$–$$$$*

3 Mansfield Hotel
A distinctive Theater District hotel, the Mansfield features a soaring lobby, copper-domed salon for free continental breakfast and afternoon tea, and original Elie Nadelman drawings in the library. Rooms have sleigh beds. ⊗ *12 West 44th Street, New York, NY 10036 • Map J4 • 212 277 8700 • www.mansfieldhotel. com • $$$*

4 Algonquin Hotel
A literary landmark, famous for the *New Yorker* "Round Table," the Algonquin remains an oasis of civility, with antique lighting fixtures and *New Yorker* cartoon wallpaper in the halls. Rooms are small but have charm. ⊗ *59 West 44th Street, New York, NY 10019 • Map J3 • 212 840 6800 • www.algonquinhotel.com • $$$*

5 Salisbury Hotel
Well-placed for visits to Carnegie Hall, shops, and theaters, the Salisbury was once an apartment-hotel and still has a quiet, low-key, ambience, with traditional American decor, good-sized accommodations, and a pleasant new breakfast room. ⊗ *123 West 57th Street, New York, NY 10019 • Map H3 • 212 246 1300 • www. nycsalisbury.com • $$$*

6 Roger Williams Hotel
An atrium with floor-to-ceiling windows, fluted zinc columns, ultra-modern maple furniture, and a mezzanine lounge for complimentary breakfast are among the features that have transformed this hotel. ⊗ *131 Madison Avenue, New York, NY 10016 • Map L4 • 212 448 7000 • www.roger williamshotel.com • $$$*

7 Hotel Elysée
The Elysée has the warmth of a small inn, serving not only breakfast, but wine and hors d'oeuvres in the evening. Room service is from the legendary Monkey Bar & Restaurant. ⊗ *60 East 54th Street, New York, NY 10022 • Map J4 • 212 753 1066 • www.elyseehotel.com • $$$–$$$$*

8 Blakely New York
The cosmopolitan mood begins in the Art Deco lobby with clocks showing the time around the world. Contemporary rooms have red lacquer furnishings and kitchenettes. ⊗ *136 West 55th Street, New York, NY 10019 • Map H3 • 212 245 1800 • www.blakelynewyork.com • $$$*

9 Shoreham
A thoroughly modern makeover has included custom cabinetry, creative use of light and textures, and guest rooms in pale tones. Complimentary breakfast and all-day refreshments included. ⊗ *33 West 55th Street, New York, NY 10019 • Map H3 • 212 247 6700 • www. shorehamhotel. com • $$$*

10 Doubletree Guest Suites
The price of an ordinary hotel room will buy you two comfortable rooms (one with a sofabed), two TVs, and a kitchenette at this Theater District hotel. Kids stay free and have their own playroom. ⊗ *1568 Broadway, New York, NY 10036 • Map J3 • 212 719 1600 • www. doubletreehotels.com • $$$*

  ***Note:** Unless otherwise stated, all hotels accept credit cards, and have en-suite bathrooms and air conditioning*

Price Categories

For a standard, double room per night (with breakfast if included), taxes, and extra charges.

$	under $150
$$	$150–$250
$$$	$250–$350
$$$$	$350–£450
$$$$$	over $450

Left **Hotel Edison** Right **Carlton Arms**

🔟 Budget Accommodations

1 Wyndham Hotel
Reserve well ahead if you hope to snag one of the large, comfortable rooms here – among the city's best buys. Furnishings are a bit threadbare, but this only adds to the home-like atmosphere. 🔌 42 West 58th Street, New York, NY 10019 • Map H3 • 212 753 3500 • www.hotel wyndham.com • $$

2 Pickwick Arms
Rooms may be small and spare, but the lobby is pleasant and the central location cannot be beat. Rooms have TV and there is a rooftop sitting area. Single rooms with shared baths are under $100. 🔌 230 East 51st, New York, NY 10022 • Map J4 • 212 355 0300 • www. pickwickarms.com • $

3 Gershwin Hotel
The bright red façade adorned with huge white abstract forms tells you that this is an arty, budget choice, popular with young visitors. Don't expect frills, but rooms do offer TV and private baths. 🔌 7 East 27th Street, New York, NY 10016 • Map L3 • 212 545 8000 • www. gershwinhotel.com • $$

4 Herald Square Hotel
A tiny, budget hideaway renovated with taste. The small rooms have been nicely decorated and baths are new. The cherub over the front door remains from the days when this Beaux Arts building was the first home of LIFE magazine. 🔌 19 West 31st Street, New York, NY 10001 • Map K3 • 212 279 4017 • www. heraldsquarehotel.com • $

5 Hotel Edison
Although the rates have gone up in recent years, this remains good value in the Theater District. It features a stunning Art Deco lobby and small but well decorated rooms with updated bathrooms. The hotel's café is a long-time, favorite, inexpensive pre-theater choice. 🔌 228 West 47th Street, New York, NY 10036 • Map J3 • 212 840 5000 • www. edisonhotelnyc.com • $$

6 La Quinta Manhattan
On a midtown block known for its Korean restaurants, this is one of several Apple Core hotels – renovated buildings offering comfortable lodging, new bathrooms, and first-class services at reasonable rates. 🔌 17 West 32nd Street, New York, NY 10001 • Map K3 • 212 736 1600 • www. applecorehotels.com • $–$$$

7 Habitat Hotel
A great midtown location for a budget hotel, renovated with care and some sophistication. Rooms are small but have modern furniture, TV, and Internet access. Those sharing baths have a sink. 🔌 130 East 57th Street, New York, NY 10022 • Map H4 • 212 753 8841 • www.stayinny.com • $

8 Carlton Arms
There's no TV or phone, but this budget haven is popular with young visitors for its hip spirit and funky halls with walls painted by young artists. Private baths are available in 20 of the 54 colorful rooms. 🔌 160 East 25th Street, New York, NY 10010 • Map L4 • 212 679 0680 • www.carltonarms. com • No air conditioning • $

9 Hostelling International
Although run by American Youth Hostels, all ages are welcome to share the clean, safe rooms, with 4 to 12 beds at budget prices. This 628-bed facility offers a coffee bar, cafeteria, and self-service kitchen. 🔌 891 Amsterdam Avenue, New York, NY 10025 • Map D2 • 212 932 2300 • www.hinewyork.org • No en-suite bathrooms • $

10 A Hospitality Company
This company offers furnished studios to 3-bedroom apartments around the city. Refrigerators are stocked with breakfast fixings. Great value, but be sure locations are near transit lines. 🔌 515 Madison Avenue, 25th floor, New York, NY 10022 • Map H4 • 212 813 2244 • www. hospitalitycompany.com • $–$$$

Left **The Muse** Center **Inn at Irving Place** Right **The Iroquois**

Boutique Hotels

Library Hotel
1 Books fill this 60-room themed hotel. Each floor is devoted to a Dewey Decimal System category, like the Arts or Philosophy, with appropriate volumes in each room. Includes a rooftop sitting room and terrace. ✆ 290 Madison Avenue, New York, NY 10017 • Map K4 • 212 983 4500 • www.libraryhotel. com • $$$–$$$$

The Muse
2 A new Theater District boutique, the Muse inspires with a smart lobby decorated with Matisse-like murals and good-size rooms painted in pale colors with bright bedcovers. Offers personalized business cards for guests. ✆ 130 West 46th Street, New York, NY 10036 • Map J3 • 212 485 2400 • www. themusehotel.com • $$$

Inn at Irving Place
3 Two Greek Revival townhouses form an elegant, 12-room inn straight from a Jane Austen novel. Rooms have fireplaces and antiques; only the VCRs and CD players bring them up to date. ✆ 56 Irving Place, New York, NY 10002 • Map M4 • 212 533 4600 • www. innatirving.com • $$$

Hotel Wales
4 There is a European feel to the genteel Wales. Fresh from renovation, the hotel has stylish, traditional furnishings and a panoramic, rooftop deck. Breakfast and tea are served in a room lined with illustrations from children's books. ✆ 1295 Madison Avenue, New York, NY 10128 • Map E4 • 212 876 6000 • www. waleshotel.com • $$$

Lowell
5 Luxurious and intimate, the Lowell exudes old-world charm in rooms and suites with wood-burning fireplaces, libraries, flowers, marble baths, and kitchens. Decor is an eclectic mix of French, Deco, and Oriental. ✆ 28 East 63rd Street, New York, NY 10021 • Map H4 • 212 838 1400 • $$$$–$$$$$

Iroquois
6 A suite is named for James Dean, who lived here from 1951 to 1953; other Hollywood guests have included Sandra Bullock and Johnny Depp. Rooms are modestly sized but deluxe, with French decor. Packages offer excellent rates. ✆ 49 West 44th Street, New York, NY 10036 • Map J3 • 212 840 3080 • www.iroquoisny. com • $$$

Casablanca
7 A Moroccan theme, complete with tiles, arches, and ceiling fans, sets this 48-room Theater District hotel apart. Rooms are small but well furnished. Continental breakfast is served in (what else?) Rick's Café. ✆ 147 West 43rd Street, New York, NY 10036 • Map J3 • 212 869 1212 • www. casablancahotel.com • $$$

Hotel Giraffe
8 A sunny glass-walled lobby leads to this newly constructed, 73-room hotel, with stylish Retro decor and a delightful roof terrace. Indulgent rooms, just seven per floor, even feature bedside controls for the shades. Breakfast, snacks, evening cheese, wine, and champagne are all complimentary. ✆ 365 Park Avenue South, New York, NY 10016 • Map L4 • 212 685 7700 • www.hotelgiraffe.com • $$$–$$$$$

Dylan
9 Although the 1903 façade has been faithfully restored, the former Chemists' Club has been transformed with serene Zen decor. The great hall is now the Virot restaurant. ✆ 52 East 41st Street, NY 10017 • Map K4 • 212 338 0500 • www.dylanhotel. com • $$$–$$$$$

Bryant Park
10 Raymond Hood's 1924 American Radiator Building has become an ultra-contemporary hotel, with giant glass windows, bold, red-lacquered lobby desks, and pale-hued rooms that are the last word in minimalist decor. ✆ 40 West 40th Street, New York, NY 10018 • Map K3 • 212 869 0100 • www. bryantparkhotel.com • $$$$$

  Note: Unless otherwise stated, all hotels accept credit cards, and have en-suite bathrooms and air conditioning

Left **Tribeca Grand Hotel** Right **Soho Grand Hotel**

⑩ Hip Hotels

1 Soho Grand Hotel

Perfectly suited to its artistic neighborhood, the hotel is housed in a landmark cast-iron building. The surroundings are dramatic and contemporary, and the Grand Bar is always hopping. ◈ *310 West Broadway, New York, NY 10013 • Map R4 • 212 965 3000 • www.sohogrand. com • $$$$–$$$$$*

2 TriBeCa Grand Hotel

TriBeCa's first hotel is a hit. All the neighborhood gathers at the Church Lounge, the dramatic lobby/bar with 70 translucent columns of light. Rooms are a calm counterpoint with an array of high-tech toys. ◈ *2 6th Avenue, New York, NY 10013 • Map P3 • 212 519 6600 • www.tribeca grand.com • $$$$–$$$$$*

3 W Union Square

Designer David Rockwell has turned a Beaux Arts building into a contemporary showstopper, complete with floating staircase. Trademark W features include a lobby with books and chess sets, and rooms with pillow-top beds. ◈ *201 Park Avenue South, New York, NY 10003 • Map M4 • 212 253 9119 • www. whotels.com • $$$–$$$$$*

4 Morgans Hotel

Ian Schrager's understated first New York hotel still has loyal fans for its clean, uncluttered look and clever, functional built-ins in the small but trendy rooms. Celebrity favorite restaurant Asia de Cuba adjoins the lobby. ◈ *237 Madison Avenue, New York, NY 10016 • Map K4 • 212 686 0300 • www.ian schragerhotels.com • $$–$$$*

5 Royalton

Media and fashion folk flock to this collaboration between Ian Schrager and Philippe Starck, with a space-age lobby, curving hallways, and cool bathrooms. Celebs are the norm in the bar and restaurant. ◈ *44 West 44th Street, New York, NY 10036 • Map J3 • 212 869 4400 • www.ianschragerhotels.com • $$$–$$$$*

6 Paramount

Appropriately in the Theater District, this hotel is like a theater, thanks to Philippe Starck's spectacular stairway and lofty lobby. Ian Schrager created the hotel for the young and hip, and they come in abundance, despite rooms that disguise their minute size with playful design. ◈ *235 West 46th Street, New York, NY 10036 • Map J2 • 212 764 5500 • www.ianschrager hotels.com • $$$*

7 Hudson Hotel

The Schrager-Starck team pulled out all the stops for this 1,000 room extravaganza, a melting pot of styles described as "organized chaos". Tiny rooms were billed low-budget, but rates went up when the hotel became a hit. ◈ *356 West 58th St, New York, NY 10019 • Map H2 • 212 554 6000 • www. hudsonhotel.com • $$*

8 Time Hotel

Bold red, bright yellow, or blue? Each of the 200 rooms in this new hotel is awash in color, courtesy of hot designer Adam Tihany. Take the glass and chrome elevator to the peaceful second-floor bar. ◈ *224 West 49th Street, New York, NY 10036 • Map J3 • 212 320 2900 • www.thetimeny.com • $$$*

9 Mercer Hotel

A hit from day one with Hollywood luminaries, the Mercer is housed in an 1890 structure built for John Jacob Astor II, and makes good use of lofty spaces and a voguish, shabby-chic look. ◈ *147 Mercer Street, New York, NY 10012 • Map N4 • 212 966 6060 • $$$$–$$$$$*

10 W Times Square

The W Hotel group has a winning formula, turning an ordinary hotel into a hip sanctuary. It features a big, open lobby, plenty of light and clever use of contemporary furnishings in a limited space. ◈ *W Times Square, 1567 Broadway and 47th St, New York, NY 10036 • 212 930 7400 • Map J3 • www.whotels.com • $$$–$$$$$*

Left **Benjamin** Center **Hilton New York** Right **Hotel Metro**

Business Hotels

1 Hilton New York

The quintessential business hotel, the 2,040-room Hilton has a central location, huge ballroom, and extensive meeting facilities. A re-design has transformed the lobby, upgraded rooms, and added a large fitness club and spa. ✆ *1335 6th Avenue, New York, NY 10019 • Map J3 • 212 586 7000 • www.hilton.com • $$$–$$$$*

2 Millennium Broadway

A postmodern skyscraper, encompassing a theater, the Millennium is sleek and streamlined. Compact rooms are well appointed with high-tech features that include voicemail in four languages. ✆ *145 West 44th Street, New York, NY 10036 • Map J3 • 212 768 4400 • $$$$*

3 Benjamin

A 1927 landmark by Emery Roth has been converted to an all-suite hotel designed for executives, with all the requisite high-tech gadgetry and the popular An American Place restaurant. ✆ *125 East 50th Street, New York, NY 10022 • Map J4 • 212 715 2500 • www.thebenjamin.com • $$$–$$$$*

4 Beekman Tower Hotel

The Beekman is an Art Deco gem. Suites are roomy and provide kitchenettes; the 26th floor Top of the Tower lounge is the perfect unwinding place. ✆ *3 Mitchell Place, 49th Street, New York, NY 10017 • Map J5 • 212 355 7300 • www.mesuite.com • $$$–$$$$*

5 Metropolitan

Newly refurbished, this mid-range property offers 722 comfortable rooms and good value suites. Amenities include a fitness center and business facilities. ✆ *569 Lexington Avenue, New York, NY 10022 • Map J4 • 212 752 7000 & 800 836 6471 • www.metropolitanhotelnyc.com • $$$*

6 Hotel Metro

Popular with the fashion industry, and good value, the Metro has a sophisticated Deco feel and good-sized rooms. Public spaces include a library, rooftop terrace, and spacious dining room. ✆ *45 West 35th Street, New York, NY 10001 • Map K3 • 212 947 2500 • www.hotelmetronyc • $$*

7 The Drake Swissotel

Business travelers appreciate the prime location, fitness center, spa, meeting facilities, and well-equipped business center of this recently refurbished 495-room hotel. Rooms have high-speed internet access, voice mail, call waiting and fax machines. ✆ *440 Park Avenue, New York, NY 10022 • Map H4 • 212 421 0900 & 800 372 5369 • www.swissotel.com • $$$*

8 Sheraton Manhattan

An indoor pool, sauna, and free continental breakfast are among the features of this 22-story hotel, a quieter sibling and neighbor of the Sheraton New York, a major convention venue. The theater district is steps away. ✆ *790 7th Avenue, New York, NY 10019 • Map J3 • 212 581 3300 & 800 223 6550 • www.sheraton.com • $$$–$$$$$*

9 Holiday Inn Wall Street

High-tech heaven, this was New York's first hotel with T-1 Internet access, plus check-in computers that dispense key cards. Comfortable rooms come with ergonomic work-spaces, a PC with DVD/CD and MS Office applications. ✆ *15 Gold Street, New York, NY 10038 • Map Q4 • 212 232 7800 & 800 465 4329 • www.holidayinnwsd.com • $$–$$$*

10 Ritz Carlton Battery Park

This luxury hotel has stunning views of the harbor and impressive attention to detail. Special touches include telescopes in rooms, feather beds, and a "bath butler." Kids will enjoy the Skyscraper Museum on site. ✆ *2 West St, New York, NY • Map Q3 • 212 344 0800 • $$$$*

Note: *Unless otherwise stated, all hotels accept credit cards, and have en-suite bathrooms and air conditioning*

Left **The Lucerne** Right **The Mayflower**

Price Categories

For a standard,
double room per
night (with breakfast
if included), taxes,
and extra charges.

$	under $150
$$	$150–$250
$$$	$250–$350
$$$$	$350–£450
$$$$$	over $450

🔟 Neighborhood Hotels

1 Lucerne

The Upper West Side offers excellent value, and the Lucerne, housed in a 1903 building, is top of the list. It has a comfortable lobby, business and fitness centers, a rooftop terrace, and tasteful rooms with many amenities. ❧ *201 West 79th St, New York, NY 10024 • Map F2 • 212 875 1000 • www. newyorkhotel.com • $$$*

2 Excelsior

A lavish, old-world lobby fronts a recently refurbished, well-appointed hotel with traditional decor, many suites, in-room computers and fax machines. A breakfast room, library, outdoor decks, and media room are among other features. ❧ *45 West 81st Street, New York, NY 10024 • Map F2 • 212 362 9200 & 800 368 4575 • www. excelsiorhotelny.com • $$*

3 Hotel Beacon

Named for the famous theater next door *(see p52)*, the Beacon is a relaxed, comfortable hotel, with generous rooms with standard decor, and, a big plus, kitchenettes with refrigerators and microwaves. ❧ *2130 Broadway, New York, NY 10023 • Map G2 • 212 787 1100 • www. beaconhotel.com • $$*

4 Mayflower

The location, a short walk from Lincoln Center, is a big attraction, drawing performers to this long-time standby.

The hotel is overdue for refurbishment, but the rooms are comfortable enough and offer kitchenettes. Views from those facing the park are prime. ❧ *15 Central Park West, New York, NY 10023 • Map H2 • 212 265 0060 • www. mayflowerhotel.com • $$*

5 Empire Hotel

Lincoln Center is across the street from this refurbished hotel with an impressive lobby and small but decently decorated rooms. There's a tape and CD library for in-room players, plus a café, good for pre-concert dining. ❧ *44 West 63rd Street, New York, NY 10023 • Map H2 • 212 265 7400 • www. empirehotel.com • $$–$$$*

6 Franklin

The most affordable lodging on the Upper East Side, the Franklin offers style rather than size, with sleek furnishings and compact rooms. The hotel serves complimentary breakfast and cappuccino, espresso, and tea all day. ❧ *164 East 87th Street, New York, NY 10128 • Map F4 • 212 369 1000 & 877 847 4444 • www. franklinhotel.com • $$$*

7 Chelsea Savoy

An excellent neighborhood lodging, close to Chelsea's shops, flea markets, cafés, and galleries. Pleasantly furnished rooms are a decent size, with all the necessary amenities, and

the bathrooms are new. ❧ *204 West 23rd Street, New York, NY 10011 • Map L2 • 212 929 9353 • www. chelseasavoynyc.com • $$*

8 Best Western Seaport Inn

Close to South Street Seaport, this restored 19th-century building has the predictable rooms of a chain hotel, but a cozy lobby. All 72 rooms have VCRs and refrigerators, and breakfast is included. ❧ *33 Peck Slip, New York, NY 10038 • Map Q4 • 212 766 6600 & 800 468 3569 • www.bestwestern.com • $$*

9 Washington Square Hotel

A haven in the heart of Greenwich Village. Rooms are tiny, hallways painfully narrow, but the decor pleasant, continental breakfast is included, and you can say you stayed where Bob Dylan and Joan Baez once hung out. ❧ *103 Waverly Place, New York, NY 10011 • Map N3 • 212 777 9515 • www. wshotel.com • $$*

10 60 Thompson

SoHo's new, 12-story luxury hotel has 100 rooms, elegantly decked out with custom furnishings. Guests can enjoy the view from the roof garden or watch the neighborhood scene from the sidewalk café. ❧ *60 Thompson Street, New York, NY 10012 • Map N3 • 212 431 0400 • www. 60thompson.com • $$$$*

General Index

Acknowledgements

The Author
Eleanor Berman is a widely published travel writer whose journeys have spanned 59 countries and six continents. A long-time New Yorker, she is New York correspondent for the Expedia travel web site, main contributor to the *DK Eyewitness New York Travel Guide* (winner, Thomas Cook award 1994), and author of *New York Neighborhoods* (winner, Independent Publishers award, 2000) and nine additional travel guides.

Project Editors Felicity Crowe, Marianne Petrou
Art Editor Gillian Andrews
Senior Editor Marcus Hardy
Senior Art Editor Marisa Renzullo
Senior Publishing Manager Louise Lang
Publishing Manager Kate Poole
Art Director Gillian Allan

Photographers David King, Tim Knox

Illustrator Chris Orr & Associates

Cartography Casper Morris

Maps John Plumer

Editor Caroline Taverne

Researcher Vivienne Foley

Picture Research Jenny Silkstone, Lilly Sellar

Proofreader Stephanie Driver

Indexer Hilary Bird

DTP Jason Little

Production
Joanna Bull, Marie Ingledew

Design and Editorial Assistance
Sonal Bhatt, Tessa Bindloss, Rebecca Carman, Sherry Collins, Gadi Farfour, Jo Gardner, James Hall, David Saldanha, Melanie Simmonds, Hayley Smith, Brett Steel, Rachael Symons, Andrew Szudek, Shawn Thomas, Karen Villabona, Ros Walford.

Additional Photography
Tony Foo, Andrew Holigan, Edvard Huember, Dave King, Norman McGrath, Michael Moran, Susan Sayler, Paul Solomon, Chuck Spang, Chris Stevens, Robert Wright.

Picture Credits
t-top, tl-top left, tlc-top left centre, tc-top centre, tr-top right, cla-centre left above, ca- centre above, cra- centre right above, cl-centre left, c- centre, cr- centre right, clb-centre left below, cb-centre below, crb-centreright below, bl-bottom left, b-bottom, bc-bottom centre, bcl-bottom centre left, br-bottom right, d-detail.

Works of art have been reproduced with the permission of the following copyright holders: *'Untitled'* Christian Boltanski (c) ADAGP, Paris and DACS, London 2002 99bl.

The publishers would like to thank the following individuals, companies and picture libraries for their kind permission to reproduce their photographs.

AMERICAN FOLK ART MUSEUM, New York: John Parnell 19c;

AMERICAN MUSEUM OF NATURAL HISTORY, Courtesy Department of Library Services: 35c, 35b, 35t, 37c, 37b, 138cr; D. Finnin 36tl, 36tc, 36tr, 36c; ASSOCIATED PRESS AP: Stephen J Boitano 49b; AXA FINANCIAL, INC.: *City Building* from America Today, Thomas Hart Benton, 1931. Distemper and egg tempera on gessoed linen with oil glaze 92 x 117 in. Collection AXA Financial, Inc. through its subsidiary The Equitable Life Assurance Society of the U.S (c) T. H. Benton and R. P. Benton Testamentary Trusts/ VAGA, New York/DACS, London 2002 14tl; MARY BOONE GALLERY: *Eric Fischl Installation* (1999) ZINDMAN/FREMONT, N.Y.C. 42tl; THE BOUTIQUE HOTEL GROUP: 174tc, 174tr; BROOKLYN MUSEUM, NEW YORK: 154tl; Adam Husted 40tr.

CENTRAL PARK CONSERVANCY: Sara Cedar Miller 26b, 27b; COACH USA: 164tc; COLORIFIC: Black Star 18b; PAULA COOPER GALLERY: *Prospective Retrospective* by Carl Andre 43c, Adam Reich 42tr; CORBIS: 17cr, 48c, 48ca, 158-159; Bettman 19t, 20tl, 20c, 20b; 25t, 48tl, 49t; Bill Ross 16t; Bob Krist 168tr; Charles O'Rear 38-39; Dave Houser 62c; David Katzenstein 62b; Duomo 63c, Duomo / Chris Trotman 63t; Gail Mooney 9t; 18cl, 22c, 64b, 128tc; James Marshall 157t; Joseph Sohm; ChromoSohm Inc 4-5; Kelly Mooney 116cr, 119t; Kit Kittle 128tr; Lawrence 70-71; Lee Snider 10cl, 74br; Lynn Goldsmith 10-11c; Michael S. Yamashita 3bl,

131; Museum of the City of New York 48tc; Nathan Benn 45cl; Patrik Giardino 167t; DEPARTMENT: 170TR; DIA CENTER FOR THE ARTS: Cathy Carver 120tl; HOTEL EDISON: 175tl; THE SOLOMON R. GUGGENHEIM FOUNDATION, NEW YORK: *Before the Mirror* Edouard Manet, 1876, Thannhauser Collection, Gift Justin K Thannhauser 1978, photo David Heald 33t; *Black Lines* Wassily Kandinsky, 1913, Gift Solomon R. Guggenheim 1937, photo David Heald (c) ADAGP, Paris and DACS, London 2002 33b; *Haere Mai* Paul Gauguin, Thannhauser Collection, Gift Justin K. Thannhauser 1978 33r; *The Hermitage at Pontoise* Camille Pissaro, Thannhauser Collection, Gift Justin K Thannhauser 1978 32c; *Woman with Yellow Hair* Pablo Picasso, December 1931, Thannhauser Collection. Gift Justin K Thannhauser, photo David Heald (c) Succession Picasso/DACS 2002 32b.

HILTONS OF NEW YORK CITY: 178TC; HULTON GETTY ARCHIVE: 20tr; Ernst Haas 20tc. THE IMAGE BANK/GETTY IMAGES: 59c; IMAGE STATE: AGE Fotostock 96-97; THE IRVING PLACE: Roy J. Wright 176tc; JAZZ PROMO SERVICES: 52tr; JOAN MARCUS: 23b, 25c, 25b; NY CITY MARRIOTT HOTELS: 173tl; THE METROPOLITAN MUSEUM OF ART, NY: The Metropolitan Museum of Art, New York: 28b, 29cb; *Cypresses* Vincent van Gogh, 1889, Rogers Fund 1949 30b; *Gertrude Stein*, Pablo

Acknowledgements

Picasso, 1905-6, Bequest of Gertrude Stein 1946 (c) Succession Picasso/DACS 2002 30tr; 'The Card Players', Paul Cezanne, Bequest of Stephen C. Clark 1960 30tl; 'Washington Crossing the Delaware' Emanuel Gottlieb Leutze, 1851, Bequest of John S. Kennedy 29t; 'Young Woman with Water Jug', Johannes Vermeer, 1664-5, Marquand Collection, Gift of Henry G. Marquand 1889 7c and 30c; 'Garden at Sainte-Adresse' Claude Monet, 1867, Monet Purchase, special contributions and funds given or bequeathed by friends of the Museum (c) ADAGP, Paris and DACS, London 2002 30tc; The Cloisters Collection/Mick Hales 31crb; Purchase The Costume Institute Fund in memory of Polaire Weissman 1989 29ca; 'Triptych with Annunciation', Robert Campin, 1425, The Cloisters Collection 1956 31b; The Cloisters Collection 1937 31t; The Cloisters Collection Gift of John D. Rockefeller 1937 31cl; THE MUSE HOTEL: 176tl; MUSEUM OF MODERN ART: ©2004 Photo Elizabeth Felicella, architectural rendering Kohn Pedersen Fox Associates, digital composite Robert Bowen 40c; NEW YORK CITY FIRE DEPARTMENT: 170tr; PACE WILDENSTEIN: Ellen Page Wilson 'Cornflake Girl', Mel Ramos (c) Mel Ramos/VAGA, New York/DACS, London 2002 42c; PRADA: 99br; REGENT HOTELS: 178tc; RENAISSANCE NEW YORK: 173tc; ROCKEFELLER CENTER ARCHIVE: 14tr, 15c, John D Rockefeller Jr 48tr; SOHO GRAND HOTEL: 177tr; SOUTH STREET SEAPORT MUSEUM: 82tc; ST. MAGGIE'S CAFE: 77tl; TRIBECA GRAND HOTEL: Michael Kleinberg 177tl; VINE RESTAURANT: 77tr.

All other images are © Dorling Kindersley. For further information see www.dkimages.com.